CONFESSIONS OF A TROLLEY DODGER FROM BROOKLYN

BY STAN FISCHLER

RESEARCH EDITORS: BOB HOFFMAN, ANGELA RADUAZZO, RICK DA CRUZ
ARTWORK: SHIRLEY FISCHLER, JOHN HENDERSON
INTRODUCTIONS: BROOKLYN BOROUGH PRESIDENT HOWARD GOLDEN
ACTOR JERRY STILLER

H&M PRODUCTIONS

(FRONT COVER, TOP RIGHT) Our gang at 582 Marcy Avenue in Brooklyn. (left to right). Ben Fischler (my dad), Simon Friedman (grandpa), Aunt Helen Friedman; Etel Friedman (grandma), Me, Molly Fischler, "Da Momma." That's the ubiquitous Brooklyn-style stoop behind us.

(FRONT COVER, LOWER LEFT) A typical five-cent "Brooklyn limousine" that graced the streets from the turn of the century to the 1940's. This model, the 500 series, had motors that groaned like cattle in a small corral. Or, like the drone of bagpipes, if you will.

(REAR COVER) The motorman of old 5081 seems as nostalgic about the sweet J.G. Brill product (born in 1912) as we were riding it. This beauty was rebuilt in the 1930's and scrapped in the late 1940's. I considered it sexy, as trolleys go; a veritable Marilyn Monroe on wheels.

TROLLEY DODGERS, BASEBALL AND BROOKLYN

The majority of baseball fans who follow the Los Angeles Dodgers would be hard-pressed to explain precisely why their Southern California representative to the National League ever got so unlikely a name as Dodgers. After all, what would one be dodging in California, if not the next mudslide or earthquake?

But as senior Los Angelinos realize, their baseball team originally was rooted in Brooklyn whence the name Dodgers originated. Ah, but what were Brooklynites dodging since it wasn't mudslides or earthquakes?

In 1884, when Brooklyn's new baseball franchise was accepted in the American Association, it was the City of Brooklyn—not one of New York's five boroughs—and boasted a population of 600,000, third largest in the United States.

To transport all these citizens, Brooklyn had created one of the world's most comprehensive horse-drawn streetcar systems. With electrification, the horsecars became trolleys and Brooklynites spent a good part of their lives getting out of the way of the newfangled cars. Hence, the good Booklyn burghers became known as "Trolley Dodgers."

Authors Donald Dewey and Nicholas Acocella (Encyclopedia of Major League Baseball Teams) point out that the baseball "Trolley Dodgers were named for an activity familiar to every resident of the bustling city."

The Brooklyn Trolley Dodgers played in the American Association from 1884 to 1889 at Washington Park, Ridgewood Park and Union Grounds. When the franchise joined the National League in 1890, it had a number of nicknames; among them the Bridegrooms (so named because a number of players on the team were married within a brief period of time in 1888), but also the Trolley Dodgers.

In time, the name would simply be shortened to Dodgers although the trolleys remained a conspicuous part of the Ebbets Field landscape. By the turn of the century no less than five lines—Tompkins, Lorimer, Franklin, Ocean and Flatbush—rolled in the immediate vicinity of the ballpark and did so until the post-World War II years. But before the Dodgers won their first World Series in 1955 all those trolleys were gone. Not long afterward the Dodgers had left Brooklyn as well. This book is about one of those trolley-dodgers and the beloved streetcars, themselves.

H & M PRODUCTIONS II INC.
193-07 45 AVE.
FLUSHING, NY 11358

ISBN 1-882608-10-0
LIBRARY OF CONGRESS 95-075024

© Copyright 1995

TABLE OF CONTENTS

My favorite riding position, just to the left of the motorman. From this vantage point I could study how he manipulated the controller. This is Brooklyn & Queens Transit car #5027 on the Ralph-Rockaway Line, at Rockaway Ave., in 1940.

(LEFT) That's Howie on the right with his mom, Sally, holding her son, then sister, Norma, and big brother Gershy

(ABOVE) Our second home, P.S. 54. (Sandford St. entrance)

FOREWORD

Howie Sparer was my best friend. Anybody who grew up in Brooklyn, circa 1932-1952, would know what that meant. The bonds were permanent, irrevocable.

We met in Kindergarten in Mrs. Fischer's class at Public School 54 on Sandford, Nostrand and Hart Streets in what was then known as Williamsburg, or if you will, "Upper Williamsburg," since those living closer to the bridge considered us outlanders of sorts.

Howie and I remained close friends until the third grade when we had a memorable spat at the Parade Grounds (Park Circle). That episode ruptured our relationship for approximately eight days, after which we figuratively kissed-and-made-up. We remained best friends until Howie died at the age of thirty in 1963.

At the time of our first meeting in Kindergarten, Howie lived a block away from me. Our house (582 Marcy Avenue) was located around the corner from the Sparer abode on Vernon Avenue. Howie lived in a four-story walk-up apartment building at the bottom of Vernon, adjoining Nostrand Avenue. There were several similar buildings next to Howie's house and across the street, filled with kids our age. Abe Yurkofsky (now Dr. Abraham Yurkofsky, top-notch allergist) lived diagonally across from Howie's place and remains a life-long friend. But Abe wasn't a best-friend only because he was two years older—ergo, "a big guy"—and therefore in a distinctly separate class which was closely observed on The Block. The Karger brothers, Norman and Stu, lived next door to Howie and were first-rate pals as was Richie Mishkin, Irving (Gots) Gottlieb and Gilbert Birnbaum.

Yet, Howie was my best friend, although we were very different. I was an only child, living in a three-story brownstone with my parents, Molly and Ben, grandparents, Etel and Simon, and spinster Aunt Helen who, on rare occasions, was like an older sister.

Howie also lived with his parents, Sidney and Sally, but had an older sister, Norma, who was both beautiful in my eyes but tough, and an older brother, Gerson, who always was called Gershy. A good fellow, Gershy nevertheless intimidated me a bit mostly because he was one of the _really_ big guys; a full four years older.

Our personalities were diametrically opposite. I was impulsive, emotional, hypersensitive and bursting with energy. Howie was cool, calm and collected; never one to race too far ahead of the world around him.

For some inexplicable reason, Howie appreciated my "qualities" more than anyone, and quietly became my biggest booster. I was the fastest runner in our group but Howie made me feel as if I was Mercury personified. He would often comment—in the most positive way—that nobody ever became more enthusiastic about a project he undertook than I did and I kind of liked that kind of talk.

Which is not to suggest that we didn't have our share of disagreements. I loved hockey but Howie couldn't have cared less about the ice game and had a way of rebuffing my attempts to turn him into a fan that thoroughly frustrated Your's Truly. I loved trolleys and subways and els while Howie wondered why I would ever get excited about a ride on the BMT. But the one thing we liked most of all was hanging out together. Sometimes it was in Al and Shirley's candy store on the corner of Nostrand and Vernon. Or, chomping on a hot dog (with mustard and sauerkraut) at the S&L Delicatessen on DeKalb and Marcy Avenues. It might mean plotting strategy for a "big" softball game against the Harts or walking to the (not so) New Hebrew School on Stockton Street near Tompkins Avenue.

We played a lot of ball together; especially punchball, the "official" game of Vernon Avenue; not to mention "Association" (football), two-hand touch and softball in the P.S. 54 schoolyard. We went to the movies together and, every December, would be shepherded by either Sally Sparer or Molly Fischler to the Loeser's Department Store (on Fulton St.) toy department for an annual Hanukkah-Christmas gift.

Howie's parents were in the pickle and mayonnaise business (Spare Way Food Products on DeKalb across from the S&L Deli.). By our Depression Era standards, the Sparers became wealthy in a relatively short time between 1940 and 1945. By the time Howie was ten years old (1942), the Sparers were "rich" enough to move out of Williamsburg to a two-story brick building at 602 Montgomery Street in what we considered posh Crown Heights.

Despite the geographical separation, our friendship remained secure. We would alternate sleeping "over" each other's home and would embark on such joint adventures as bicycle excursions to the wilds of Staten Island (via the 69th St. ferry) or a Saturday matinee at Manhattan's Paramount Theater for a live stage show and a movie.

During the last years of World War II, Howie's parents moved yet again to an even larger house (with a lawn, no less!) on East 28th Street in Flatbush. Like the Montgomery St. home (adjoining the Tompkins Ave. trolley line), the Sparer's house in Flatbush was streetcar-convenient. Only this time I rode the Nostrand Ave. line to get there.

Howie and I trolleyed everywhere, including a memorab;le trip on the Tompkins route that went over the Williamsburg Bridge and down into the labyrinth of tracks at the underground Delancey St. terminal.

In 1944 and 1945, at the very zenith of the Sparer's wealth cycle, Sidney and Sally rented a summer home in exclusive Sea Gate, at the western tip of Coney Island. Howie and I shared many adventures there, including the near-kidnapping of a Norton's Point trolley.

Howie and Gershy on Montgomery Street.

Howie the collegian in 1954.

Our paths briefly parted when Howie went to Michigan State University and I remained at Brooklyn College. Nevertheless, our bonds had been forged and we hooked up at every opportunity. After college, Howie eventually returned to New York, became a stockbroker, married Liz and moved to a middle-income development near Pratt Institute on Clinton Hill.

In the meantime, I went from a job as assistant publicist for the New York Rangers ice hockey team to columnist for the New York Journal-American newspaper and a hockey chronicler for assorted publications including The Hockey News.

Curiously, Howie, who had never given hockey a tumble in our earlier years, suddenly became, as they say, involved. To my amazement, he even bought season tickets to Rangers' games at old Madison Square Garden at Eighth Avenue and 50th Street and occupied a front row mezzanine seat which was directly behind my campground in the press box which overhung the mezzanine. Howie and I saw lots of each other in this milieu. Our friendship was tighter than ever although he was consumed with family activities. He had two young sons and was also very attentive to his nephew (Norma's son) Marc Gold. I recall visiting Marc's home with Howie and giving Marc a pep talk about getting into the writing business.

On a Wednesday night during the 1962-1963 season, I had made my way up to the press box for yet another Ranger game and, instinctively, looked for Howie in his usual seat. There was no one there so I assumed that an excess of work had kept him from the game. The next day I learned he was in bed with the flu. After work on Friday, I took the train down to Baltimore for a visit with my old Ranger friend Aldo Guidolin who was now coaching the Clippers in the

American Hockey League. After the match, I stayed at Aldo's house and on Saturday joined the Clippers for the team bus ride to Hershey, Pennsylvania for a Saturday night AHL contest.

To return home after that, I had to grab a 1 a.m. milk run out of Harrisburg that got me into New York at about 5 a.m.. I had just fallen asleep early Sunday Morning in my apartment on East 19th Street when the phone jangled me to consciousness, and the fateful message.

Our mutual friend, Dave Perlmutter, was on the other end. His voice was ominously and uncharacteristically grim. "Stan, I got bad news. Howie died early this morning!"

In my state of semi-consciousness, I couldn't quite comprehend whether I was suffering through a nightmare or was on the wrong end of reality. I couldn't think of anything better to say than, "Are you kidding?" Dave repeated what I didn't want to hear. "He died in the hospital—pneumonia."

Howie was gone; just like that.

Of course, he never was gone from memory. Howie was the most special of the gang and everyone knew it, felt it, and accepted it as fact. It was the same for Jack Goldstein, Dave Perlmutter, Seymour Foner, Marc Gold and anyone who had the good fortune to know the fellow I affectionately nicknamed "Sparer—The Old Crow."

Howie was terribly caring about others but never enough about himself. He was an extraordinarily likeable, amusing, entertaining, insightful, beautiful and sensitive guy—even though he rarely was on time. He loved the mamalouchen (mother tongue) and he loved music, even though he banged out " It Had To Be You" on the piano until it came out of our ears. Howie was my best friend and, as such, he was irreplaceable. His death left a void in my life that never has been filled; and I'm certain that Jack, Doov, Marc and Seymour will underline the point.

My Father, who revered Howie, had an expression he reserved only for the most very special people in his life. "He was a prince." Such a kudo certainly was applicable to Howie who was so much a part of my life, as CONFESSIONS OF A TROLLEY DODGER FROM BROOKLYN reveals.

This book is dedicated to the memory of Howie Sparer in belated but nonetheless sincere appreciation for all the happiness he brought to me and all the others around him.

A Bridge Plaza-bound Wilson Ave. Line Peter Witt-type car passes children contemporary with my childhood. They're playing traditional Brooklyn street games of either stoopball or Ace-King-Queen.

ACKNOWLEDGMENTS

To adequately thank all those responsible for this book would take about as long as it took to ride the Nostrand Avenue trolley from Delancey Street in Manhattan to Avenue U near Sheepshead Bay.

Let's begin at the beginning: The book never would have been possible had it not been for the good folks (Barbara Cohen, Judith Stonehill, and Francis Morrone) at New York Bound Books, who liked my subway book, Uptown, Downtown.

Fortuitously, I was invited to speak at one of the NYBB'S TRANSIT WRITER SYMPOSIUMS in September 1992. During the post-lecture question-and-answer period, somebody wondered whether I had planned to write another book about trains. "To tell you the truth," I replied, "my ambition is to write a trolley book but I don't expect to find a publisher willing to do it."

And that seemed to be that. But as I was leaving, a gentleman named John Henderson introduced himself and mentioned that he was both a publisher of train books as well as a hockey fan. (The fact that he rooted for the Rangers was a bit disturbing, but since this is a free country, I didn't argue with him.) And a good thing too; Henderson said he'd like to talk to me about my streetcar project. The rest is history as you can tell from the following pages.

What made it even better, as I soon learned, was John's sensitivity to the subject and myself, particularly during my son's hospitalization in the summer of 1993. (I'll never forget that the first bouquet of good luck flowers came from the Hendersons).

To get the project on track—if you'll excuse the expression—intense research was needed. Words cannot adequately describe the superb job Bob Hoffman did as a catalyst in the first months of research. Bob was a veritable ferret on the spoor of trolley reference works and literally switched me onto the express track as the project developed steam. Bob also received splended assistance from the Electric Railroaders Association, as knowledgeable and dedicated a group as you'll ever find.

Unfortunately, Hoffman's NYU internship ended in June 1993 and he wasn't around for completion of the book. (Bob, wherever you are, thanks!)

CONFESSIONS OF A TROLLEY DODGER FROM BROOKLYN was heavily dependent on photos. Bob Presbrey not only made his incomparable collection available, but also entertained me with the finest collection of pop music from the 20's, 30's, and 40's that I could've wished for, while spending hours analyzing his archives. Without Bob, the project would have been derailed.

My friendship with Don Harold dates back to my journalistic days when I covered the Transit Authority in the late 1950's and 1960's for the New York Journal-American newspaper. Don contributed many photos and cordially sat for an interview with Bob Hoffman. I fully planned to include Don among the Trolley Superstars because he deserves the recognition. However, space limitations compelled me to shunt the interview to a literary siding. Since I had included Harold in my book, UPTOWN-DOWNTOWN, as a Subway Superstar, I felt just a bit less guilty about scratching his excellent profile from this book. I hope he understands and realizes how deeply I'm appreciative of him.

Before his untimely death, the late Al Hirsch provided a fund of information that was critical to the history. I've never met more intense trolley historians than Al, Bob, and Don. After Hirsch's death, his son Billy, a loyal Islanders fan, provided me with some priceless photos which are included in this volume.

Bill Meyers, another member of the circle of trolley devotees, also opened up his photo collection for our use.

Once I headed into the homestretch, two vibrant, young researchers helped put the finishing touches on the manuscript. Angela Raduazzo and Ricardo Da Cruz not only were genial and encouraging supporters, but plunged into the project with the enthusiasm of old trolley hands. To borrow a baseball bromide, they were both "clutch hitters."

I would be remiss without thanking transit buff, Bernie Ente, for his unflagging encouragement and Marc Gold, who supplied some vital pictures of his uncle Howie Sparer, and Marc's mother, Norma Sparer-Gold.

Many dear friends opened their archives to find precious photos of yesteryear. Special thanks to Abe Yurkofsky, Ralph Hubbard, Anne Yearwood, Norma Gold, Lew Klotz and those I'm sure I've forgotten.

Members of both the Friedman (my mother's) and Fischler (my dad's) families were typically helpful in providing memories, details and photos. Thanks to Uncle Joe and Aunt Lottie Friedman, Uncle Ben and Aunt Lucie Friedman, Aunt Frances Friedman, Cousin Ira Sheier, Cousin Joan Friedman, Cousin Lois Friedman, Cousin Richard Friedman, Cousin Paul Friedman, Cousin Daisy Singer, Cousin Judith Pelton and Cousin Judd Fischler. My mom's cousin, Miriam Reisberg, made a valiant attempt to find a photo of hand-crunching Muttle Bernstein and friend John Landers was equally vigorous in our futile search for a photo of shop teacher, Mister Montague.

John Landers also devoted countless hours to other types of research for which I am grateful.

I am indebted to all of you for the contributions, but especially my wife, Shirley, for her help in the crunch.

The vast resources of the Electric Railroaders' Association were of immesurable assistance in the research. The ERA is a trolley buff's dream-come-true.

The photo collection of the Brooklyn Public Library provided interesting photos of early trolley cars and scenes.

Likewise, the superb book BROOKLYN TROLLEYS by James C. Greller and Edward B. Watson not only was a treat to peruse but also provided considerable background information and pictorial inspiration. Having it at my side made the streetcars come alive. Greller and Watson's car rosters proved invaluable in studying the Brooklyn trolley evolution.

Added thanks to Gil Zimet for the loan of BROOKLYN TROLLEYS and to William D. Middleton, author of the splended work, THE TIME OF THE TROLLEY, which provided invaluable information for my project.

DEDICATION

There always was one overriding purpose of this book; I wanted my two children, Ben and Simon, to get a first-hand knowledge of what life was like in Brooklyn from 1936 to 1946—or from my fourth to my fourteenth birthday—during my most formative years. I wanted them to know how much I loved trolleys, how they impacted on my life, and what life was like in the land of the Brooklyn Dodgers.

Sadly, I never seemed to have enough time to tell them all of the stories from my childhood during their earlier years and I felt it was important that they knew and understood what it was all about to grow up at 582 Marcy Avenue.

As it happened, I had hardly begun writing the first chapter in June 1993 when Simon was stricken with cardio-myopathy (heart disease).

From the end of June through early August, my wife and I lived day by day wondering whether Simon would survive, as he needed a heart transplant if he was going to live.

In those painful days, several things enabled me to continue functioning and one of them was this book. Every morning, after walking Cleo the dog and before leaving for the hospital, I would sit down at the computer and work on a chapter. Transferring my thoughts back half a century provided a significant moment of relief until the night came on August 6, 1993 when Simon received his new heart.

So this book is dedicated to the boys, to Shirley, who was at Simon's bedside whenever he needed her, and one who was especially attentive to us during Simon's ordeal. That would be my pal, Howie Sparer's nephew, Marc Gold. Howie's spirit lives on through his nephew, Marc, who has become as close to me as Howie had been and proved it many times over during that critical summer of 1993.

If there could be a latter-day Howie Sparer it would be a fellow we encountered at Columbia-Presbyterian Hospital during Simon's crisis and thereafter. Larry Swasey of the New York Regional Transplant Program was a remarkable inspiration both to Shirley and I as well as Simon and has become a close friend and constant source of positive thinking and laughs. The book also is dedicated to the memory of Howie, and the friendship of Marc and Larry.

INTRODUCTIONS

Most youngsters growing up in Brooklyn today know about the trolley car only through old movies and history books. However, there was a time when real trolleys were a presence in every part of Brooklyn, the "hometown" of one in every seven Americans.

The diesel bus, which supplanted the trolley on our streets, is a poor substitute for stimulating the boyhood imagination that Stan Fischler captures so well in this delightful memoir.
In describing his trolley adventures while growing up in Brooklyn, Stan reveals the origins of his life-long preoccupation with the New York City transit system. Fischler chronicles the central role that the trolley car played in the vitality of Brooklyn and captures the spirit of an era when this particular means of transportation was an integral part of the lives of the millions of our citizens.

At the time Stan grew up, there were few destinations in Brooklyn you could not reach by trolley. The trolley was a vital means of travel for residents of every part of the Borough, and there were probably more trolley cars in Brooklyn than any other major metropolis in the world. With the pole raised from the back of the car to draw power from the electric wires overhead, these steel cars swayed down the middle of every major thoroughfare, connecting neighborhoods from Greenpoint and Williamsburg to Coney Island and Flatlands.

In addition to its important role in carrying people to work in factories, warehouses and offices, the trolley opened a whole world of leisure and recreation to people of all ages for just a nickel. It took them to visit family and friends; it took them Downtown to shop or go to the movies; it took them to Coney Island for fun or the ferry at 69th Street for a quick voyage to Staten Island; it also took them to watch the Brooklyn Dodgers play at Ebbets Field.

The trolley car, in fact, was responsible for naming the legendary Brooklyn baseball team. With these "monsters on rails" roaming the major streets, particularly in the earlier parts of this century when they became popular, survival meant learning to be a "trolley dodger" to stay out of their way.

Like other stalwart Brooklynites, Stan learned how to be a "trolley dodger." He also learned how to write skillfully to tell the world about his love for both the trolley and his native Brooklyn. In this book, as he weaves his personal reminiscences into a definitive history of the growth of the trolley in Brooklyn, Stan also writes about its demise. However, I am pleased to note that in urban areas in the U.S. and around the world, the virtues of the trolley are once again being recognized. Perhaps the trolley will be as much a part of our future as it is our past.

During the era that is the subject of this book, Brooklyn's vast network of trolleys seemed indestructible. Unfortunately, that proved to be an illusion, as "progress" replaced the trolley with a more prosaic means of transportation. What is true, however, is that the Brooklynites who rode the trolleys absorbed a strength of character, determination and resilience from those old steel cars and rails. The trolleys may not have survived, but the Brooklyn character has. In this marvelous book, Stan Fischler helps us understand why.

Howard Golden
Borough President of Brooklyn

Stan Fischler called to say, "I'm doing a book on trolleys. Didn't you mention that your father drove a bus in New York City?" "Sure, " I said, "but what's that got to do with streetcars?" He said, "I'm sending over some photographs." The photos of trolley cars immediately evoked memories.

My Father, all 5-foot-3 of him, was possibly the shortest bus driver in New York City. He used a cushion on the seat to lift him. If he were a street car conductor he would've had to stand on a milk box. So my father became a bus driver. Next to the subway or taxi the trolley was a tortoise. Trolley lines extended endlessly and linked the boroughs of the city. They were the veins of transportation.

At age 14 we had moved from East New York, Brooklyn to the Lower East Side. I entered a PAL track meet to be held at an armory on Throop Avenue in Brooklyn. It was a snowy day and the trolley cars were running late. Nevertheless I boarded one at Bridge Plaza. I saw electrical sparks shooting out from the poles disengaging from the power lines. The trolley car stopped and the conductor reattached the lines. They kept disconnecting. I finally gave up and started to jog to the Armory. I figured I could beat the trolley. I did and also arrived for the race exhausted. I had run at least two miles. Needless to say I lost the race.

Williamsburg was one of the eleven places our family moved to in the 30's. At the foot of the Williamsburg Bridge was Bridge Plaza. For me the trolley that travelled into Manhattan and its bright lights was the railway to a better life.

When I mentioned this to my older cousin Sandra she laughed and said, "I'll never forget my first ride on a trolley. It was a wintery day and my father had wrapped his coat around me to keep me warm. Suddenly the street was alive with people screaming. They leapt off the streetcar. John D. Rockefeller was throwing dimes out of his limousine and people were going crazy trying to pick them up."

According to my older cousin Sandra, the streetcar must've had a mysterious fascination for my mother. According to her, my mom took the streetcar to Unity Hospital as she went into labor with me in her womb. "Was it possible she was timing her contractions as the conductor announced streets like Kosciusko, Halsey and Chauncey?" I asked "That's how you learned timing Jerry," she announced with the authority of a shaman. No doubt my mother felt confident that the conductor could've delivered me in case her water burst.

Sandra lived in a remote section of Canarsie that might still have been inhabited by the Indians who sold the island of Manhattan to the Dutch. Getting to where she lived you took a subway to Rockaway Parkway. You than transferred to a trolley which burrowed its way through wild grass which brushed against the windows of the car obscuring everything in sight. The station stops were dirt paths that cut through the fields. The conductor let you off upon request.

Going to Sandra's house meant adventure. She'd somehow manage to scrape up enough pennies to take us on trips. her favorite haunt was an amusement park at Jamaica Bay where she worked as a shill. Tony, the owner, had a concession where you'd show your strength by hitting the bell with a sledgehammer. He'd spot my fourteen-year-old, 85-pound cousin, pull her out of the crowd, hand her the hammer and invite her to take a crack at hitting the gong. She obliged by rolling up her sleeves like a longshoreman and proceed to unerringly ring the bell again and again to everyone's amazement. Of course it was all fixed. Tony would then dare any guy in the crowd to match her. The muscle boys, eager to impress their girlfriends paid the price. When the humiliation ended and the crowd dispersed Tony'd slip Sandra a couple of bucks. She'd then take us for hot dogs or to a movie. It was what having a cousin was all about.

One day she arrived at our house in East New York and said she was taking me to see "Snow White and the Seven Dwarfs at Radio City Music Hall." I had never been to Times Square, let alone Radio City with its 5000 seats. I sat in awe as Snow White kissed Grumpy, Sneezy, Doc, Happy, Sleepy and Bashful. When the film ended the traveller curtain swept across the giant stage as lights flooded the theatre. On our left an organ silently sprouted out of the wall like a mushroom. The organist, his body swaying like a marionette in the wind played "Hi-ho-hi-ho it's off to work we go." The notes reverberated like in an ancient cathedral. Every molecule in my body was affected. I was incredibly alive. The organist was suddenly swallowed back into the wall as the Radio City Orchestra led by Erno Rapee rose from the pit on a hydraulic lift segueing into "Hi, ho, hi, ho." The Rockettes danced on followed by the Corps de Ballet in perfect synchronicity. When the show ended I knew I wanted to be an actor. (Ironically years later Anne Meara and I were offered a booking at Radio City which we had to turn down.)

My cousin and I walked on to the street. we were back to reality. On the ride home to Canarsie I knew my life had changed. It was the mother of all trolley rides for me. To this day whenever I hear Judy Garland sing "The Trolley Song," I'm back on the Canarsie Trolley on my way to Sandra's house.

Jerry Stiller

CAST OF CHARACTERS

HOWIE SPARER—He was the quintessential "best friend," who was involved in more trolley escapades with me than any other neighborhood chum. It has been said that Howie was "the nicest guy you'll ever want to meet." Few would argue that point.

NORMA SPARER—She was everything a "big sister" is supposed to be; vigilant, concerned, tough, loving and beautiful. Norma had a mesmerizing effect on us and was not amused when I stayed out too late with Howie or we tried to kidnap a trolley car.

LEW KLOTZ—Lew and I were such close pals that a dozen years went by before I realized he really <u>wasn't</u> my cousin. He was amazingly like Howie in personality and disposition, Lew was a favorite to visit because it meant I would ride the Ocean Ave. speed cars to Sheepshead Bay.

SELMA KLOTZ—"Aunt" Selma's high-intensity temper would have been intimidating had she not been so hospitable to me whenever I visited Klotz Manor. That is, except for the time Lew and I engaged in a devastating pillow fight that eventually removed a lamp and pounds of plaster from Lew's bedroom wall.

ETEL FRIEDMAN—My very Hungarian grandmother was nicknamed "Gram." She ruled 582 Marcy Avenue with Queen Victorian elegance and vehemence. A DeKalb Ave. trolley ride to Loew's Metropolitan with Gram always was a treat; except when she did her end run around the Loew's Met usher who mistakenly insisted that there were "no seats down front." We got the seats but I was crimson with embarassment.

SIMON FRIEDMAN—Otherwise known as "Gramp," my grandfather was one of the wittiest men although "Gram" would have disagreed. His putty factory on Lorimer St. was a regular terminal for me. This meant a ride on the Lorimer Street line. He was affectionately known as "Uncle Sziga" (Jigger), Hungarian for Simon.

MOLLY FISCHLER—"Da Momma," as Howie referred to her, worked very hard to turn her son into a "mensch." It was a futile pursuit but she was a wise, warm and the best broiler of lamb chops in Williamsburg. Mom inadvertently got me started in sports with a trolley ride to Ebbets Field, circa 1937.

BEN FISCHLER—Oozing with energy, my dad worked harder than most while complaining the least. He never owned a car and as a result, streetcars became my limousines. Pop had one of the most infectious laughs and some of the best descriptive phrases ("I'll fix your wagon!") and, despite a sharp temper, never, uttered an obscenity (to me) as long as he lived. And this was a World War I sailor who served on a mine-layer in the North Sea.

ANNE YEARWOOD—Our splendid sixth-grade teacher at P.S. 54, kissed me in class on the day I completed an especially difficult crossword puzzle. She was strict but in a warm effective, teacherly way. A visit to her house on the Putnam Ave. line was memorable for her warmth and piano-playing.

LOTTIE FRIEDMAN—Aunt Lottie taught me how to play gin rummy and on one memorable Sunday shepherded me to Riis Park. Then, via the Flatbush Ave. trolley, we visited the RKO Kenmore on Church Ave. for a sidesplitting movie called "Prairie Chickens." On Election Day 1944, Lottie had me distributing Norman Thomas-for-president leaflets on behalf of the Socialist Party.

JOE FRIEDMAN—My mother's kid brother (Lottie's husband) maintained the family's naval tradition in World War II as a member of the Seabees. Joe and my "Catholic Uncle," John Cooke, taught me all there is to know about brotherhood and ethnic equality merely by their splendid relationship. Joe loved to say, "Let's maintain revolutionary decorum."

MUTTLE BERNSTEIN—King of the Handshake, he was my mom's uncle who operated a hardware store under the Broadway (Brooklyn) BMT el. From the front of Muttle's store, a streetcar buff could enjoy an endless cavalcade of trolleys including Utica-Reid, Sumner-Sackett and Ralph-Rockaway, to name a few.

MORRIS GOLD—The soldier with the John Hodiak moustache and the endless collection of magic tricks wooed Norma Sparer at the memorable Sparer VJ-Day party in Sea Gate. He later turned to making horseradish in the shadows of the McDonald Ave. Trolley. He's still magically making it very well, I might add.

SALLY SPARER—Howie's mom was a consummate professional—unconsciously a woman's libber four decades ahead of time—helping to run Spare-Way Food Products on DeKalb Ave. One of my all-time favorite people, Sally had humor, good nature and a 1937 Packard.

SIDNEY SPARER—It always was comforting to know someone like Sidney could make the American Dream work. Howie's dad built a pickle and mayonnaise empire right across from the DeKalb Ave. trolley. I knew he was an empire builder the day I went to Howie's bar mitzvah at Brooklyn Jewish Center and set my eyes on the swans carved out of ice and chopped liver.

NAT KLOTZ—Here was the ultimate gentleman–as in gentle man–who often hit the road, selling women's gloves in Upstate New York. Nat and my dad were like Damon and Pythias, which proved that my father had good taste in friends.

RALPH HUBBARD—We met and laughed our way through P.S. 54. Ralph lived around the corner on Myrtle Ave. and was involved in many an adventure, including the notorious Mister Montague demerit incidents.

CANTOR KWARTIN—A kid like me whose mastery of Hebrew was less than Talmudic required a patient, loving bar mitzvah teacher. Cantor Kwartin was all of that and the proof is that I actually <u>did</u> get bar mitzvahed.

ABE YURKOFSKY—Some of the "big guys" on the block could be officious and offensive but not Abe. Our only disagreement was over whether I should–or should not–scrawl the hockey score on Mrs. Yurkofsky's icy kitchen window pane. Mrs. Yurkovsky ruled against me but only after I had committed the sin.

NEIL BROWN—Classmate from third-grade through Eastern District High School and Brooklyn College, Brownie was the best all-around athlete in the neighborhood and regular partner in classroom pranks. Neil and I once nearly lost our bookends to shop teacher Montague.

One-half of the Passover table in 1948. (left to right) My mother, Aunt Helen, Aunt Hattie, Uncle Paul, Cousin Ira and Your's Truly.

SIDNEY GOODMAN—Aunt Charlotte's husband had been a semi-pro baseball player and bought me my first catcher's mitt. I can still feel the sting from the first pitch Uncle Sid hurled at me. Either he had the best arm on Vernon Avenue or I had the most tender palms.

DOCTOR SONENSHEIN—In the days when doctors still made house-calls, Dr. Sonenshein thought nothing of travelling all the way from Flatbush to our Williamsburg home. He had the ultimate "bedside manner," warm, soothing, dulcet toned and, most of all, competent. His office overlooked the Coney Island Ave. streamliner trolley route.

CHARLOTTE GOODMAN—She was one of my father's kid sisters; the mother of Cousin Sandee who had a vivaciousness about her that was shared by her sisters, my Aunts Beatrice and Natalie; otherwise known as Beadie and Tillie. Sandee taught me how to ride a two-wheeler bike which at the time—in 1942—was a major advance in my transportation growth.

ED FRIEDMAN—The most avid baseball fan in the family, my mom's brother was a partner in Lorimer Paint Works (the putty factory) and loaned me the company's 1939 Chevrolet for weekend use when I was in college. (I quickly blew the clutch.) He was a very sweet guy although Ed and my pop had a tiff at the plant that left a lasting scar.

FRANCES FRIEDMAN—Aunt Frances became my heroine when I discovered that she worked in an auto supply shop just a block from Ebbets Field. Visits to the Ed-Frances apartment on Linden Blvd. were treats thanks, in part, to the Flatbush Avenue trolley ride.

BEN FRIEDMAN—Sitting across from me at the Passover table, Uncle Ben invariably would provoke a smile by making silly faces just when Gramp was beginning his prayers. In a room full of funnymen, Ben could inspire laughter in me faster than anyone. After the trolleys disappeared, he patiently taught me to drive.

LUCIE FRIEDMAN—A native of Antwerp, Belgium, Aunt Lucie reeked with class. She blended an air of sophistication with down-to-earth humor and was the first to: a. offer me a cigarette (I refused); b. mix me a gin-and-tonic (I accepted); c. take me to the 1939 World's Fair; d. bake me a chicken a la king and, e. let me baby-sit (for daughter Joan).

Uncle Ed and Aunt Frances, in 1943. They never failed to give me the royal treatment after I rode the Flatbush Ave. trolley to their Linden Blvd. apartment.

SARAH AND JOSEPH FISCHLER—I vaguely recall riding the Ocean Ave. Line to see my father's parents, both extremely warm and sweet people. Grandpa Fischler, a very talented tailor, died in 1938, when I was six, before I really got to know him. Grandma, who soon moved to the Brooklyn Hebrew Home for the Aged, died a few years later. I remember one trolley ride on the Utica-Reid Line to see Grandma Sarah with my dad a few months before her passing.

GERSON SPARER—Gershy–or Goo–was Howie's big brother by about four years and, therefore, held in awe. He was the one who personally picked out the ox-blood-colored first baseman's mitt which became my punchball staple and nest for several sure-hits I somehow caught. Gershy's new post-war Buick established him as a Hall of Famer in our eyes.

HELEN FRIEDMAN—My mother's younger sister lived a floor below us at 582 Marcy and was like an older sister to me. The family athlete–she skied long before it was fashionable–Aunt Helen loved to take me on hikes with the New York Hiking Club. She once invited me to an overnight at NYHC's lodge in Budd Lake, New Jersey where I met my first outhouse (with flies large enough to have been supplied by Central Casting.) She died too young of a brain tumor.

JUDD FISCHLER—My East New York cousin, Judd was a couple of years older but not too old that I couldn't enjoy a visit to Ralph-Rockaway trolley country. No question, Judd had me rolling on the floor faster than the best funnymen on either side of the family, except for Uncle Ben. By the way, he still does!

Uncle Ben, who always made me laugh at Passover dinners, and Aunt Lucie, who made the best chicken a la king I ever tasted at my Marcy Ave. home in 1938.

JUDITH PELTON—Cousin Judy to me, Uncle Sam and Aunt Bea's daughter was a class act who lived for a time on the Ocean Ave. Line. Her dad, replete with wax moustache and rapier wit, was such a tonic to me, he was one of the few I allowed to visit when I was hospitalized with hepatitis. Humor-wise, Judith is a chip-off-the-old-block in the best sense of the term.

SANDEE GOODMAN—Uncle Sid and Aunt Charlotte's daughter was my age and so avid a baseball fan that she had eight-by-ten glossy photos of Brooklyn Dodgers heroes Pete Reiser and Peewee Reese hung in her bedroom. The Church Ave. trolley ran near Sandee's house. Her untimely death from diabetes was as much a crusher as Howie's and Aunt Helen's.

DAISY FISCHLER—Not many can claim to have a Daisy Blossom for a cousin. The daughter of Uncle Julius and Aunt Ceil–a couple of my top relatives–Daisy was, and still is, the most ebullient member of either family. I sometimes think that Good Health Seltzer is mixed among her veins and arteries. Judd's older sister is a winner; a tender, loving beauty.

HATTIE, PAUL AND IRA SHEIER—Three of the most vital, wonderful people in my life, Aunt, Uncle and Cousin lived in Albany. The home of the Toonerville-type Birney Safety Trolley that passed Uncle Paul's clothing store on South Pearl Street.

NON-TROLLEY COUSINS—Unfortunately, Lois, Richard and Paul Friedman were too young to have seen the trolleys. I love them anyhow.

CAST OF (TROLLEY) CHARACTERS

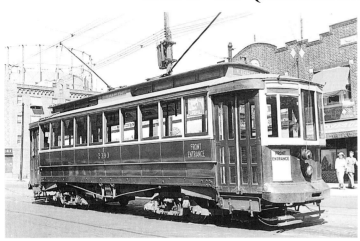
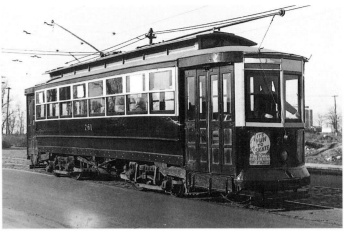

DOUBLE TRUCK CLOSED CARS & SEMI-CONVERTIBLES:
(THE GROANERS)

Their motors emitted a noise that sounded very much like the plaintive groan of cattle enroute to the slaughterhouse yet these old cars had a classic beauty about them. In their senior years, they carried themselves like royalty. I always fancied a car like the 761 as the Queen Mother of the rolling stock. (England's Queen Mother Mary had been a distant favorite of mine during the late 1930's and early 1940's).

Some of these patrician streetcars had open sides (semi-convertibles) in the summer while others were distinguished by the extended snout as in the the case of 761. But they had several beauty marks in common; the roof lines being one and the retractible front step being another; not to mention the motor sound which, at best, also could charitibly be described as the trolley version of the drone of bagpipes.

The ordinary closed cars, either single or double truck, were by far the most common in the history of the trolleys. These cars were unique in that the entrances and exits were arranged in a number of different configurations, depending on car size and the method of fare collection.

The main allure of the semi-convertible, built in 1900 by Eugene Chamberlain, was that the windows could either be removed and stored, or slid into wall pockets during inclement weather. The first five ever built were developed by the Brooklyn Heights railroad shops. These cars also featured push-buttons for passengers to signal the motorman to stop and Chamberlain seating, chairs that swung from the side of the car out to the aisle. Due to the installation of newer-style windows that could open, the semi-convertible look was discontinued.

CONVERTIBLES: (THE BREEZE CARS)

Long before air conditioning was even considered for surface transit lines, the Brooklyn trolley system had a better solution—genuine free air.

This was made possible by the convertible cars which offered enough open space to allow the balmy summer breezes to waft through the cars once the motorman pushed the controller into the speed position.

The convertible eliminated the need for separate cars for both winter and summer operation. Convertibles had two sets of side panels, both window panels and open bars for the summer. Panels were simply removed and stored, enabling a closed car to make the conversion into an open one. Either way, they too were groaners.

The cars themselves were large and powerful, most all were made of wood and steel. An all-steel car was built by Pressed Steel Car but the cars were too weighty. The convertibles lasted well into the fifties and never ceased to fascinate me. Unfortunately, very few ran in my neighborhood.

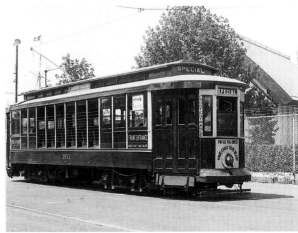

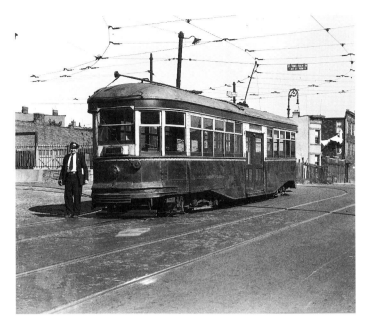

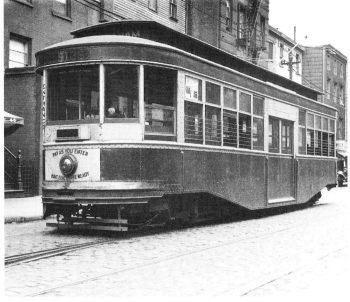

5000'S: (THE SEXPOTS)

Incongruous as it may sound, the 5000 series cars—with either the curved or square roofs—had a sexy quality about them. It had everything to do with their buxom dimensions coupled with curvy lines and other zesty features such as the roof ladder curving down over the left front of 5038. It reminded me of the distinctive over-the-eye wave of actress Veronica Lake's hair style.

In terms of body dimensions, the 5000's oozed all the brashness and brass of Mae West. You could almost hear the cars saying, in Westian tones, "Hey, young fella, why don't you step up and ride me some time?" Perhaps that's why when it came time for my friend Howie and I to kidnap a trolley, we chose the sexiest car on the lot.

The 5000's began a trend of entrances and exits located at the center of the body rather than at the ends. The doors were sliding, subway type, in design and were intended to increase the speed of passenger boarding. The car was large enough to seat 58 passengers, and folding seats were available at the center doors for riders if necessary. After Mayor Hylan put a stop to trolley trains in 1924, all 100 5000's were rebuilt into one-man cars. The unused center door was sealed shut and permanent seating was set up in front of it. They served most lines and were retired in 1946-48.

6000's TRAILERS: (THE SENSUOUS COUSINS)

Long before I began riding trolleys, the system would operate double-cars; the first with a motor and the second–the trailer–without means of propulsion but pulled by the lead car. I rode them most often on the Flushing Ave. Line.

These cars were similar in design to the successful 5000's except for the missing feature of a deck roof. These trailers were added due to the heavy flow of traffic on certain lines. After World War I, in 1919, 100 trailers were ordered from J.G. Brill and were numbered 6000-6099. Unfortunately the usage of these trolley cars was stopped in 1924, so 54 of the cars were renumbered, motorized and put into use. The rest were scrapped in 1932. They should not be confused with the more modern 6000's, built in 1931-32.

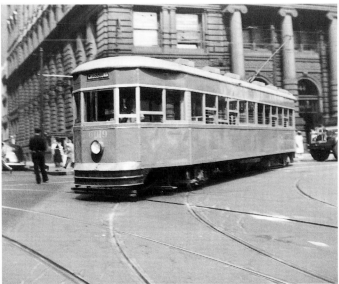

6000-6199: (THE PRETENDERS)

The more modern 6000 series car suggests an actor who aspired to an Oscar but never quite made it because—even though he looked good—he lacked the depth to be a star. Ubiquitous in Brooklyn during the 1930's and 1940's, the newer 6000 wanted to be a streamliner but fell short of the goal and also figured to be a smoothy and, again, just missed.

Which is not to suggest that it was thoroughly bereft of qualities. It did betray a handsomeness of sorts, had some neat interior appointments and could produce an arresting sprint on a long straightaway. Yet the 6000 promised more than it delivered and will always be remembered here as The Great Pretender.

Brooklyn and Queens Transit Company had ordered 100 cars built by J.G. Brill and one year later ordered 100 more, this time 50 were built by Brill with the other 50 from Osgood-Bradley. The two sets of cars had only minor differences. 6000-6099 were built with leather seats and 6100-6199 had wood seats and an electric "NEXT CAR" sign on the front side. The cars were comfortable and scenic due to the large windows. The automatic exit doors in the rear of the trolley were innovative. The 6000 cars motored along almost every main line and were all retired in 1951.

 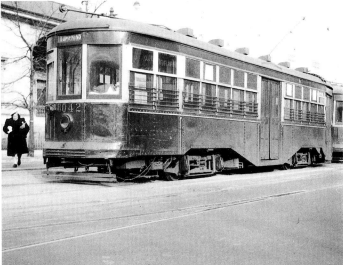

PETER WITTS (8000's): (THE DEBONAIRS)

A Cleveland streetcar engineer came up with a design for a drop-center entrance car and, lo and behold, Peter Witt's name became permanently attached to a genre that included a number of designs. But the best—and most common— belonged to Brooklyn's trolley network. As a kid, we all knew these well-proportioned, smartly-crafted trams deserved a name other than "the Kingston Avenue car," or "the Nostrand trolley."

They displayed all the airs of a sophisticated, lyrical gentleman as they danced along the tracks. Fred Astaire's name often came to mind until I learned that in trolley buff's lexicon they're known as the Peter Witts. That's a very gentlemanly name that befits this trim, terrific vehicle. Peter Witt. Fred Astaire. Same thing when it came to the 8000 series.

The Brooklyn City Railroad Company introduced the Peter Witts to Kings County. Originally, the passengers paid the fare to the conductor at the center before they exited the car. A special feature that set the original Peter Witt car apart from most other trolleys was the distinctive paint scheme called a spider's web or sunburst that was applied to the front, attracting full attention of travelers on Brooklyn lines.

Cars 8100-8199 and 8500-8534 were speed cars, well-designed and providing Brooklyn riders with an exceptionally fast run along Ocean Avenue.

PCC car 1095 is a Coney Island Ave. Car at Brighton Beach. 1071, going away, is a McDonald Ave. car near its West 4th St. terminal.

PCC'S: (THE ZEPHYRS)

Brooklyn led the nation in its development and use of the streamliners. Known in the trade as the PCC Car, the 1000 series had a unique personality that at the very least could be called attractive and at the very best could be described as ultra-beauteous. Yet, the most striking aspects of the 1000's, compared with her cousins, were its speed and sound.

The streamliners moved as fast as the fastest cars on city streets. Yet while its accelleration was a marvel, the silent motor and virtually inaudible wheel friction created an ironically sweet sound that could best be compared with a zephyr. (Not surprisingly, the top-of-the-line Lincoln automobile of 1940, when the PCC car was in its heyday, also was called The Zephyr.) The 1000 series trolley seemed so etherial that it appeared to be from another world. Perhaps zephyr is an understatement.

Developed by the Presidents' Conference Committee in the 1930's, these cars were not only ultra-modern in design but focused on improving performance. The PCC was built in numerous arrangements but most often they had a front entrance and center exit. The St. Louis Car Company was selected to build the first 100 cars. Ridership skyrocketed on those lines that received PCC's but the response fell on deaf ears; no more were built for Brooklyn. The original 100 lasted through 20 years of service and were scrapped in 1956.

It's a tribute to PCC design and sturdiness that many are still regularly operating in cities such as Newark, New Jersey and Toronto, Ontario and often provide better rides than their newly-built contemporaries.

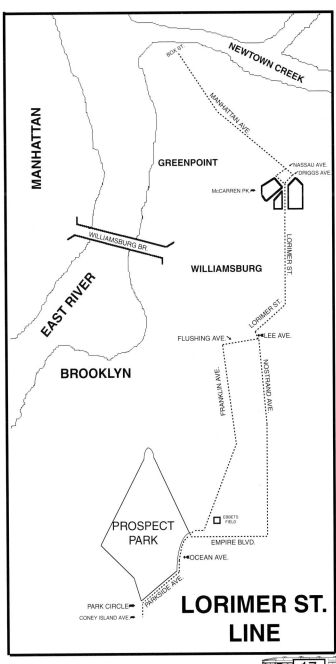

LORIMER ST. LINE

That's not me, but it's what I dreamed of doing on the ride to Grandpa Simon's putty factory on Lorimer Street.

CHAPTER ONE:
THE LORIMER STREET LINE

In many ways the Lorimer Street Line was my favorite and three destinations explain why. They would be grandfather's paint and putty factory, Ebbets Field, home of the Brooklyn Dodgers, and the McCarren Park swimm pool in Greenpoint. The Lorimer Street trolley took one to each of these destinations and I visited them quite often.
I will begin with Lorimer Paint Works because that's the first place I remember. My grandfather (on my mother's sic Simon Friedman, owned the paint-and-putty business on Lorimer Street between Marcy and Lee Avenues in Williamsburg section of the borough, On a good day, the plant was within walking distance of our three-sto brownstone (owned by my grandfather) at 582 Marcy Avenue, between Myrtle and Vernon Avenues, but on not-so-days, you took the trolley.

The Lorimer Street trolley, in our neighborhood, ran along Nostrand Avenue which was one very long block aw from our house. One strolled to the corner of Marcy and Vernon Avenues, turned right and then plied Vernon, which v my "home" block, to its dead end at Nostrand. I loved walking down Vernon because there was always a chance that encounter any one of several good pals, starting with my best friend—except for a brief interlude of ma unfriendliness—Howie Sparer, or other good chums like Abe Yurkofsky or Norman Kramer. When I got to the end Vernon, I hung a right turn at Al and Shirley's candy store (our favorite hangout by far) and walked past Katzma kosher butcher shop and John Mastromarino's barber shop, as well as John Buscemi's barber shop. (Can you imagine t barber shops rubbing shoulders on one block?) Finally, I'd arrive at the corner of Myrtle and Nostrand. I was now in shadow of the wonderfully slow but fantastically rhythmical Myrtle Avenue elevated line with its Victorian (Nostra Avenue) station just above.

While awaiting the trolley at Myrtle at Nostrand, a lot of exciting things could happen—or, at least they were excit for a rail fan like me. There was, for example, the possibility that a Myrtle Avenue trolley might thunder along a

Now I should point out that there was a major difference between a Lorimer Street streetcar and the Myrtle Avenue version. The Lorimer car was what the pros call a "Peter Witt Car," or 8000 series, which means it was designed in the early 1920's by a Cleveland trolley engineer of the same name. It featured, among other things, a drop center design at the middle doors. The Witt Car had very trim lines–almost perfectly symmetrical from stem to stern–and would be a marvel of design even today.

The car could be operated from both ends so that when it reached a destination, such as Empire Boulevard (Ebbets Field), the motorman merely got out, pulled down one trolley pole and put up the other. He then operated the car from the other end. By contrast, the Myrtle Avenue version, or 6000 series, was a one-ender. It was a more recent model and boasted its own brand of sleekness, particularly the sweep of the rear and its broader bow. But, in my mind, the Myrtle Avenue cars couldn't cut it, style-wise, with the Peter Witts on the Lorimer line.

What I liked most about waiting at the Myrtle-Nostrand junction was the possibility of the old, open-platform el cars braking into the wood-platformed station. Above all, or better still, I delighted in seeing a Myrtle Avenue car doing the crossover through the Nostrand-Lorimer tracks. My fascination over the crossover sounds is directly attributable to my intuitive drumming-rhythm psyche. I often think in terms of drum sounds and the report of steel wheels bouncing over the four-tracks tickled my ears. All crossovers are essentially the same, yet different, if you pay close attention to the nuances of their sounds, which, of course, I did with a passion. The Myrtle-Nostrand crossover lacked the smoothness of, say, Tompkins-Dekalb, which meant it sounded a loud, staccato--bum-bum-bum, bum-bum-bum, bum-bum-bum. This always had the hint of a derailment, although I never witnessed one.

When the Lorimer Street car loomed in view from three blocks away, (Hart Street–across from Public School 54, my second home), I immediately wondered whether my favorite seating location would be available in the trolley. That particular spot was the jump seat, a wooden slat that was directly to the left, behind the motorman's round wooden seat, or disk. This disk sat on a long thin pole which passed for his "chair."

Just out of the shop, 8283 of the Flatbush Line, sports the spider web logo which adorned the front of Brooklyn's Peter Witt cars in the 1920's before the 6000 series arrived. The Dracula poster was a less-permanent adornment.

The upraised slab of wood at the bottom left marked the end of the jump seat; my favotrite location next to the motormen.

From the jump seat, I had a perfect view of all the motorman's materiel, from the iron controller, which he operated with his left hand, to the brake handle on the right side and the bell pedal that stuck out of the floor next to his right foot and produced the trolley's "clang-clang-clang." If you sat right up there, you could learn how to run a trolley pretty quickly, especially when you paid as much attention as I did.

After the age of five, (1937), I wanted very much to be a motorman, so I did my best to imitate the operator from my jump seat. A vertical wooden piece was attached to the jump seat and it moved about an inch in either direction, as the trolley stopped and started. By gripping the upper part of the wooden piece with my left hand, I could push it forward to "start" the trolley and, of course, pull it back to apply the brakes. (No such wonderful contraptions were available in the more streamlined Myrtle Avenue cars.) I was like a second motorman.

The Lorimer Street trolleys alternated on Nostrand Avenue with the regular Nostrand Avenue cars. Since both were Peter Witt-style cars, you never knew which was coming until it was about half a block away and you could read the sign above the middle front window.

One thing I always liked about the Lorimer line was its destination sign "LORIMER–BOX." Lorimer was a lyrical sounding name that somehow reminded me of the actor Ronald Coleman, who happened to be my mother's second favorite, after Leslie Howard. The word "BOX" always intrigued me. "Why would a street be called BOX?" What was it like, all the way at the end of the line, in distant Greenpoint? (Eventually, I would explore Box Street on a trip to McCarren Park Pool which was not far from Box Street.) Only recently did I meet Newsday columnist Steve Zipay who actually grew up near Box Street.

The trip to Gramp's putty factory took me past the huge Sperry Gyroscope-Norden Bombsight plant that sprawled along Nostrand Avenue, from Stockton to Floyd Streets. This was followed by an assortment of small businesses all the way to Flushing Avenue where the tracks crossed both the Graham Avenue and the Flushing Avenue trolley lines. The cars on these lines were considerably older than the Peter Witts. They were one-enders but with a truly majestic look.

To the left, down Flushing Avenue, sat the enormous Brooklyn Naval Shipyard (Navy Yard to us). The Flushing crossover was smoother–almost imperceptible–than the one at Myrtle and Nostrand. We then wheeled ahead to Wallabout Street where, again, to the left was the Wallabout Canal, (soon to give way to enlargement of the Navy Yard), and the Wallabout Market which had an old-world

This is the corner of Lee and Flushing Avenues, a block from my grandfather's putty factory, which was around the corner from the trolley in the background. The Nostrand Line also used these tracks but without switching.

charm of its own. After passing Wallabout, I could see the red brick building that housed the Slattery Stove Company. It was then that the trolley pole rolled over the device attached to the overhead wire which automatically moved the switch from its straightway (ahead to Lee Avenue for the Nostrand Avenue car) to the right-hand curve, on to Lorimer Street. I got out of my seat and walked to the door as the motorman applied the brakes with three or four back-and-forth tugs on his brake handle, before he finally pushed it all the way to the left. He then pushed one of four big black buttons near the bottom of the coin machine and the wooden doors flew open. I trotted down the steps and on to Lorimer Street for the half-block walk to my grandfather's shop.

26 Lorimer Street was a rather unimposing structure. It had a gray, wooden door in front that always looked like it needed a good dusting. That was probably because one of the main ingredients in putty-making is a dusty white substance called "whiting" which was constantly being carted into the factory.

Once inside, I made a right turn into the glass-enclosed office where I'd usually find my mother poring over books. (She was the company secretary). My uncles Ed and Ben Friedman could be found, too, either on the phone talking to customers or chatting with the "Boss," my grandfather, Simon. Simon Friedman was christened "The Boss" by one of my favorite people, Uncle John Cooke who, at the time, was the company's bookkeeper. Uncle John, as I called him, had been virtually raised by grandmother, Etel Friedman, ever since kindergarten when his father died and his mother was unable to care for him. John Cooke and my Uncle Joe Friedman had become brothers so to speak and, as far as I was concerned, John Cooke was as much an uncle of mine as Ed, Ben or Joe, despite the fact he was Catholic.

Here's the entrance to the Lorimer car. I turned left past my favorite seat straight ahead. Notice the fare box with door buttons underneath.

Cooke was renowned for his sense of humor, dialect jokes and imitations of Lou Holtz, one of the most popular Jewish story-tellers of the day. But Uncle John kept his humor in check at "The Shop." My grandfather, Simon–himself a loving and witty man at home–was all business at Lorimer Paint Works so there was precious little time for comedy around the office.

After saying my "hellos" to everyone, I was granted my usual tour of the putty and paint machines. At one time, (1939), my father worked in the plant alongside a rugged, affable, Irishman named John Tracy, who could easily have been a double for James Cagney, the actor.

Dad and Tracy would bring me over to the putty-making machine which resembled a gigantic pot with an equally enormous roller–like an immense steel roller skate–that rumbled around the pot crushing the mixture of whiting, linseed oil and other aromatic elements which go into the making of putty. When the mixture was complete, either my dad or Tracy would pull a large silver lever that opened a chute. The fresh putty slid out into gleaming tin buckets which were lined up and pushed into place by one of the workers.

That's my Jewish Uncle Joe on the left and my Catholic Uncle John on the right.

In another part of the plant, a product called red lead paint was being manufactured. That didn't have the same appeal to me as the putty-making, partly because the machinery wasn't as much fun to watch and partly because I always was given a fresh, small can of putty to take home with me for play, as one would with a pack of molding clay.

Although others may not have thought that Lorimer Paint Works was a particularly wholesome place in which to work, I always enjoyed my visits there as a kid because: a. I was treated royally; b. I loved the smell of the place; c. The putty-maker never ceased to intrigue me; d. people like Tracy and my Uncle John were neat; e. I liked seeing my dad in his working venue; and f. I got a free can of putty to take home.

It was a short walk from the streetcar stop to the ballpark.

The very best way for me to get to Ebbets Field was by riding the Lorimer Street trolley. True, the BMT Brighton Line stopped at Prospect Park Station, only a couple of blocks from the ballpark, and the Tompkins Avenue trolley also went there, but it always seemed easier just to turn the corner and walk the one block to Nostrand where the Lorimer line ran. Thus, the Lorimer Street trolley figured prominently in this story. It was 1942 and the Brooklyn Dodgers were defending the National League championship which they had won the previous year. My friend, Howie Sparer, who had since moved from Vernon Avenue to 602 Montgomery Street in the Crown Heights section, was an avid Dodgers fan, while I–in a usual spirit of contrariness–had switched my allegiance over the winter to the St. Louis Cardinals, starring Stan (The Man) Musial and Whitey Kurowski.

This was a very hot summer day and I decided that it would be a good idea to take my Lone Ranger lunchbox with my grandmother's usual baloney sandwich on rye. "Gram," as I called her, also would fill the Thermos bottle with chocolate milk, but on this day, I suggested it would be interesting to fill the Thermos with ice cold Pepsi-Cola from the bottle.

"You can't do that!" Gram insisted. "The Pepsi will explode on the trolley." Darn! I couldn't figure out the logic of that but, half-Hungarian that I am, I surreptitiously poured the Pepsi out of the bottle and into my Thermos, quickly secured the lid, bade good-bye to Gram, and hustled out of the house, down Vernon Avenue to Nostrand. This time I hung a left at the corner of Nostrand and walked past Ralph's Shoe Repair Shop. Ralph was a jovial Italian-American who loved to sing opera and charm the ladies. He also was especially nice to the kids and always had a big "Hello" for me. I reached the corner of Willoughby Avenue and Nostrand, where marvelously, an old and well-preserved mansion guarded the southeast corner. We always regarded the mansion with a special reverence, because of its size and because whoever lived there—I was never quite sure who—was definitely rich.

I crossed Nostrand and, in no time at all, my Lorimer Street car had arrived. After handing the motorman the three cents–kids didn't have to pay the customary nickel fare–I decided to bypass the upright fare box with the fat, black buttons on the side, ignore the jump seat and take the step up to the regular passenger section of the car because something was on my mind–the Thermos of Pepsi and grandmother's warning. The passenger section of a Peter Witt car had brown, wood-slatted seats, each with an accompanying window. With luck, one could press the two handles on each side of the window and get it up to head-height which would guarantee a full view of the street and the possibility of a breeze as the trolley moved along.

I chose to move to the rear of the trolley because I was becoming increasingly worried. Perhaps my grandmother was right and the Pepsi would explode in the Thermos. But how great would the explosion be? As the Lorimer Street car crossed Dekalb Avenue and headed towards Gates Avenue, I had a vision of a headline in the next day's New York Daily Mirror: "MYSTERY EXPLOSION ROCKS BROOKLYN TROLLEY CAR— MANY INJURED." And all because I didn't listen to Gram. We had now reached Fulton Street and then Atlantic Avenue. Little droplets of sweat had crossed my brow as I convinced myself that a liquid time bomb was sitting in my Lone Ranger lunchbox. The entire trip to Empire Boulevard and Bedford Avenue consumed no more than a half-hour but it seemed like a lifetime to me. When the trolley finally reached Ebbets Field, I rushed out, dashed up the Bedford Avenue hill and met Howie in front of the bleacher box office. (The Dodgers always called the bleachers "The Pavilion.") We bought our tickets, hustled up the wonderfully long concrete ramps inside the stadium and got our front row seats in the bleachers.

Ebbets Field was called a "bandbox ballpark" for good reason. It was a bandbox. The stadium held about 32,000 seats and, except for right field and a bit of right center, these seats surrounded the grass with a closeness you wouldn't find in other ballfields. This was specifically true of the Ebbets Field bleachers which overhung center field. The first two rows, which usually were available to those who ran up the ramp fastest,

After the game we'd walk over to the Flatbush Avenue terminal for the hot-dogs at the stand (under the Coke sign; far left) near the BMT station. Then I'd hop on the Lorimer for the ride home. I once got a spanking exactly where the folks are walking across the street. The moment the BMT Franklin Ave. train surfaced from the tunnel portal beyond the fence, I instantly stopped crying. Trolleys and trains always had that mesmerizing effect, especially after my mother had given me a licking.

actually were once meant to be box seats but now cost the same 55 cents as any other bleacher seats. When you sat in the front row, as Howie and I did that day, you actually felt as if you were peering right over the pitcher's shoulder; that's how close it was.

A Cardinals-Dodgers game always was special in those days but this one had an extra added quality to it because the best pitcher on each team–Whitlow Wyatt of Brooklyn and Morton Cooper of St. Louis–was facing the other. That, however, was secondary to our capturing our seats and then my opening the Lone Ranger lunchbox and, most importantly, its Thermos bottle. I gingerly flipped the clamp on the outside, lifted the lunchbox cover and then grasped the Thermos. At that moment, I felt like a bomb squad expert who was trying to defuse an unexploded blockbuster. With extraordinary slowness and great care, I turned the Thermos cover until it was removed and then warily I unscrewed the inner cork, wondering if, at any second, the Pepsi would explode, as Gram had predicted. Finally, I heaved a sigh of relief as the cork came off. Inside I could see the amber, sparkling cola which I eagerly poured into the cup. The explosion was defused; the baloney sandwich was superb and the Pepsi the best I had ever tasted! The same could be said of the ball game. The Cards and Dodgers were tied 0-0 going into the top of the ninth, when St. Louis third baseman Whitey Kurowski, one of my favorites, belted a Wyatt fastball into the lower left field grandstand. Cooper shut out the Brooks in the bottom of the ninth and it ended 1-0 for the Cardinals.

I did a bit of childhood gloating with Howie. Then we ambled back to Empire Boulevard for the trolley ride home.

It was customary for Ebbets Field patrons to stroll out of the ballpark toward Bedford Avenue along the outfield grass. We exited via a big opening to the left of the Botany sign.

The trip to McCarren Park on the Lorimer line was exciting in another way. It marked the first time I had ever ventured with a bunch of friends to a public swimming pool, far out of my neighborhood. McCarren Park was one of those WPA Depression projects which provided some excellent recreation facilities for lower class families. It was located in the heart of Greenpoint, a neighborhood I had never before explored, since it was a good distance from our house and we had no friends or relatives living there.

The big feature of McCarren Park was its swimming pools; no pools were available in our neighborhood. If you wanted to cool off on a hot summer day, there were few choices for a Williamsburg kid: you could take the train to Coney Island, (a good hour's ride), or, take the Nostrand Avenue trolley to Flatbush Avenue and then a Green Bus Line fume-belcher to Jacob Riis Park, (a good hour-plus); or, you could visit a new, well-chlorinated public pool such as McCarren or Betsy Head Park which was in East New York.

My friends chose McCarren because it was closer and, once again, the Lorimer Street Line would deliver. The adventure here was taking it past my grandfather's shop for the first time in my life. That meant moving on to Lorimer Street, past Marcy Avenue, Tompkins Avenue, eventually to Broadway and on to Greenpoint, which was a world unto itself, at least in my eyes.

We reached McCarren Park in about a half-hour and I was truly dazzled by the size of the pools–much bigger than I had expected–and the vast number of swimmers. Until that day, I had never actually dived off the side of a pool into the water but but my buddies did it with such ease, I felt obliged to copy them–which I did, but not very well. Bellywhopping was more like it for me!

Before leaving McCarren, I made a point of looking for Box Street, which was far beyond the end of the park, as I remember it, and not particularly different from Nostrand Avenue or Tompkins Avenue or any other unimposing Brooklyn Street. It just happened to be at the end of the line where the trolley stopped; the poles were changed and the trolley went back in the other direction.

On the ride home, I was less interested in the Peter Witt car than I was in having survived my most intense afternoon at a swimming pool in my young life. It was a rousing day; I was exhausted and just happy to get home to show my parents that I could do very well at a Brooklyn swimming hole. Thanks, of course, to the Lorimer Street trolley which went to the destination of all destinations, Box Street.

Here's what the inside of a Lorimer Street car looked like en route to McCarren pool. With the windows wide open, you'd get a wonderful breeze. That is, if you were lucky enough to get the window to lift. The odds were usually 3-1 in your favor.

Moving closer to the front we observed the motorman's lair with the controller on the left. My unfulfilled ambition was to be a full-time trolley-driver.

CHAPTER TWO:
THE NORTON'S POINT LINE

Of all of Brooklyn's trolley lines, the Norton's Point route was one of the more obscure, not to mention shortest. Why then, you may be wondering, is it placed in such a high position in the book?

Actually, for two reasons, the first of which is that it was tangentially involved in what I like to call "The A[...] Trolley Car Kidnapping." The second being that for all it shortness, the Norton's Point line was a curiosity [...] Fontaine Fox's cartoon characters in "The Toonerville Trolley That Meets All the Trains," which I loved to read [...] York Sun newspaper.

To begin with, the Norton's Point line never even reached Norton's Point in those wonderful years of 194[...] when I rode it. Norton's Point is at the very tip of Sea Gate, which happens to be at the very western tip of Co[...] As its name implies, Sea Gate was surrounded by a gate—actually a formidable toll gate-type entrance which [...] undesirables from entering. Sea Gate was a private community of middle and upper middle class famili[...] Norton's Point on its far side.

(ABOVE) T[...]
Point car sp[...]
the right of [...]
Sea Gate.

(LEFT) That'[...]
of Sea G[...]
distance o[...]
Norton's Po[...]
beyond. Th[...]
favored poin[...]
Howie and I.

Where else but in Sea Gate could there be trolley tracks on your front lawn?

For a period of time, the trolleys emanating from the Stillwell Avenue, Coney Island BMT terminal actually entered Sea Gate and plied the tracks past the hotels and rooming houses all the way to Norton's Point and then returned to Coney Island. However, in 1944, when my friend Howie Sparer and his family began renting a house by the shore, the Norton's Point car ended its run outside the gate.

Nevertheless, the tracks inside Sea Gate were still in place and the Brooklyn and Queens Transit Company, which operated the trolley lines, had stored a number of the old Norton's Point cars inside Sea Gate. Not only that, but they stored them without fencing or any other protection. In other words, they were there for any twelve-year-olds to mess around with as long as no cops were present; which they usually weren't—Sea Gate being a forgotten part of the world.

To reach Howie's house from my home in Williamsburg entailed a grand tour de force of the Brooklyn transit system. It started with my getting on the GG (Brooklyn-Queens Crosstown) subway line at Myrtle-Willoughby station which was directly below our brownstone at 582 Marcy Avenue. In my room on the third floor to the rear (farthest away from Marcy), at about 10 PM, I usually was in bed. When I put my ear to the pillow, I not only could hear the GG local roll into the station but actually could hear the hiss and opening of the doors.

Forgive the digression. The GG line had been completed in 1937, directly under our house. It was virtually brand new and a delightful line to ride in many ways although I resented the fact that the front windows on the R-1-9 cars didn't open. Nevertheless they were big and afforded a good view.

The trip from Myrtle-Willoughby went past Bedford-Nostrand (subway station), Classon Avenue, Clinton-Washington, Fulton Street and then the huge express station called Hoyt-Schermerhorn in Downtown Brooklyn. At that point I alighted, crossed over to the other platform and took the A train to Franklin Avenue. From there it was up to street level and then a free transfer to the ancient Franklin Avenue shuttle which began its run at Franklin and Fulton.

In the summer of 1944 the Franklin Avenue line actually was a full-fledged express that ran all the way to Coney Island. After beginning its above-ground run at Franklin, it remained an el until it began its descent into the notorious S curve (that's where the 1918 Malbone Street wreck, killing 97 people, took place) and into the Prospect Park express-local station. The Franklin train left Prospect Park on the local tracks and then switched to the express rails about 100 yards south of the station. From there it was a deliriously joyful ride to Coney Island.

What made it so special for a rail fan like me was the jump seat by the front window and the fact that front windows on those 67-foot BMT "Standards" actually opened. That meant that you could either stand on a jump seat, or, if you were big enough, simply stand on the floor of the car and stick your head right out of the window, as the train rushed toward Brighton Beach.

The Brighton run began in an open cut, taking you with staccato click-clack speed past Parkside Avenue local station and into the Church Avenue express-local stop. From there, the run was especially picturesque, rolling around the Beverly Road curve with the tsuka-tsuka, tsuka-tsuka sound of wheels over rail joints that had the rhythm of Benny Goodman's "China Boy." It was then past Cortelyou Road and into Newkirk Avenue express-local station before the climb out of the cut and up to the above-ground embankment at Avenue H.

At this point you had a super vista of Flatbush as the train hurtled toward Kings Highway Station. To the left was the vast George Wingate Stadium, then the old Vitagraph Movie Studios and the remnants of the Long Island Rail Road line that once went to the Sheepshead Bay Race Track.

The next express stop was Sheepshead Bay from where the tracks went from the embankment onto the traditional street el structure which led to the 90-degree curve into Brighton Beach Station. Just before the curve, you could catch a good view of the Atlantic Ocean and Brighton Beach Baths.

Now the el moved on to Coney, past the Brighton extra-track "yards," Ocean Parkway's grand concrete station, and over the L.M. Thompson Roller Coaster, which adjoined Luna Park, and into West 8th Street Station. The train then crawled around another curve and into the multi-tracked Stillwell Avenue terminal which also received the West End, Sea Beach and Culver lines from other exotic parts of Brooklyn.

A ramp at Stillwell Avenue station led directly to the elevated Norton's Point line and, naturally, the trolley was sitting there awaiting the BMT's arrivals.

Here's where we got on and off at the Stillwell Ave. Terminal. It was a very exciting station because of the many converging lines.

The Norton's Point car is rolling up the ramp past Tony's Coney Island rooming house. I'd have been on that car leaving Howie's Sea Gate home for the BMT Stillwell Ave. Station at the top of the ramp.

Although the Norton's Point line occasionally had the 8000 series (Nostrand, Lorimer, Tompkins) cars that ran in my neighborhood or the 6000 series (Myrtle Avenue, Gates Avenue) more modern version, the Norton's Point car I remember was truly from a bygone era. It was a bulky but beautiful hunk of machinery that reminded one of a buxom burlesque stripper.

Rather than the simple lines of the Peter Witt car, the Norton's Point trolley had an assortment of geegaws including the hobbleskirt middle door and bizarre (at least to me) window arrangements.

But the strangest aspect of the Norton's Point line was the route itself. Instead of rolling on traditional trolley tracks on a normal street, it moved on regular railroad rails in what amounted to a back alley dirt-covered road past old Coney Island bungalows.

When I compare the Norton's Point run to the

(ABOVE) We'd often pass young bathers returning from the Coney Island beach to their summer bungalow colonies.

(LEFT) Unlike other lines, the Norton's Pointer felt more like a Toonerville Trolley than a normal streetcar.

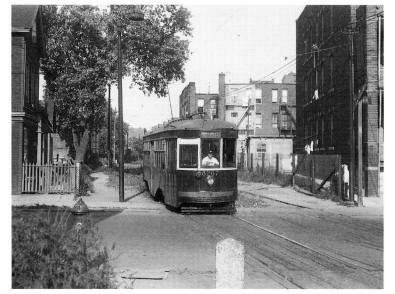

fictional Toonerville Trolley, I am hardly exaggerating. The tracks were supposed to be straight but the ride suggested that there were curves within the straight rails and the swing-and-sway and endless bounces of the car made one wonder what miraculous law of gravity kept it on the tracks. A Dramamine vendor would have made a fortune riding between Stillwell Avenue and Sea Gate.

By the time we reached Sea Gate at the end of the line, I felt as if I had gotten the kind of money's worth in thrills that one obtained from the Cyclone Roller Coaster, except that the Norton's Point car managed to turn crawling into an exciting art form.

(ABOVE) The Norton's Point car had its own special gate for entering Sea Gate.

(BELOW) This is precisely the car we wanted to hijack. To this day, the sign on the right puzzles me as it did in 1944.

At Sea Gate I walked over to the guarded entrance and told the security man that I was visiting Howie Sparer. He immediately lifted the gate, from where I walked a couple of blocks to Howie's house-by-the-sea.

Since Uncle Sam was still in the midst of World War II and rationing was at its height and such luxuries as bicycles and bicycle tires were in short supply, Howie and I had to make do with one old bike that was kept at his house. Which meant that we would ride each other around on the crossbar or take individual rides.

On one such double-ride, Howie rolled over a jagged walnut shell which was hard enough to pierce the tire and produce a hiss that was heard across Sea Gate; or at least so we thought.

In any event the tire was flat and there was no bike shop around to repair it so Howie and I disconsolately walked back to his house. As it happened, our stroll took us right past the storage area where the unused, old Norton's Point cars were basking in the son.

"Hey," I said, "why don't we stop and inspect the cars?"

Since there was nothing better to do, Howie, although not a train or trolley buff like me, agreed. So, he put down the bike and we walked over to the front door of the lead car.

It was slightly ajar and we soon discovered that with a sharp tug we could open it wide——which we did.

After looking both ways to determine that nobody was watching us, we climbed the steps that took us right up to the motorman's location. I sized up the controls and immediately got the feel of what was there to play around with, presuming that any playing would be done.

The controller's handle was to the left. It was different from the kind I was used to seeing on the Peter Witt Cars but it moved easily from right to left into the high position and was easy to push down from the "dead-man's" position.

To the right was the braking equipment with one notable exception—the brake handle was missing. I knew the motormen carried the brake handle with them and simply fitted it into place when they were ready to operate the trolley. For some reason, I had the notion that some motorman might have left his brake handle for us to use.

That presented a problem but I didn't mention it to Howie who wouldn't have known a brake handle from a brake shoe.

"Lets go in the back," I suggested, "and see if we can hook this baby up."

We climbed out of the Norton's Point car, looked both ways to see if anyone had seen us—the coast was still clear—and then walked along the dirt and gravel to the rear of the car. The trolley pole in back was being held in place by the roof hook.

"I think I can get it free," I said.
"Are you sure it's a good idea?" Howie said with surprising (for him) anxiety.
"What's life without a little adventure?" I shot back, stealing one of Howie's favorite lines.

I grabbed the thin but strong rope that rose, like a snake, out of a round steel container affixed to the rear of the car.

This is what it looked like once we opened the door and peered inside. Notice the brake handle is missing.

The trolley pole you're looking at is the one we tried to connect. It wasn't an easy maneuver

After getting a good grip on it, I pulled down and then to the side to enable the pole to clear the retaining hook on the roof.

Eureka! The pole was now free and clear and I could actually see the little wheel on the top of it. Now the trick was to connect the trolley with the overhead wire. Of course, the power may have been cut and it would all have been a waste of time if that were the case.

Connecting the wheel was more difficult than I had imagined. But I finally got it in the vicinity of the wire and—Just like that!--a loud singing of the trolley's motor could be heard. I had made the electrical connection; now the Norton's Point car was our's to kidnap.

Howie and I trotted back to the front of the trolley and climbed back into the cab. "I can move it," I said, "but I won't be able to stop the damn thing."

"What do you mean?" said Howie, who remained eminently trolley-ignorant.

"What I mean is that we can get the car going but I don't have a brake handle that can make it stop?"

"That's dangerous."

"That's right."

"I don't think we should take it for a ride," Howie insisted with impeccable logic. "What happens if some kid runs across the tracks and you can't stop the trolley?"

"You'll run in front and warn people away."

"Yeah, but what if you come to a hill and it starts running out of control?"

I thought for a moment. Sadly, I concluded, "you're right."

We glumly climbed down from the cab, walked back to the rear of the car. I tugged at the rope and gingerly pulled the wheel off the overhead wire. Just as suddenly, the hum-a-hum-a-hum of the electric motor stopped.

Eventually, I worked the trolley pole back into its stationary position under the hook, took one last look at the Norton's Point Car that promised us a wild adventure and then walked back home with Howie pushing his forlorn flat-tired bike.

I consoled myself with a bromide my mother had taught me; discretion is the better part of valor. To close the adventure, Howie and I walked to the end of the line where the tracks fell into the sea and wondered about what might have been if the trolley had a brake handle in its proper place. Our conclusion was that Stan Fischler would have been Brooklyn's answer to Casey Jones!

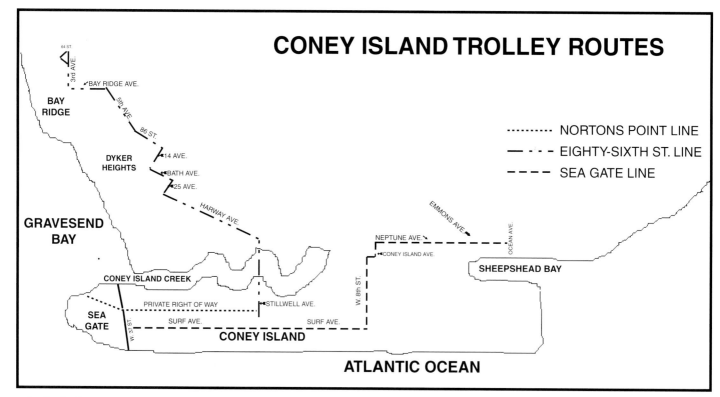

This is Norton's Point. The pilings in the distance were part of a wharf that ocean going steamers could dock at. During World War I soldiers embarked to Europe from this pier after riding the trolley.

CONEY ISLAND TROLLEY ROUTES

64 ST.
3rd AVE.
BAY RIDGE AVE.
BAY RIDGE
5th AVE.
86 ST.
DYKER HEIGHTS
14 AVE.
BATH AVE.
25 AVE.
HARWAY AVE.

GRAVESEND BAY

·········· NORTONS POINT LINE
— · — · — EIGHTY-SIXTH ST. LINE
— — — — SEA GATE LINE

EMMONS AVE.
NEPTUNE AVE.
OCEAN AVE.
CONEY ISLAND AVE.
W. 8th ST.
SHEEPSHEAD BAY

CONEY ISLAND CREEK
PRIVATE RIGHT OF WAY
STILLWELL AVE.
SEA GATE
W. 37 ST.
SURF AVE.
SURF AVE.
CONEY ISLAND

ATLANTIC OCEAN

CHAPTER THREE:
THE TROLLEYS OF CONEY ISLAND

roadway of Coney Island is called Surf Avenue, which is well-named since it runs parallel to the Atlant
block from the Coney Island Boardwalk and the surf beyond.

since my first visit to Coney Island in 1937, Surf Avenue has had a mesmerizing effect on me, mostly b
s, sounds and smells. Surf Avenue means the Cyclone Roller Coaster, The Wonder Wheel, the world
Nathan's Hot Dogs and, in an earlier part of my life, Feltman's Pavilion and Luna Park.

rolleys that ran along Surf Avenue covered the Coney Island gamut, starting with the public handball co
rkway and moving west past the Cyclone, Faber's Poker, the electric bump cars, Nathan's, the Stillwe
way terminal, Loew's Coney Island and incredible Steeplechase (The Funny Place), the ultimate an
s time.

rt of its route the trolleys of Surf Avenue paralleled the Norton's Point Line and eventually terminated
: of Sea Gate. It featured both the traditional Peter Witt and several older model cars and was memora
al incidents including one involving a remarkable day of childhood gambling and another being the cel
ay in August 1945 when Sally Sparer treated her son, Howie, and I to the ultimate spend-all-y
on.

ambling episode was rather strange in that neither Howie nor I were particularly interested in cards, cra
h betting pursuit. However, on this not-particularly-hot summer day in July 1944, we walked from Su
ardwalk and noticed an interesting establishment called Faber's Poker.

e first explain that our traditional game of chance in Coney was Skee-Ball. For a nickel, which was ins
depository to the right of a bowling type surface, you pulled a lever and five wooden balls rumbled
nged together with a hearty "CLUNK!" and you were ready to roll. The idea in Skee-Ball (I always
as to roll the ball up the ramp and into the center of three bullseye-type receptacles. If you missed th
), you had a chance at the next-best (50), the next-next-best (30) or the worst (10. It also was possible to
han	whereupon the ball fell into the bottom receptacle and you got nothing

If you reached a certain level of points you received a coupon or two which could be redeemed for some relatively chintzy item such as a rabbit's foot or toy dog. To win anything worthwhile–like a portable radio–you'd have to spend two weeks at Skee-Ball and get a whole bunch of 100s.

For some inexplicable reason, Howie and I decided to bypass Skee-Ball and headed towards Faber's Poker more out of curiosity, I guess, than anything else. The poker game–also called Pokerino at another establishment down at the Boardwalk–always seemed a more adult kind of pastime and didn't have the mildly athletic quality of Skee-Ball.

In any event it was 11 A.M. and Faber's poker was virtually empty

except for Howie and I. We timidly walked in and ambled over to the row of candy store-type stools and studied the game.

For a nickel you received five Spalding-type black rubber balls which were rolled under a glass partition into any one of an array of large holes which had card signs–from Jack of Clubs to King of Hearts–next to them. The trick was to get a winning poker hand and for that you received coupons.

Howie and I did not expect to stay very long at Faber's Poker because it appeared very intimidating and not that much fun, but we still figured we'd give it a try.

We began rolling the balls under the glass and were fascinated at the manner in which they caromed from one hole to another, off the backboard and, almost inexplicably, into one of the holes. There seemed to be little rhyme or reason for the direction taken by the balls and with very little strategy applied, one could get the balls to where you hoped they'd do some good.

But lo and behold, on the very first try, Howie got three Jacks and I did something equally good and we both wound up with a pair of coupons. Just for the hell of it, we decided to check and see what we could get with them and it turned out that a Faber's Poker coupon was worth a lot more than one for Skee-Ball.

(RIGHT) There's the poker arcade on the left in the shadow of the awesome Cyclone with Feltman's Pavilion in the background. Although Nathan's Famous, further down Surf Ave., got the publicity, Feltman's was first with the great-tasting hot dogs in Coney Island.

(BELOW) After collecting my Coney Island bounty, I headed for the BMT at the Surf Avenue entrance on the left. The modest facade hardly did justice to the massive terminal beyond. When it originally opened as part of the vast Brooklyn Rapid Transit empire, Coney Island became a haven for the masses.

Hey, we figured, why not try our luck again. So, we returned to the tables and won and won and won and won. It seemed as if every time we rolled a ball, something good happened until we ran out of nickels.

Taking our coupons to the prize area, we both decided that it would be a good idea to bring home some items to make our mothers happy. I remember picking out a sugar dispenser with a special red plastic cap that guaranteed to measure one teaspoonful with every turn. I also picked out some kitchen glassware, a salt-and-pepper set and some other <u>chotchkes</u> (items of no special use but which looked like fun) that would persuade mom that a poker game was worthwhile.

I considered this a remarkably fruitful bonanza and could hardly contain it all on the BMT ride home. It was also difficult to contain my emotions. I was sure that my mother would consider me a saint for delivering so many vital items for her kitchen use so when I finally made it home with the bounty, climbed up the stairs to our house and showed her what I had in the bags, I expected a grateful hug and kiss.

To my utter amazement–not to mention dismay–-my mom was less than thrilled. It wasn't that she bawled me out–that didn't happen too often–but she hardly appreciated the luck of Faber's nor did she really believe that the sugar dispenser that guaranteed one teaspoonful with every pour was one of the world's greatest inventions. As for the other items, her general reaction was, <u>EH</u>! It left me with only one reaction: back to Skee-Ball.

Easily the best Skee-Ball night of all took place in the summer of 1945 as World War II roared to a close. Howie and I had been Bar Mitzvahed that spring and the Sparers once again were renting their house in Sea Gate.

It was the last year of the War and the tide had clearly turned in the Allies' favor. Our Marines were mopping up in the Pacific and the Nazis had finally capitulated in Europe. A rare feeling of patriotic euphoria gripped the country and, of course, Howie and I shared it, having lived the most important parts of our lives from the war's beginning (1941) through the dénouement.

Now in mid-summer we all sensed that the end was near. The atom bomb had devastated Hiroshima, followed by the H-bomb that wasted Nagasaki. On this morning, after Howie and I had spent some time at the Sea Gate Beach, word came over the radio that the Japanese had finally surrendered.

It's difficult to convey to a youngster of today what an emotional involvement we had in World War II. The feeling of patriotism experienced then is no longer a part of our lives and the intensity with which we followed the battles–from El Alamein, to D-Day to the Battle of the Bulge–was unmatched in my life except, perhaps, for some Stanley Cup playoff thrills.

News of the Japanese surrender set off a chain reaction of celebrations with people unabashedly hugging in the streets, dancing on sidewalks and, of course, planning the party of all parties.

In Sea Gate, we celebrated two ways. First, there was an adult party at the Sparer's house that got underway about 6 P.M. and ran on into the night. At about 7 P.M. Sally Sparer gathered Howie and I, stuffed us in her 1937 Packard and drove to Brighton Beach Avenue, where the BMT el rumbled over the seaside shopping district.

Brighton Beach Ave. sizzled with a vibrancy that was at once a product of its diverse shops and the famed Brighton Beach Baths at the corner of Coney Island Avenue where the BMT el turned north toward Manhattan. One of the shops on Brighton Beach Ave. was Aufrichtig's Grocery Store, run by Max and Ted Aufrichtig. The former would become father of eventually-to-be broadcasters Marv, Al and Steve Albert, not to mention grandfather of play-by-play man Kenny Albert. (Interestingly, the Aufrichtig grocery is still family-run and remains at the same Brighton Beach Avenue location.)

Sally, a delightful, business-like woman, spirited us to a Chinese restaurant for dinner. Until then, a Chinese meal for me consisted of egg drop soup, chicken chow mein–with plenty of Chinese mustard–and tea with almond cookie. It usually cost 85 cents at Yee Ping Hing on Tompkins Avenue. To this day it was the best meal for the money in the universe.

But this was to be the Chinese dinner of my life. Sally ordered the works but the star attraction for me was shrimp with lobster sauce. I had never seen a shrimp in my life, let alone ate one. Lobster sauce was an accompaniment so romantic and aromatic, I could hardly believe that I was being graced with such a plate.

The meal was beyond words and I savored every moment of it but especially the arrival of the lobster itself. Why it seemed so beautiful in its red hue and well-sculpted claws and fuselage to even eat. But the Sparers wasted no time desecrating the crustacean so I soon joined in and became a lobster fan for life.

After dinner, Sally drove the Packard a few blocks to Coney Island where the air was crisp and ever-so-slightly cool. Horns were blowing, people were celebrating and the rides were banging and clattering all over Surf Avenue.

Until that night I had never had the experience of riding a roller coaster although the thought had entered my mind from time to time. A merry-go-round or bumping cars had been our speed until then but V-J Day had come and now I was to move up a notch in the Coney thrill department.

Sally walked us over to the L.M. Thompson Scenic Railway which was directly across Surf Avenue from the Cyclone. We entered Thompson on Surf but the ride itself described a northerly route under the BMT el and then out in the direction of Coney Island Creek.

I was awfully frightened about the roller coaster. Howie didn't betray any emotion. Sally had bought our tickets and now we were on line awaiting our fate. Naturally, I was trying to figure out every possible way out of this mess but I knew that there was no backing down.

My first roller-coaster ride was on the Thompson Scenic Railway right behind the rear of the trolley (twin towers in the distance.) The spires of Luna Park adjoin B&B carousel, the best merry-go-round in Coney.

At last the five-car coaster rumbled in from its run, the riders climbed out and we walked the wooden plank to get into our seats. We were located in the rear which I thought might make a difference although I did not know how. The attendant locked us in and then, with a slight jerk, the cars rumbled off, under the el and then up and up and up toward the Thompson's peak.

We now were away from the lights of Surf Avenue. The roller coaster clattered so sharply you could practically count every <u>click-clack</u> as the grips underneath bit into the steel pulley. It was dark, wonderful and scary. I unconsciously held my breath as the click-clack had stopped and we reached the top. There was nothing but blackness and the outline of factories on the other side of Coney Island Creek. I assumed that once we headed down the incline, it would be the last sight on earth for me.

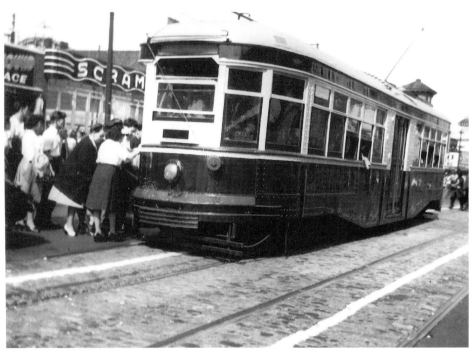

This is what we looked at from the top of the roller-coaster. The trolley riders are doing what the sign on the building suggests. Scramble was a good ride but the Bobsled, Cyclone and Wonder Wheel were the best. Right behind was the carousel with gold rings. Grabbing a brass ring—which we occasionally did—guaranteed a free ride.

The five-car coaster train plunged over the edge and I saw nothing but an abyss in which a part of my body seemed to be flying. I gulped the gulp of Gulliver as the car rushed downward and just as suddenly reached the bottom, climbed and then veered to the right.

Remarkably, I was still alive. That was one good thing. The other was that I actually was enjoying this ride. I knew that after the first hurdle, the worst was over—and it was. From there, the Thompson was a breeze and just to prove it, Howie and I did a second trip right after the first. We had been hooked on roller coasters.

After that, Sally ushered us to the Skee-Ball where there was no limit on the amount of nickels we could obtain. It was a Skee-Ball freak's delight and we had enough coupons for some cockamamee oversize mug or something–nothing that I would dare bring home to mother on another night, but what the hell, this was V-J Day.

Now, it was on to the Steeplechase--The Funny Place.

Unlike most of the Coney Island attractions which were individual rides, like the Bobsled, Thunderbolt or the Whip, Steeplechase–the Funny Place—was a self-contained amusement park under an enormous white shed. Its logo featured a large, toothy smiling head of a man and it was sprawled over enough different places to have it embedded in one's mind. When you thought of the Steeplechase, you immediately envisioned the smiling man and the founder of the Funny Place, George C. Tilyou.

To get into the Steeplechase, you purchased a large round coupon which had about 20 separate rides listed. Each time you went to a ride, your card was punched until you had completed the run of attractions.

By far the best part of the Steeplechase was the ride that gave the amusement park its name. It consisted of five merry-go-round type horses which were lined up next to each other on metal monorails. Each horse sat on a rail which snaked around the entire perimeter of Steeplechase, from Surf Avenue to the Boardwalk and back.

The idea, of course, was to have your horse win the race. When all five horses were occupied, the riders were strapped in, a bell went off along with the electrical current which propelled the nags.

While "The Horses," which is what we called them, didn't have the up and down thrill of a roller coaster, they did have a special quality all their own because of their speed and the fact that you rode them in open air through all of interesting nooks and crannies of the amusement park. And, on top of that, there was the excitement of a race itself.

Although each of us was strapped on the horses, there also was the fear of being thrown off, particularly at some of the sharp turns which were taken at what we thought was high speed.

On this night, Howie and I got a special kick out of the ride because we normally rode the horses in the afternoon. In the evening, with the amusement park buzzing, Steeplechase had an aura all its own. Don't ask me if my horse won that night, because it really didn't matter to me. What mattered was the breathtaking event itself.

Steeplechase had a few other winners. One was what seemed to be the world's highest sliding-pond; an expanse of undulating wood that began at the roof of the shed and sent you sliding endlessly down to the bottom. I needed an awful lot of nerve to negotiate it because heights and I don't get along that well.

Another feature that was more intriguing than fun was a curved, sliding tunnel that began about 40 feet above and deposited you on to a series of moving, circular wooden plates that eventually dumped you off to the side. The slide was great fun but I always seemed to cut my arm while moving from disk to disk. My memories of that one are not very fond.

We spent an hour at Steeplechase and then gathered around Sally, returned to the Packard which headed along Surf Avenue to Sea Gate. When we got there the V-J Day party was in full swing at the Sparer villa by the sea. Sidney, Howie's, dad, was there. Howie's older sister, Norma, who I had known very well, was arm and arm with a handsome man with a moustache who reminded me of the actor John Hodiak. For some reason, I got the feeling that they really liked each other. He was introduced to me as Morris Gold, a tall, nice man, who obviously had fallen in love with Norma Sparer.

Eventually she became Mrs. Morris Gold and that was my last memory of V-J Day, 1945 and the Surf Avenue trolleys.

Norma's wedding picture with her brother Howie on the left and her parents on the right. At the time of the nuptials, Sally and Sidney Sparer had become big-time food product tycoons.

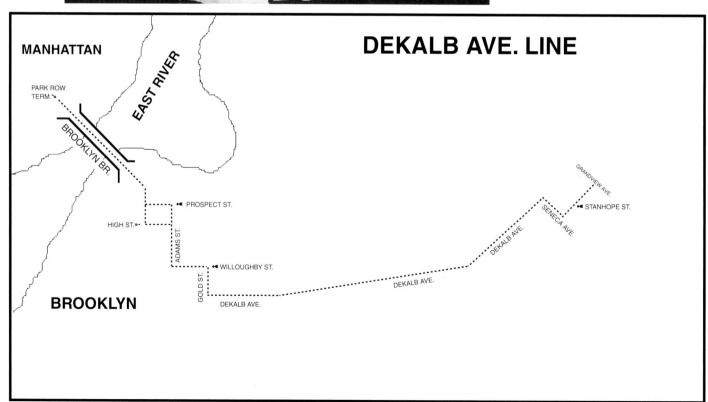

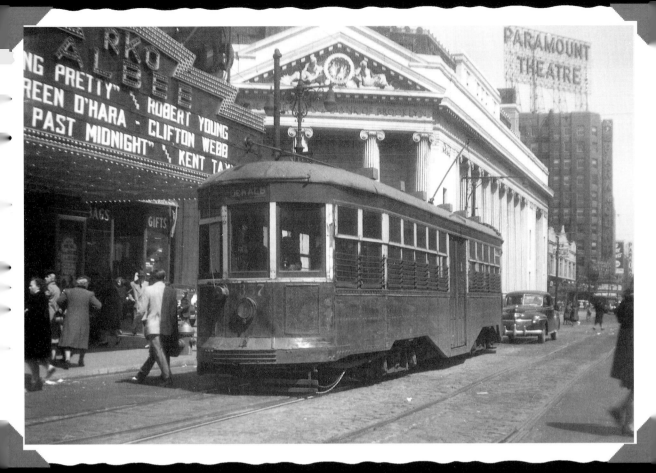

The DeKalb was a favorite because it took us to Downtown Brooklyn and some of the best movie houses in the world.

CHAPTER FOUR:
THE DEKALB AVENUE LINE

he DeKalb Avenue Line, which ran four blocks from my house, was responsible for one of the worst bawlings-
suffered in my young life.

t was the result of a rather wonderful adventure in Downtown Brooklyn that eventually led to the discovery
ie house and the further discovery of four very funny people known as The Marx Brothers.

Here's how it happened: On Saturday afternoons, Howie and I often frequented the Kismet Theater, which was
movie house on DeKalb near Tompkins Avenue, around the corner from one of our favorite drops-ins, The Airp
.

perated by a husband-and-wife team, the Airplane Store really wasn't called that by its owner. The sign in front
'LER'S HOBBIES, and, in fact, the Airplane Store was a typical–though miniscule–hobby shop that feat
ything from electric trains to model boat kits to you-name-it.

ut the most popular item, according to us, was hanging in the front window display. It was a Supermarine Sp
sh fighter plane which was one of the mainstays of the Battle of Britain. The Spitfire symbolized the Airplane S
use model aircraft was one of the most important things in our young lives, in 1944, when World War II was a
nt.

Perhaps the most amazing thing about the Airplane Store was its size. It was one of those, you-have-to-take-
-down-to-get-inside kind of places. It had only two aisles which reached the counter at the end where Mr. or

Neither was particularly nice but, on the other hand, they weren't bad people either. What really mattered was their inventory which featured a healthy stock of model plane kits, which I would buy on a regular basis and then slave over on the living room table while the piercing aroma of airplane cement–or the Duco variety–wafted into my nostrils. Little did I realize in those naively youthful days that one could get high on that stuff.

More about the Airplane Store and model-making another time. Back to DeKalb Avenue. On this particular Saturday afternoon there was a lousy movie playing at the Kismet Theater so Howie and I decided to venture Downtown and, perhaps, find a good flick there.

I met Howie at his house, on Vernon Avenue, just a couple of buildings east of Nostrand. At that

A half a block from the corner of DeKalb and Tompkins sat the greatest little toy store in Brooklyn. Cutler's Hobbies is that tiny shop right behind the woman at the rear of the trolley.

point in time, both of his parents, Sally and Sidney Sparer, worked at their pickle-and-mayonnaise plant on DeKalb near Marcy Avenue. When his parents were away, Howie was supervised by his older sister, Norma, who was a very attractive woman, then in her late teens. For all her beauty, Norma also was a very intense and tough female, although none of her anger ever had been vented on me—at least not until this fateful day.

After meeting Howie at his apartment, two stories up, we strolled over to DeKalb, passing Willoughby Avenue, a street on which neither of us had any friends—I never could figure that out—then Hart Street which was our rival in punchball, softball and whatever other sport we happened to be playing. Next was Pulaski Street, where our school chum, Harvey Mandel, lived and, finally, DeKalb.

The DeKalb Avenue trolley came all the way from Ridgewood, which was a section of Brooklyn that was virtually foreign to me. I vaguely knew that there had been a German population there at one point in time but in the midst of World War II, no German-American wanted anything known about his heritage; if he knew what was good for him.

I did know that the DeKalb Avenue line eventually crossed Broadway (Brooklyn) and then headed west past Lewis Avenue, Sumner Avenue, Throop Avenue, the Kismet Theater, Tompkins Avenue, Marcy Avenue and finally, Nostrand where we boarded.

DeKalb cars usually were the same 8000 series Peter Witt-style trolleys that rolled along the Tompkins, Nostrand and Lorimer lines so the fascination was not so much in the equipment as it was in the areas through which it operated.

What made DeKalb special was the variety of scenery during the trip. We passed the East Brooklyn Savings Bank at Bedford Avenue. That was my home bank; the one that started me saving with bankbooks at P.S. 54

Looking sharp as ever, DeKalb 8442 rolls to its right off the Brooklyn Bridge.

back in the second grade. Seeing that sprawling, pillared bank building always gave me a sense of security.

At Franklin Avenue we passed the State Theater which, like the Kismet, was owned by the Interboro Theater chain. It had virtually the same style of marquee as the Kismet but always ran films at least two weeks after they had appeared at "our" theater. We enjoyed comparing films but, somehow, never ever went to the State Theater. It was, in a sense, considered below us although the price for a ticket was exactly the same as the Kismet.

After passing a row of factory buildings, we approached Pratt Institute, an oasis near Hall Street, where my mother

frequently wheeled me in a baby carriage during my earliest years. That was followed by the approach of Fort Greene Park, the imposing Revolutionary War Prison Monument and a long downhill sprint to Flatbush Avenue Extension and the Paramount Theater with its longer-than-long marquee that extended from well into DeKalb Avenue all the way around to Flatbush Avenue Extension.

The Paramount was one of my favorite first-run theaters, partly because it was there that I saw my first basketball game. If you can believe this, in 1942 the Brooklyn Dodgers baseball team formed an off-season barnstorming basketball squad and played semi-pro teams. One such game was played on the enormous Paramount stage, and I was there to witness it with my dad. It was more of a novelty act than a game but seeing the Dodgers anywhere was a kick.

(ABOVE) That endless marquee of the Brooklyn Paramount hooked all the way around to Flatbush Extension. By this time we were within striking distance of the spiffy Fulton Street department stores.
(BELOW LEFT) This is what I saw ahead of me as we passed the DeKalb-Flatbush crossing with Ben Tucker's Hudson Bay Fur Company on the far left.
(BELOW RIGHT) Loeser's Department store is standing right behind the bus. It had a terrific toy department at Christmas time and was the first stop for Howie and I during gift-buying expeditions led by our mothers.

The corner of DeKalb and Flatbush Avenue Extension also was the gateway to Downtown Brooklyn. At this point one's excitement level rose as did the sense of sight and smell. The aroma of hot dogs emanated from the Dodgers Cafe. There was the rumble from the ancient Fulton Street elevated line heard more distinctly as the DeKalb Avenue trolley passed the white, domed Dime Savings Bank building. The trolley skirted the RKO Albee Theater (on a par with the Paramount), and then switched on to the Gold Street tracks, after facing Frederick Loeser's department store, one of Brooklyn's finest.

(left) One of the most impressive sights visible out of the right side windows was the handsome Dime Savings Bank building.

(below) The Lido and Paris-Court Theaters were straight ahead down Court Street on the right behind Borough Hall and the big Municipal Building.

Loeser's was followed by Namm's Department store, which was just as big but not as popular in our eyes because its toy department didn't match up as well as Loeser's. But the biggest department store of all–a brand-new building–was next. That would be Abraham & Straus, otherwise known as A&S. At the far end of Fulton Street sat the Loew's Metropolitan Theater, a favorite of my grandmother's, Gage & Tollner's splendid restaurant and, finally, stately Brooklyn Borough HalThe DeKalb Avenue Line headed to the Brooklyn Bridge. But Howie and I got off and walked to Court Street, where we began our search for something interesting. None of the flicks at either the Paramount, Albee or Loew's Met interested us and, frankly, we had given up hope of finding any movie to see.

We took a left turn at Court and walked south. This was new turf for Howie but not for me. My Aunt Helen Friedman had for years worked for a goggles-maker named Harry Biegeleisen in a plant on Bergen Street not far from Court, so I had ventured around there a few times and was especially taken by a Pyramid Auto Supply Store which also carried some especially neat toys and games in its windows. (I was always attracted to stores that carried more than one item–such as auto tires and toys.)

As Howie and I walked along Court, we became taken by a difference in ambience. There was a foreign element that was strikingly different from our Williamsburg community and also a perceptible sense of toughness. This did not appear to be the most hospitable of neighborhoods but, what the hell, we plowed on to see what there was to see, fully expecting to be attacked by a gang.

Across the street to the right we noticed a movie theater with the strange name, Paris-Court, or maybe it was Para-Court. Whatever, it was featuring a picture that did not interest us so we moved further south. Lo and behold, there was another little movie house on the next block, the Lido.

The marquee proclaimed, "Double Feature–John Tierney as Dillinger and The Marx Brothers in Horsefeathers."

This was as weird a double-bill as anyone could imagine. Dillinger was a relatively new film while Horsefeathers dated back to the early 1930s. Neither Howie nor I had ever seen The Marx Brothers and were only vaguely aware of them. The Lido Theater was worth a try.

We entered early into Horsefeathers and never laughed so hard in our lives. This was the spoof on college life with Groucho as Professor Wagstaff of Huxley College. Line after line had us on the floor as the characters of Groucho, Chico, Harpo and Zeppo were like no comedians we had ever experienced. Groucho opened with an address to the students. "Any questions?" he asks. "Any answers? Let's have some action around here. Who'll say 76? Who'll say 17.76? That's the spirit! 1776!" He starts a conversation with Zeppo, playing his student son. The retiring president of the college interrupts to tell Groucho. "I am sure the students would appreciate a brief outline of your plans for the future." "What?" barks Groucho. The man repeats himself, word for word. "You just said that! That's the trouble around here: talk, talk, talk!" exclaims Groucho. And so it went.

Howie and I laughed so much we decided to see Horsefeathers over again after Dillinger (a good movie) had ended. By the time we had left the Lido it was late afternoon, but we didn't think much of it. We retraced our steps toward Fulton Street and then walked past all the department stores to the Albee Theater where DeKalb Avenue begins.

(ABOVE) Here's where we turned around to see a trolley coming across from Fort Greene Park, but we decided to walk the rest of the way.

(BELOW) The DeKalb Ave. trolley has just passed the Brooklyn Technical High School at Clinton and DeKalb. It's one of New York's largest.

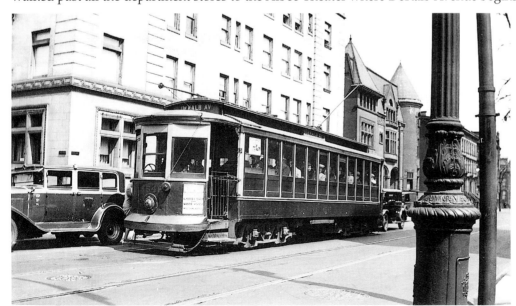

"Why don't we walk until a trolley comes?" I suggested.

"Good idea," said Howie, and off we went, eastward toward home.

The air was crisp. It was walk-type weather and we moved along DeKalb, turning every so often to see whether the DeKalb Avenue car was coming into view. Without saying anything, both of us expected to walk maybe a block or three at most before getting on the trolley. The DeKalb streetcar usually was one of the most reliable in the borough.

By this time we were retelling Marx Brothers' routines, occasionally dissecting Lawrence Tierney's performance in Dillinger and forgetting that we were supposed to be looking for a trolley. A good five minutes had passed and still no DeKalb Avenue car, but we didn't care. We had become so engrossed in talk that the ride home was the farthest thing from our minds.

Now it was dark and Howie apparently had forgotten that his sister Norma was home waiting for him, that she appreciated punctuality and, most important of all, that Norma's temper could be wrathful, to say the least.

We had already passed Fort Greene Park, Brooklyn Technical High School and Washington Avenue, when finally a trolley's brakes could be heard. We turned back and sure enough the DeKalb Avenue car was approaching.

When we reached the corner of Clinton and DeKalb, I said, "We walked this far, why don't we just walk the rest of the way home?"

Howie agreed. We resumed the conversation, almost oblivious to the darkness. We were at least an hour late for our appointed return to Vernon Avenue.

When we finally turned off DeKalb to Nostrand and stepped up our pace to Vernon I intuitively sensed that we had moved into the trouble zone, but it remained a somewhat vague feeling until I walked Howie up to his apartment and Norma opened the door.

It wasn't so much that Norma exonerated her brother as much as the fact that she held me mostly responsible for keeping Howie out so late. Norma's decibel count was matched only by the vehemence in her body language. Pacific typhoons could not have blown me out of that apartment and down Vernon Avenue faster than the intensity of Norma Sparer's words.

By the time I reached home Norma had already phoned my mother and informed her of the awful expedition that Howie and I had undertaken. It was quite clear that Norma had blamed me for luring her kid brother into the wilds of Court Street and, the fact is, she was half-right. The other part of the blame belonged to Howie. We did it by mutual consent but, by the same token, I now can appreciate Norma's concern. While her parents were at work, she was Howie's guardian and she had expected him home before dark.

For my misdemeanor, I was officially banned from seeing Howie

This is the way "Gram" and I looked prior to a movie excursion to Loew's Metropolitan via the DeKalb Ave. trolley.

(by nobody in particular) for a week. After that it was status quo ante, except for the fact that I never–ever–trifled with Norma Sparer again.

The DeKalb Avenue Trolley

Howie and his sister, Norma. Both Howie's parents and my parents work, which meant that we had to be overseen by elders. Norma did the job for the Sparer family while my grandmother did it for the Fischlers.

was woven into my life fabric in many other ways. especially trips to the movies with my grandmother. I would see it often when I visited the S&L Delicatessen on the corner of Marcy and DeKalb, the scene of good friend Abe Yurkofsky's Bar Mitzvah.

We had many kosher delis in our neighborhood; one, Goodman's, was just a block away on the corner of Vernon and Tompkins but the S&L, four blocks from our house at 582 Marcy Avenue, was the king of them all for several reasons.

For starters, Messrs. Shevinsky and Levinton (the S&L of S&L Deli) sold high quality food, Secondly, the deli was comfortable in the sense that it had a long aisle full of tables and a back section which always could handle an overflow crowd on weekends. Finally, there was Max the waiter.

Max was the quintessential Jewish deli waiter–right out of Central Casting. Slightly bald, he walked with a slight tilt when he delivered the dishes and, most of all, had an intriguing way of calling his orders into the kitchen, always bellowing the number of orders both at the start and finish of his roar.

If, by any chance, I ordered a corned beef sandwich, Max the waiter would intone, "ONE CORNED BEEF, ONNNNE!" Or, if someone else wanted two pastrami on club, it would be, "TWO PASTRAMI ON CLUB, TWOOOOO!"

Max the waiter was both gruff and avuncular at the same time. I speak firsthand because during the war, when both my parents were working, it was customary for me to have a weekly lunch at S&L instead of coming home from school where my grandmother would have a sandwich waiting for me. (This S&L break was an occasion for Gram to have a vacation and go downtown shopping.)

I loved going to the S&L for the food but there was also a bit of fear involved as well, thanks to Max the waiter. You must remember that this was wartime and there were all manner of shortages, including ketchup. Normally, every table at the S&L had a large bottle of Heinz ketchup sitting alongside the jar of horseradish deli mustard and the usual salt and pepper.

Since I enjoyed eating french fried potatoes with my ketchup, it was customary for me to pump as much of the thick, liquidy red condiment out of the bottle as I possibly could so that the french fries themselves were thoroughly blanketed by the crimson covering and were virtually invisible to the naked eye.

On this day, I began batting the bottom of the ketchup bottle to get that little extra out of it when Max shouted over my shoulder. "DON'T YOU KNOW THERE'S A WAR ON. KETCHUP IS HARD TO GET."

Max's voice set off tremors inside my stomach. I got the message, and from that point on it was very easy to notice the yellow-brown french fries on my plate. But the day after the war ended I emptied my ketchup bottle as I had always done before Max the waiter had bawled me out.

S&L was notable for other things. Nuances like the sign that overhung the cash register, "SEND A SALAMI TO YOUR BOY IN THE ARMY." I often wondered whether a kosher salami ever was sent and what it tasted like at Fort Dix or the Normandy beachhead, for that matter.

The S&L Deli outlasted the DeKalb Avenue trolley and still was in business in the early 1960s which was the last time I had seen the establishment. But the multi-aromas of knishes, Specials (oversized frankfurters), kishke and smoked meat are still a part of me; as well as Max the waiter shouting, "ONE CORNED BEEF, ONNNNE!"

**It's mid-summer which means the side slats are down on a
DeKalb Avenue convertible, the coolest ride in town.**

The time-honored ritual of the conductor or motorman, changing the poles at the end of the run. In this case it's the eastern terminus of the DeKalb Line at Stanhope St. and Grandview Avenue.

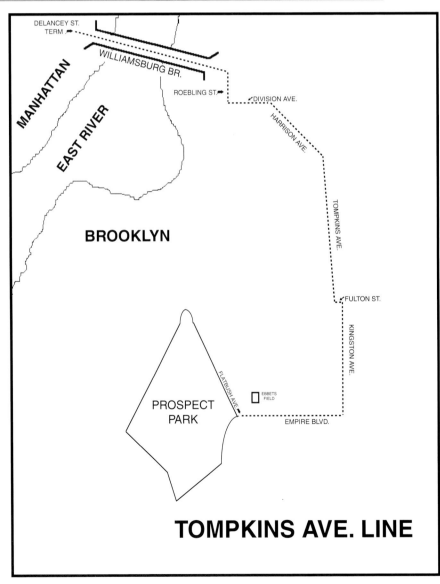

DELANCEY ST. TERM.

WILLIAMSBURG BR.

MANHATTAN

EAST RIVER

ROEBLING ST.

DIVISION AVE.

HARRISON AVE.

BROOKLYN

TOMPKINS AVE.

FULTON ST.

KINGSTON AVE.

PROSPECT PARK

FLATBUSH AVE.

EBBETS FIELD

EMPIRE BLVD.

TOMPKINS AVE. LINE

My Bar Mitzvah home is Temple Shaari Zedek
(Gates of Righteousness). I entered through
the side door hidden by the rear of the trolley.

CHAPTER FIVE:
THE TOMPKINS AVENUE LINE

a purely religious standpoint, the Tompkins Avenue Line was the most important to me because
for two years to prepare for my Bar Mitzvah with lessons at Temple Shaari Zedek which was far
ood. The Tompkins Avenue trolley also was important for my unpleasant adventures at the New
well as my first solo Chinese meal, but we'll get to that later.

e say up front that my family was mildly religious. My grandparents on my mother's side—Etel a
—who occupied the first two floors in our three-story Marcy Avenue brownstone, attended an
e only on the high holy days. Although there were at least two major shuls much closer to our house,
traipsed from 582 Marcy Avenue, down Vernon Avenue (remember it was a long city block), then a l
y, then a right turn at Willoughby for the final walk to shul. That took us past the Griffin Shoe Polis
ancient cobblestone pavement beyond Walworth Street, Spencer Street and at last to Bedford Aven
ion Beth Jehuda stood alongside an old firehouse which featured an ancient Walter hook-and-ladde
e Walter would become my favorite truck company because of their long-snouted engine housings.)
rents went to Congregation Beth Jehuda only on the high holy days but from time to time they woul
Avenue trolley to a much larger synagogue called Temple Shaari Zedek which was of the con
n. That meant that the services were more anglicized and, wonder of wonders, the shul also had an c
n enormous structure, this shul struck me as a veritable Jewish Radio City Music Hall!

r distinction was in the dietary observance at our house. My grandparents, whose large kitchen was l
d floor facing the backyard, kept a kosher home. That mean such delicacies as bacon and ham were
rs." However, in my mother's very tiny kitchen on the third floor, there were no distinctions betwe
osher. Bacon-and-eggs were the order of the day almost every Sunday morning.

I mention this only to point out that my parents had no particular urgency about my obtaining a deep religious education and the thought of attending Hebrew School never entered my mind until I walked to P.S. 54 one day with my friend Jay Koslo who lived a couple of blocks away on Marcy Avenue between Hart and Pulaski Streets. Jay was one of several guys in our P.S. 54 gang.

Jay was an amusing fellow who I numbered among my better friends (Howie Sparer was my "best" friend), and who was in my fourth grade class at P. S. 54 on the corner of Hart Street and Nostrand Avenues. On this walk to school, Jay mentioned that he had just enrolled in the New Hebrew School on Stockton Street near Tompkins Avenue and suggested that I join him there.

It wasn't so much that Koslo painted a rosy picture of the New Hebrew School but he did make it seem like a worthwhile way of passing a late afternoon after P.S. 54, and, what the heck, he was there so why shouldn't I join as well?

That's me with my head between Gil Birnbaum (left) and Jay Koslo (right). Joe Vetere and Ed Flores round out the front with Ralph Hubbard standing tall behind Flores. This was a P.S. 54 trip to Wallabout Market, near the Navy Yard, via the Lorimer St. Line.

Hmmm. I thought about it on the walk home from school that afternoon and by the time I reached 582 Marcy I had convinced myself that if the New Hebrew School was good for Jay Koslo then it would also be good for me. I made a beeline for the telephone and called my mother who was working at my grandfather's putty factory.

"Mom," I said, "I gotta go to Hebrew School."

My mother wouldn't have been more surprised had I said I wanted to become the Pope.

"Why Hebrew School?" Molly Fischler calmly replied.

To that I offered the most valuable piece of logic at my command. "Because Jay Koslo is going!"

"That," my mother insisted, "is not a reason to go to Hebrew School." Then a pause. "You wait 'til I get home and we'll discuss it with your father."

A few hours later the Fischler clan huddled in the living room and I pointed out that Jay Koslo had told me some wonderful things about the New Hebrew School and it seemed to me worth a try. To my utter amazement, my folks raised hardly an objection. After school the next day, I accompanied Jay along Marcy Avenue, past the huge Cascade Laundry building under the el at the corner of Marcy and Myrtle Avenues, then another block to Stockton Street, a right turn and one long block in enemy territory until we reached the New Hebrew School.

At one glance I could tell that the New Hebrew School had not been new for a long, long time. Maybe in 1900 it was new, but now it was a rather homely, unimposing three-story building surrounded by an open picket-fence made of iron that resembled a string of black lances side by side all around the building.

I could never tell whether the iron fencing was meant to repulse invaders as in the Italian gangs that occasionally would harass us on our long walk from the New Hebrew School to Marcy Avenue, but I knew that once I got inside the fence I felt a lot more secure than I did walking along Stockton Street between Marcy and Tompkins Avenues.

Having officially enrolled in the New Hebrew School, I enjoyed my last moments of after-P.S. 54 pleasure. The next thing I knew I was placed in a class different from Jay Koslo's and with a bunch of fellows with names like Honshel Sperber and with an instructor called Ma (not as in mother but as in Mister) Rosenberg.

Rosenberg was of modest dimensions but had a very intimidating pair of eyes and a voice that cut right to the heart. It required about two seconds to realize that: a. Ma Rosenberg was not a very nice man; b. he was going to work my ass off; and, c. following Jay Koslo's lead was the worst mistake of my young life.

But I was there and now I had to make the best of it. My next move, of course, was to line-up other friends to enroll at the New Hebrew School as Jay Koslo had done with me and, naturally, the most likely victim was Howie Sparer. A day later I gave Howie the same sales pitch that Jay Koslo had given me and–Shazam!–Mr. and Mrs. Sparer gave their son

This is the corner of Tompkins and Myrtle under the el station. Jay Koslo and I would be heading in the same direction as the chap on the left, toward the New Hebrew School just a block away.

approval to become a latter-Theodore Herzl as well. Howie wound up not in our class but with soft-voiced Ma Shofar, a very sweet lady.

Unfortunately, the New Hebrew School fulfilled none of our expectations and, for the most part, was a disappointment. But, for a time, it was very much a part of my life. I would return home from P.S. 54 at 3:15 PM, have my chocolate milk and graham crackers in my grandmother's kitchen, then buzz off for Ma Rosenberg's penitentiary.

We had to be at the New Hebrew School by 3:45 PM so there was little room for dalliance. I generally met Jay Koslo in front of 582 Marcy and we then walked under the Myrtle Avenue El, past Cascade Laundry towards Tompkins Avenue.

Stockton Street, from Marcy to Tompkins, was unfriendly territory for me. It was like another country and we Jews heading for Hebrew School were not exactly welcome. There were at least two loosely-knit groups of Italian gangs that occasionally marauded along Stockton but the harassment was more mental than physical and the insults ("Kike" was the most-used) were difficult to take although they almost became an accepted part of life.

The New Hebrew School had a policy of having its students sell books of raffle tickets which were actually contributions to buy trees for planting in Palestine, which at the time we considered the Jewish National Homeland. The twenty or so kids who sold the most tickets each season were given prizes which could be a highly-coveted game such as Jim Prentice's Electric Baseball.

The day when prizes were given out was one of the rare enjoyable times at the New Hebrew School. Nonetheless, we were also warned by veteran students that on that particular day we had to be very wary en route home because the "goyim" always knew the details of "Prize Day" and were waiting to ambush us on the walk along Stockton to Marcy. Of course this was a never a big problem for me since I never sold enough tickets to win a major prize.

The New Hebrew School was an orthodox institution and succeeded in elevating my knowledge of Hebrew to the extent that I learned to read the language, learned a bit of Jewish History and was forever bonded to a religion. The stumbling blocks were Ma Rosenberg and the Saturday services.

We were required to come to shul on Saturday mornings and participate in the prayers. That part was all right but what frustrated many of us was that they were conducted entirely in Hebrew, at high speed and nobody ever bothered to help us keep up with the pace. As a result, I was lost from the first day I attended to the last and considered the school's inability to help me bridge that gap the major flaw in the Hebrew educational process. Had it been otherwise, who knows, I may have become a rabbi!

Ma Rosenberg was simply too strict for my tastes. After a long day at P.S. 54 I simply wasn't up for a harsh Hebrew schoolroom scene. And since I knew full well that my parents never wanted me to go to The New Hebrew School, I did not care as much for his harangues as I normally would. What made matters even worse was the fact that neither Howie nor Jay Koslo were in my class.

I lasted two years at The New Hebrew School. My exit was hastened by two factors; the Boy Scouts of America and my parents. Shortly after my ninth year, I became a Cub Scout, graduated to Boy Scouts and was an active member of Troop 320. A feature of scouting was Sunday hikes to any number of exotic places including the Ten Mile River Boy Scout Camp in Alpine, New York.

Sunday hikes directly conflicted with The New Hebrew School since we were expected to attend classes on Sunday mornings and that's when the hikes took place. I put the question to my parents: do you want me to be a good Boy Scout or a bad rabbi? The problem was resolved with a one year parental reprieve. They would allow me to take a year off from The New Hebrew School but when it came within a year-and-a-half of my Bar Mitzvah I would be enrolled at Temple Shaari Zedek for Bar Mitzvah lessons and that would be that.

I left The New Hebrew School with mixed emotions. On the one hand, I was disappointed that the Jay Koslo Plan never worked out. As it happened, Jay had long since left the neighborhood (and The New Hebrew School) as did Howie. I was virtually lost in the intricacies of Orthodox Judaism and much more interested in the great outdoors, hiking and having my Sundays free of Ma Rosenberg.

When the game ended the cars would take this left turn on to Empire Boulevard where they'd pick up passengers in front of the hot-dog stand (Ebbets Field is two blocks away on the left).

Before Dodgers games concluded at Ebbets Field, Tompkins cars would sit on a layover track alongside Prospect Park on Flatbush Avenue. Later, they'd cross to Empire Boulevard.

My most intense relationship with the Tompkins Avenue Trolley began in 1943, at age 11, when I began my Bar Mitzvah lessons at Temple Shaari Zedek, located at the intersection of Park Place and Kingston Avenue in what then was a peaceful, middle class Bedford-Stuyvesant neighborhood. The shul was diagonally across from Brower Park featuring the already legendary Brooklyn Children's Museum which our classes at P.S. 54 would frequent at least once a year.

Riding the Tompkins Avenue Line had kicks that were not available on, say, the Nostrand route. The latter essentially was a straight line run from our neighborhood all the way out to Avenue U and Sheepshead Bay. By contrast, the Tompkins line offered some interesting 90 degree turns such as the one on to Fulton Street and then off Fulton Street to Kingston Avenue, not to mention the colossal 90-degree swing from the bottom of Kingston Avenue hill onto Empire Boulevard for the long-blocks dash to a layover at Ebbets Field and the terminal at Prospect Park

My Bar Mitzvah teacher at Temple Shaari Zedek was a somewhat portly gentleman who was the "chazan" of the shul. Cantor Abraham Kwartin was in his fifties; a man who immediately won me over on my first visit to the synagogue.

Cantor Kwartin said we would meet every Sunday at 7:30 A.M. in the organ loft of Shaari Zedek and the lessons would consume an hour. The cantor's English was flecked with a Jewish accent and some of his expressions amused me no end; although I never would let on to him about it. My favorite was his insistence that, "you must be here at seven-<u>surty</u>. Remember, seven-<u>surty</u>."

Apart from the warm relationship I developed with Cantor Kwartin, the best part of going for Bar Mitzvah lessons was the trolley ride. Early on a Sunday morning, the trip took no more than fifteen minutes and could have been even shorter had we made most of the lights.

I would leave my house at about 6:45 A.M. (breakfast would come later), cross Marcy Avenue and head east up Vernon Avenue. Because Marcy was a relatively busy two-way street with traffic coming off the Williamsburg Bridge and then heading south toward Flatbush, the avenue tended to be a line of demarcation in the neighborhood. The "other" side of Marcy was regarded as "Upper Vernon Avenue" as opposed to "Lower Vernon" where all my friends lived.

That big wide structure behind the trolley at the corner of Tompkins and Willoughby is an Orthodox Shul which I rarely attended. The overhanging sign on the next corner (Vernon and Tompkins) is for Corin's Drug Store. That's where I got on the trolley for my Bar Mitzvah lessons. And that's the Myrtle Ave. el station on the right in the background. The record store behind the trolley lasted only a few years but was there long enough for me to purchase Yank Lawson's classic rendition of Sensation Rag.

"Upper Vernon" was virtually foreign turf despite its proximity. When I walked up to Tompkins I invariably had a feeling that I needed a passport to cross through this part of Williamsburg. The fellows I knew from Upper Vernon–Marvin Berger was one–were more acquaintances than friends. When I reached the corner of Tompkins and Vernon I would peer down toward the Myrtle Avenue El to see if a trolley was coming. If it wasn't, which usually was the case, I walked right past, past Corin's Drug Store to the next block which was Willoughby.

A huge orthodox shul dominated the northwest corner of Tompkins and Willoughby and I often wondered why my grandparents hadn't chosen that one as their home synagogue instead of Congregation Beth Jehuda but, then again, it was on the "other" side of Marcy Avenue and maybe that was their reason.

Since I almost always arrived at Tompkins and Willoughby at the same time every Sunday morning, I usually found myself riding the same trolley with the same motorman. At 7 A.M. on Sunday very few people rode the Tompkins Avenue trolley and it was not uncommon for me to be the only one on the car when it picked me up at Willoughby.

The fare was three cents for kids in those days and as soon as I handed my pennies to the motorman, I immediately deposited myself in the jump seat immediately to his left where I could both get a good look at the tracks ahead as well as study his moves behind the equipment.

Easily, the two most fascinating devices were the controller and brakes. Operated by his left hand, the controller was a sculpted hunk of iron that had an elephantine silhouette. At the tip of what would be the elephant's trunk was a circular handle which the motorman gripped when he wanted to move the trolley.

He would press down on the handle and then move it to his left, clock-wise. That would turn the circular iron base from speed point to speed point until the motorman reached the high-position which was about four points from the start.

The controller made interesting sounds as it clicked into the points and then hit the iron block at the end when it reached high. The sound was even louder when he had to shut off the power and swing it hard in the other direction until the controller hit the other iron block with a fairly loud report.

The brake mechanism is straight ahead just beneath the middle window in the front. Note the folded slats on either side of the door. They open into seats which I usually avoided..

On Peter Witt 8000 series cars, which ran along Tompkins Avenue, the motor sound was a rather subdued whine even in its highest pitch and was not nearly as piercing as the wail of the old Bergen Street cars (which we will deal with later). Not that you could hit any really high speeds on the Tompkins Avenue Peter Witt. For one thing, the blocks were short along the route until you reached Empire Blvd. where they stretched out. Over most of the line, there was little opportunity for the motorman to really open up and get good speed.

There was, however, an advantage on Sunday morning because there was virtually no one on the street at that time— neither prospective passengers nor traffic—which meant that the trolley could run for long stretches without stopping, provided that it made all the green lights.

After setting myself up in the front, I also studied the brake mechanism. The brake handle was portable. The motorman took it with him when he finished his run and, conversely, when he began, he would fit the device into place like putting a piece of a puzzle in the middle of the jigsaw. The handle fitted neatly over a prong that was surrounded by grease-covered metal. Once the brake was in place, it sat atop a semi-circular metal plate and would be moved from side to side in order to obtain proper air pressure to apply the brakes.

The best motormen were those who could bring the trolley to a smooth stop by jiggling the brake handle several times before the brakes finally had made their final grip. The lousy motormen were those who applied the brakes too hard, too fast, causing the trolley to lurch to a stop. It was not easy to apply a "soft" brake and that is why I admired the competent brake-applier as much as any artist anywhere.

Like every trolley, the Tompkins Avenue Line had a music all of its own. This was a blend of the motor sound and the rhythm produced by the wheels going over the tracks, especially when it rolled over a crossover, a switch or banged through gaps in the track.

The downhill run toward Brooklyn on the Williamsburg Bridge was where #8384 moved like a rocket. The real kick was when it sped past the automobiles in the adjoining lanes.

For some reason, the Tompkins Avenue tracks were not as well-maintained as those on the Nostrand Avenue line, which meant that the rhythm was even sharper to the ear. I can still remember seeing one chipped rail joint which had a gap almost four inches wide (very large, and potentially dangerous) and produced a very pronounced "TUK-TUK, TUK-TUK, TUK-TUK, TUK-TUK" as the trolley's wheels bounced over it.

En route to shul, the Tompkins Avenue trolley passed such land-marks as the Classic Theater (a run-down movie house which we militantly avoided), the Airplane Store and the Sugar Bowl, a very popular ice cream parlor–lunch-eonette on the corner of Tompkins and Dekalb Avenues just across from the Kismet Theater.

During World War II the Sugar Bowl was one of two very important hang-outs, the other being on the corner of Willoughby and Tompkins across from the shul. Each was famous for having photos of just about every neighborhood serviceman, mounted either in the front window or on the walls inside.

The Tompkins Avenue trolley banged across the DeKalb crossover heading for Tompkins Park which bordered on Lafayette, Marcy and Tompkins. It had the usual playground facilities but by far the most important attraction was the Tompkins Park Public Library where I was first introduced to genuine literature. (John F. Tunis' "The Kid From Tompkinsville" was the first book I ever borrowed from the Tompkins Public Library.)

Easily the most amazing aspect about the library was the number of books it carried in relation into its size. A one-story square structure, the library was built with dark brick, adorned with ivy and covered with shingles on top. It exuded warmth and made you want to go inside. Once there, the library was hardly imposing until you got to the card catalogue; the Tompkins Park Library seemed to carry every book that was ever published. This led me to the conclusion that it was really built with 25 stories underneath, where all those wonderful volumes were stored because there surely wasn't that much room on the main–and only–floor.

The chief librarian was a rather stern, thin woman, who combed her grey-flecked hair back into a bun and, despite her apparent coldness, actually was always helpful and hardly offensive.

The Sugar-Bowl is just around the corner to the right on DeKalb Avenue. As the trolley heads for Tompkins Park it rolls past St. Ambrose Roman Catholic Church. The famed Airplane Store is on the next block at the left..

Not far from the library was the Lexington Avenue El, the oldest in Brooklyn, which eventually hooked up with the Broadway Brooklyn Line and ran to the Eastern Parkway junction. Like my neighborhood Myrtle Avenue El, the Lex featured the ancient but delightful open-ended cars with conductors between each car opening the iron gates.

The Tompkins trolley encountered another crossover at Gates Avenue–usually quite loud–and then headed for Fulton Street where it made the sharp left turn on to Fulton and then hung a right on to Kingston Avenue. Looming directly ahead was the Long Island Rail Road's elevated structure which carried the Atlantic Avenue Line from Downtown Brooklyn to Jamaica terminal.

Sitting atop Tompkins Avenue is the ancient Lexington Ave. el station, one of the oldest of its kind in the city. The trolley is crossing Greene Avenue in Bedford-Stuyvesant heading for Fulton Street.

There's nothing like a 90° curve. The wheels are squeaking as the streetcar swerves to its left on Fulton Street. I often wondered how it kept from derailing but it never left the tracks.

Any time I passed either the Lexington Avenue El or the Long Island viaduct, there always was a possibility of actually seeing a train go by, especially the LIRR which was a legitimate railroad, as opposed to the dinky el or the subways. In those days, the Long Island Rail Road operated what they called "Ping Pong" cars--passenger coaches with two circular windows on either side in the front which looked like oversized ping pong balls. The LIRR viaduct did not have a workman's walkway on either side of the tracks in the manner of the Myrtle Avenue or Lexington Avenue El. Thus, when the Long Island trains thundered by, the cars virtually hung over the side of the el and gave the distinct impression that with one bad swerve they would plunge to Atlantic Avenue below. (They never did.)

The other aspect of the LIRR that was so gripping was the relative velocity of the trains. Once they got to speed, they moved considerably faster than our subway trains. Thus, a Long Island Rail Road "watch" was almost as exciting as riding a roller coaster.

Once past Atlantic Avenue, the Tompkins Avenue Trolley headed for Bergen Street which was a favorite crossroads of mine. Unlike most of my neighborhood routes (Nostrand, Lorimer, et. al.), Bergen Street featured the oldest trolleys I had ever seen in regular use.

Dating back to the early part of the 20th Century these cars had undergone several rebuildings (as recently as 1929) but still looked ancient. Some of them in the 2000 series (2935) had trucks with a pair of large wheels and an accompanying pair of smaller wheels giving the trolley an even stranger look. Others, like 761, were rebuilt jobs that had a snout-type three front window set which overhung the front light. The 1000 series, which closely resembled the others in basic design, also was part of the rebuilding program. Ditto for the 3000 series (3301) which were hauled out of storage during World War II because of the increased ridership and need for more cars.

No doubt because of their age, the old Bergen cars had a distinct motor sound that almost sounded like the mooing of a cow. When the motorman pulled on his controller and the trolley began moving, even if you were two blocks away, you could hear the "UHHHHHHHHHHH" moaning of the old streetcar motor.

Although other lines (Summer-Sackett, Ralph-Rockaway) used these lumbering classics, I always associated them with Bergen Street and treated them with the curiosity that a bird-watcher might hold for a yellow-bellied sapsucker. Every so often the need for trolleys was so desperate on the Lorimer or Nostrand Lines that one of the old 2000s rolled past Vernon Avenue. The first time it happened, I actually thought I was dreaming and ran all the way from the middle of Vernon to the corner of Nostrand to be sure I wasn't seeing things. From that point on until the end of the war, I kept a sharp eye on Nostrand Avenue for other such curios but I can think of only two other such sightings.

From Bergen, the ride to Shaari Zedek was short and by this time there may have been two or three other passengers in the car. I hopped off at Park Place, stared briefly at the handsome, four-pillared entrance to the shul on Park Place and then crossed Kingston Avenue and walked in through the side entrance on Kingston Avenue. I took the stairs two at a time and always was at least five minutes early for the lesson with Cantor Kwartin.

Unlike the sessions at The New Hebrew School, my classes at Shaari Zedek were unpressured and bordered on fun. Cantor Kwartin taught me at a leisurely pace in the very comfortable quarters of the organ loft which struck me as the squirrel's nest of conservative synagogues.

The lessons consumed an hour and then I bade Cantor Kwartin good-bye, sped down the stairs and got on the first Tompkins Avenue trolley that came along for the trip past St. John's Place, Bergen Street and eventually home. It still was very early on Sunday morning when the streetcar dropped me off at Vernon in front of the Traffic K police precinct. I headed west to Marcy and stopped at the corner to make a purchase at Stoller's Bakery.

Already the aromatic odors of freshly baked breads were wafting from the vents out to Vernon Avenue and I couldn't wait to open the bakery door for a real whiff of the stuff. Mrs. Stoller, a handsome woman with an accent not unlike Cantor Kwartin's, was behind the counter and I delivered my usual order, "Small rye, sliced, without seeds."

Mrs. Stoller would take a caramel-colored loaf off the shelf and place it in a new contraption that looked like the open jaws of a strange metallic monster. Into the jaws she placed the loaf, pressed a button and the jaws slowly closed, slicing the bread in the process. It was wrapped in wax paper, slipped into a brown paper bag and placed into my hands. And all of this for only a mere dime (as I remember it).

My reward for bringing home the warm bread was the right to peel off what my grandmother called the "schpek," or the crusted pieces at the end, and eat them before I got to the house. A second reward was having a baloney sandwich made with that delicious rye to take to the Sunday afternoon hockey game at Madison Square Garden.

After several rides for my Bar Mitzvah lessons, I got to know the trolley car motorman pretty well although he never actually befriended me in the manner that I had hoped. I carefully studied how he manipulated the brake handle with his right hand pushing it back and forth, left-to-right, several times before actually bringing the car to a stop.

On some of the Peter Witt cars, the front door was actually opened by pushing the brake handle all the way to the right after the car had stopped. But others had a small metal lever sitting below the brake handle that the motorman merely flicked to the right to open and to the left to close.

The rear doors were opened and closed by pressing the large black buttons at the base of the Johnson Fare Box. They had a succulent sound–almost like the sound one creates while sucking on a peach–when applied and distinctly contrasted with the banging sound created when the big wooden doors slammed open and closed.

For an observer like me in the jump seat, the big kick was speed. Even though the standard 8000 series Peter Witt on the Tompkins Line couldn't go very fast in the automobile sense, it was all relative. Thus, the big hope in any ride to Temple Shaari Zedek was for the motorman to "make" as many green lights as possible and therefore keep the Peter Witt in on the highest controller point en route to shul.

One morning above all others stands out in my mind in this regard. It was in February 1945 and this Sunday morning was the coldest of the winter. The freeze never bothered me. By this time, I had become so involved in hockey that I equated the coldest days with ice forming in Prospect Park and any other place so that hockey could be played. It was, as we say, "good hockey weather" and that pleased me no end as I traipsed up Vernon Avenue to my usual destination at Tompkins and Willoughby.

I'd be sitting just to the right of the motorman's left arm in this picture. This section of Tompkins Avenue is part of my old stamping grounds, near Yee Ping Hing Chinese restaurant.

On this day it was gray and overcast. Snow had begun to fall at about 6 A.M., just as I was getting dressed. By the time I left the house there was more than a good dusting. Furthermore, the snow was sticking and I loved that best of all.

The trolley arrived within minutes of my arriving at the corner of Willoughby. I climbed the two steps into the Peter Witt, nodded hello to my regular motorman–I never did learn his name, which was a big mistake for shy little me–and sat down on the wooden jump seat.

Just then I realized that there was something different about this ride; for the first time in memory I was the only passenger in the car; it was virtually a private trolley car or streetcar limousine or whatever you want to imagine a trolley all your own.

As the motorman swung the controller into the high point, and I gazed around at DeKalb Avenue, I wondered how long this phenomenon of the exclusive trolley ride could last. Would somebody get on Lafayette Avenue? Or Lexington? Or could we make it all the way to Fulton without taking on a passenger?

The prospects intrigued me, especially since the snow was coming down harder and it seemed hardly a morning for anyone to come out for a trolley ride; unless, of course, he had a meeting with Cantor Kwartin for a Bar Mitzvah lesson.

Now the motorman had the car up to speed and the light was green at DeKalb. We rumbled over the crossover with a cushiony feeling because the snow already had gathered enough to muffle the normal BAM-BAM, BAM-BAM, BAM-

BAM sounds as the wheels jounced through the steel track openings.

The next light was at Lafayette Avenue and that, too, was green. Furthermore, there wasn't another soul in sight and now the old Peter Witt was moving as fast as it could go, occasionally swaying from side to side and always pounding out the rhythmical, BUM-BUM, BUM-BUM as it rolled over the track gaps.

When we reached Gates Avenue I was in a state of high excitement and glee. This was easily the farthest I had ever travelled on a Brooklyn streetcar without it having to stop for either a light or a passenger and it had now become a personal contest to see how far we could go without making the stop. I sensed that the motorman was almost as excited as I was.

Bedford-Stuyvesant was beautifully blanketed in snow as we rumbled past Putnam Avenue. There was virtually no automobile traffic and this enabled the snow to gather naturally without any tire marks. Meanwhile the trolley tracks had been totally covered and as a Tompkins car rolled toward us from the other direction it left a white wake in its path, giving it an ethereal effect one does not normally associate with trolley cars.

We had reached Fulton Street which meant that, at last, the motorman had to bring the controller back to its starting position in order to slow down for the sharp left turn on to Fulton. He began swinging the wooden brake handle back and forth, causing a CH-CH-CH-CH sound of the air and slowed the car almost to a stop. The light was green as he eased into the turn and then pulled the controller to the left, one, two, three points past the Borden Dairy plant and into high for the run to Kingston Avenue.

Alas, the light was red at Kingston and Fulton, so he quickly slammed the controller back to first position and applied the brakes in the hopes that he wouldn't be forced to stop altogether. There were no passengers waiting for the car and in the next couple of seconds—well before we got to the corner—the green flashed and he pulled the controller to the first point for the slow ninety-degree turn on to Kingston.

By this time I actually imagined that we could do the entire trip to Park Place without another passenger joining us. He might avoid red lights forever.

At Atlantic Avenue there was nobody and we breezed under the Long Island Rail Road el with ease, moving smartly toward Bergen. I did a double-take when I peered ahead and, through the snow, detected a body standing at the corner of Bergen and Kingston.

Incredibly, there was a passenger–a real, live man who wanted to ride the Tompkins Avenue trolley. Our dream ride had ended. The motorman banged the controller against the iron start block, wiggled the brake handle and gradually brought the Peter Witt to a halt. The man climbed aboard completely oblivious to the significance of his arrival; and how could he know otherwise? My grand excursion was over and now we hit at least two more red lights before I got off the trolley at Park Place. Still, it was a marvelous run and the reason I know that to be fact is that I remember it to this day.

My Bar Mitzvah lessons ended in April, 1945, just about the time comedian Sam Levenson had popularized his monologue "The Story of the Bar Mitzvah boy." Levenson concluded his routine with a bit about the pre-Bar Mitzvah walk to the shul with the youngster's uncle whispering in his ear, "You'll gets presents. You'll get presents. You'll get presents." And finally, the lad walks up to the altar, gives his Bar Mitzvah speech and concludes, TODAY I AM A FOUNTAIN PEN."

This a Tompkins car turning from Kingston on to Empire Blvd. I had hoped our uninterrupted ride could have reached Park Place which is less than a mile up the hill. By the way that downhill run was scarier than it looks.

There were no fountain pens for Stanley but we had a good crowd at Shaari Zedek for my fete. What I remember from my speech was, "My dear parents, grandparents, relatives and friends; this is the most important day of my life because today I enter the portals of Israel. No longer am I a thoughtless child who knows not or cares not..."

Thanks to Cantor Kwartin, I pulled it all off without any major hitch, enjoyed the Bar Mitzvah party down the street at a second story tea room and, after it was all over, my friends, led by Howie Sparer, and I walked over to a local candy store where I bought a New York Daily Mirror newspaper and read about the Toronto Maple Leafs' latest victory over Detroit in the 1945 Stanley Cup finals.

I celebrated the end of my Bar Mitzvah day in the most appropriate possible way, a ride home on the Tompkins Avenue trolley.

(LEFT) The Bar Mitzvah boy with parents, April, 1945. (The zoot-suit had peg pants and the required long key chain.)

(RIGHT) Bar Mitzvah lineup, (left to right): Howie Sparer, Me, Lew Klotz, Cousins Judd and Sandee. In the rear, Dad, Gram, Gramp and Mom. The Tompkins Ave. trolley is right behind the venetian blinds.

It was also possible for me to utilize the Tompkins line to reach the hallowed halls of Ebbets Field. Here a Tompkins car on Empire Blvd. has just passed the field, whose light towers and first base side grandstand are visible over the trolley. The cross tracks are on Rogers Avenue where the Ocean Avenue speed-car ran.

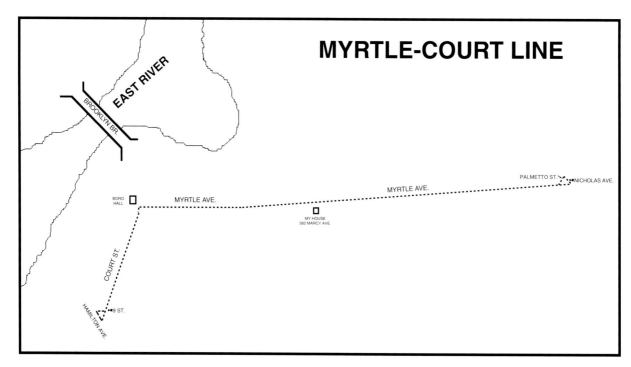

MYRTLE-COURT LINE

CHAPTER SIX:
THE MYRTLE AVENUE LINE

here was a special irony about the Myrtle Ave. Line and me. For starters, a Myrtle Avenue streetcar came within of ending my life at a very early age.

finisher's, you should know that although the Myrtle Avenue route was the closest of all trolley lines to our house st never rode the darn thing. Yet, I saw more of it than the Nostrand, Tompkins and Lorimer Street lines which arther away. Let me explain:

lived in a three story brownstone that was part of a three-house unit, starting with 586 Marcy, at the very corner o n, then 584 in the middle and finally, 582 which adjoined a pair of five-story walk-ups–I guess you could call them ents--followed by a two-story home and then the three-story building at the corner of Marcy and Myrtle, which ccupied by the Friedman family who ran a wholesale shoe findings business on the ground floor.

ere was a sense of community on the block. We were friendly with the Meyers family who lived at 586. Mr. Meyers successful plumber and kept a well-manicured garden with shrubs around the perimeter of the house. There were rothers, Larry and Melvin Meyers, both significantly older (about four to six years) than me and a daughter ce (always called "Florie"), who was about two years older and for whom I had a crush for several years, and a younger daughter, Harriet, who was about three years younger than me.

ut next door neighbors were not unlike ourselves in that the house was shared by the Grubers, who were parents (bottom floor and second floor), and the Finger family on the third floor. The Fingers had two sons abou ge, Marvin and Irwin. We occasionally played together but for reasons that I never could identify, we never reall ose, despite the fact that we lived right next door.

I had to put any reason to it, my best guess is that it had everything to do with my grandmother's low opinion o "Gram" was the Queen Victoria of 582, a pure Hungarian who considered any non-Hungarian several notche her. This was particularly true if the other party happened to be a "Litvak," a Jew from Russia or Latvia. As a , the Grubers and Fingers, who happened to be Litvaks, fell somewhere between subterranean and unthinkable i ook; to be avoided at all costs.

his was evident from the grimace that grossed Gram's face when we discussed the Grubers or her names used to to them: "The Grubuhchus" (Grubers, and spoken with utter disdain) or "The Litvachkies," (the Litvaks, spoken disdain-to-the-radical fifty).

were not particularly friendly with anyone in the two tenements, except for the Friedmans at the end of the block Mr. and Mrs. Friedman, no relation to my grandparents, were sweet people, but a couple with whom I had only a

The Myrtle Ave. Line also traversed Court St. in downtown Brooklyn.

nodding relationship. The family also had three adult sons: Barney and Booney, who helped run the business (Barney later became my trusted algebra tutor when I realized I was flunking the course at Eastern District High School) and Izzy, who was mentally retarded but extremely likeable and who could converse on a near-adult level, despite his problems.

The Friedman's Shoe Findings shop sat right on the corner of Myrtle and Marcy. Next to it, was a luncheonette which changed hands innumerable times and that rubbed shoulders with Dave's Pharmacy run by a very friendly chap who eventually lured us away from Corin's drug store on the corner of Vernon and Tompkins, although that would come much later.

However, the key business, in terms of this story, actually was a newsstand which sat on the other side of Myrtle Avenue directly across from Friedman's Shoe Findings.

Because there were so many newspapers in those days–Times, Tribune, Mirror, News, World-Telegram, Journal-American, Brooklyn Eagle, Post and Sun–as well as magazines and comic books, a newsstand could do a hefty business without the need to sell other items such as chewing gum, candy and aspirins.

The Myrtle-Marcy newsstand was across from Friedman Shoe Findings directly adjoined the entrance to the Myrtle-Willoughby subway station of the GG, Brooklyn-Queens Crosstown Line Actually, there were three entrances to the GG Myrtle-Willoughby subway station. For those heading for Downtown Brooklyn or Manhattan, which meant most people who took the subway to work in the morning, there was the entrance on Willoughby and Marcy as well as the one at Myrtle and Marcy. Considerably fewer people used the Willoughby entrance and eventually the change-booth was removed and replaced by a coin-operated automatic gate. The third entrance was on the northeast side of the Myrtle-Marcy intersection, adjoining the vast, wide-windowed engine room of the Cascade Laundry. This was the one used for trains heading northeast into Lower Williamsburg, Greenpoint and then on to Queens with its final destination being Continental Avenue in Forest Hills. This was also the entrance used if one wanted to get to Madison Square Garden by changing at Queens Plaza for the E train which stopped at 50th Street and Eighth Avenue right under the Garden.

But because so many people came from the other side of Myrtle, heading for work in Manhattan, the entrance across from Cascade Laundry was the most frequently-used and that's why Mister Davis put his newsstand there. Mister Davis was an amiable man who had become friendly with my Dad and I kind of liked him, too. It was not uncommon for my father or grandfather to send me over to the Davis newsstand to pick up a paper which, in our house, usually happened to be the New York World-Telegram or The Sun. Mr. Davis had one son my age, whose name was William but whom we always referred to as "Velvil," or "Velvilluh," both Jewish ways of describing a William. Because of William Davis' nickname, his father's newsstand became known in our crowd as "Velvilluh's." No further explanation was needed.

On this November day in 1938, which was almost the last day of my young life, I was dispatched by my grandfather, Simon, to get a newspaper for him. For some reason, I recall it being the New York Sun, which was a somewhat conservative daily with some fun features, the best of them being the one-large-box cartoon: "The Toonerville Trolley That Meets All The Trains," drawn and written by Fontaine Fox.

In any event, it was 5 P.M. and neither my mother nor father had returned from work when Gramp sent me on this routine mission. I walked out of their living room, through the windowed door connecting the living room to the hall, made a right turn at the hall, proceeded to the two doors (don't ask me whey they were there except to keep out the cold) leading to the vestibule which had the feel of a rock cave, then a right turn to open the iron gate, up two steps and out onto the miniature plaza that was our "garden," then out the front gate and a left turn to the Marcy Avenue sidewalk and the short jaunt to Myrtle.

Since the Independent System's Myrtle-Willoughby station was directly under our house, there were subway grates all along that strip of Marcy Avenue and I invariably peered down through the latticed iron coverings to see if there were any coins below. If there were, I would round up a friend or two and attempt to nab them with either a thin wooden pole with a well-chewed piece of gum at the end or by dropping a long, strong string, also with gum. The hope, naturally, was that the gum would land on the coin, stick, and then carry the coin back to the surface as we gingerly tugged on either the string or the thin stick.

In any event, I saw no coins and proceeded to the corner to Myrtle and Marcy. It was dark and chilly and I remember that I wanted to return home as soon as possible to hear the various radio serials that were soon to come on WOR Radio, starting with Jack Armstrong, "The All-American Boy," followed by Tom Mix.

The graceful lines of car #6024 are evident as it heads downhill under the Myrtle Avenue el passing the Fort Greene housing projects.

The Myrtle Avenue Line featured a very interesting streetcar in those days, known to the trade as the 6000 series, or more particularly, 6000-6199. They were the last Brooklyn cars designed and built in the early 1930's before the various trolley companies joined forces to create the official streamliner, the President's Conference Car or PCC car.

Designed by the Brooklyn and Queens Transit Company, which ran all the trolleys in Brooklyn for the BMT in the 1920s and 1930s, the 6000 series differed remarkably from the Peter Witts on Nostrand, Tompkins and Lorimer Street lines in that the 6000s were not reversible. That is, the car was only operated from one end with the rear tapering off like the observation car on a railroad streamliner.

The 6000 was a handsome car with a distinct angular front and large windows along the side, set-off by thin window posts. This particular aspect gave passengers the most visibility they could obtain from any trolley in those days. Also interesting was the fact the cars featured a turnstile directly behind the motorman. This meant that after climbing the two entrance steps, the passenger turned left and faced a metal white railing that funneled him to the thin turnstile that stood about three feet high along the right wall. The turning part of the turnstile was a yellowish metal prong with a large gap in the middle. You would put your nickel in the slot, push and the turnstile clanged sharply.

The interiors of the 6000 series made it the best looking of any trolley to date. Unlike the Nostrand Avenue Peter Witts, the Myrtle Avenue cars, 6000-6099, were outfitted with plush leather, both along the side (longitudinal) seats up front and the regular double seats facing forward that began just before the rear exit door and filled the car all the way to the end where there was a long circular (almost like a couch) lounge-type leather arrangement that went all around the rear of the car.

The lighting was also modern for its time. While the Peter Witts featured the bare bulbs, the 6000's had large frosted, semi-circular coverings over the bulbs. In place of straps, the straphangers grabbed on to white metal poles that ran just below the ceiling for the length of the car.

Easily the most advanced aspect of the 6000 series—at least to my youthful eyes—was the magical rear doors. They were magical to me because they were automatic. All you had to do was step on one of two large metal plates—called treadles by the B&QT—and when the car came to a stop, the doors flung open. A sign above the doors read, "To Open Doors, Step On Treadle." I imagined that 2,000,000 Brooklynites who had never heard the word before, added treadle to their vocabulary. Whereas the Peter Witt motorman was confined to a hard wooden disk for a seat, the 6000 series offered the motorman a leather-backed chair which was the ultimate in comfort for the trolley operator.

The controller resembled that of the Peter Witt, except that it was recessed to the left to accommodate a seated motorman whereas the brake handle, directly in front of the motorman's seat, was about two inches higher than the controller.

Despite its obvious modernity, the 6000 series car never struck me as any big deal, apart from the

Notice the soft leather seats, the capped overhead lamps, not to mention the oversized controller and brake handle in front of the motorman's seat. The turnstile was an interesting fillip on the relatively modern 6000 cars.

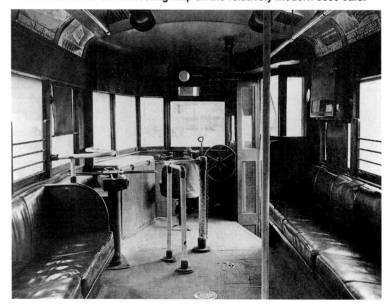

turnstile and the leather seats. I always regarded the Peter Witt as more a trolley-type trolley. The fact that there was only a front compartment for the 6000 driver and that he couldn't operate it from either end, as one could the Peter Witt, seemed to me more a disadvantage rather than an advantage.

Moreover, the 6000 series was not capable of any great speeds. It seemed to accelerate, perhaps, just a little bit faster than the Peter Witts (with the exception of the "speed cars" on Ocean Avenue) but otherwise the ride didn't seem much different.

I rode the 6000s on the Flatbush, Church, Putnam, Gates and Fulton lines and, as I already mentioned, only occasionally on the Myrtle. The main reason being that the Myrtle Avenue trolley, for the most part, paralleled the Myrtle Avenue El which ran above it. If I wanted to go downtown I would take the el, not the trolley, and if I wanted to go toward Ridgewood, once again, I preferred taking the el.

However, my story about the Myrtle Avenue Trolley really is about my near-to-death experience with it. There I was standing at the corner of Myrtle and Marcy, waiting for a green light so that I could cross to Velvilluh's newsstand. At last, the light turned green and I crossed with a number of other people. It was rush hour at Marcy and Myrtle. Workers were leaving the Cascade Laundry while others were coming out of the subway entrance on the other side from the train with the Manhattan passengers.

I was wearing a plaid mackinaw, and my brown corduroy knickers, which was standard kids' attire in those days. As always, I ran across the cobblestones of Myrtle Avenue, over the shiny silver trolley tracks and on to the sidewalk on the other side.

Velvilluh's newsstand had all the papers stacked side-by-side, I greeted Mister Davis, picked up the New York Sun, deposited the three cents and then tucked the paper under my arm like a football player.

Then it dawned on me that Jack Armstrong, one of my favorite radio programs, would be coming on the air and I'd better hustle home. When I reached the curbside to cross Myrtle again, I was completely oblivious to the traffic lights. I may have subconsciously remembered that it had been green when I crossed to the newsstand but now I was consumed with getting home and turning on the radio to 710 on the dial.

As I stepped onto the cobblestones, I noticed that a big 6000 Myrtle Avenue trolley had stopped at the corner of Marcy and Myrtle, heading for Tompkins. It was on the far side of Myrtle as I crossed and I assumed (wrongly, of course) that it had stopped for a red light, meaning I had the green.

In addition, it didn't dawn on me that I was the only person crossing. I began running into the gutter and dashed directly in front of the trolley, which was still stopped. I ran past the "Pay As You Enter, Have Exact Fare Ready" lettering over and below the trolley's front light and headed for the sidewalk, a dozen feet ahead.

Since I was consumed with Jack Armstrong and not with what was on the other side of the trolley, I never imagined that the Myrtle Avenue car actually was "hiding" a fast-moving truck which had come along on the stopped-trolley's right and was speeding to cross Marcy Avenue and move ahead to Tompkins.

As I trotted past the streetcar I peripherally peered to the right only to see the Mack Truck bearing down on me. I never broke stride, but pumped twice as hard and made it to the curb with the truck whizzing by—he never had time to even brake—about two inches from my corduroy knickers.

As I landed on the sidewalk, a horrified onlooker (some guy I had never seen before or since) launched into a lengthy harangue about how stupid I was and how I should have watched for the lights while delivering other pearls of wisdom, all of which went right past my ears.

By instinct and with the latent fear of the near-fatal accident, I was carried by my feet to 582 Marcy. Shaken and chastened by the close call, I wobbled into the "courtyard," pushed open the iron gate and huffed and puffed my way into the house.

Neither my grandmother nor my grandfather managed a good enough glimpse of me to see the fear in my eyes. I hustled up two flights of stairs, pulled off my mackinaw and quickly turned on Jack Armstrong, The All-American Boy.

I had made it by a minute, thanks to sheer luck. And no thanks to the Myrtle Avenue Trolley!

Myrtle Ave. was distinctive among our neighborhood blocks because of the elevated structure, one of the oldest in the city, and the shadow it literally cast over the street. Sunlight never came easy to those who lived under the El and most who resided in the ancient tenements between Nostrand and Tompkins Avenues suffered a harsh life.

It would be fair to say that virtually none of them owned telephones. As a matter of fact, in 1941, when I was nine years old, about half of our neighbors could not afford phones. But there was an alternative and that was the Candy Store Courier.

Every candy store in the community boasted a pay telephone which was used for both outgoing and incoming calls. If you didn't have a phone at home, you simply gave friends and relatives the number at Al and Shirleys candy store. When friends wanted to reach you, they simply phoned the candy store where at least one, two or three kids were hanging out, waiting to be a Candy Store Courier. Richie Mishkin, who was a regular at that job, would then rush to the apartment of whomever was receiving the call and advise that the other should rush down to Al and Shirley's for the message.

Being a Candy Store Courier was already a big deal in the neighborhood. A kid could make anywhere from a penny to a dime while hanging out and maybe a buck on a good day. "The only thing I didn't like," Mishkin always complained, "was traipsing up four flights. Those long climbs weren't quite worth a penny." Al and Shirley didn't mind because it meant that whomever came down for the call might remain in the candy store and make a purchase or two.

As for the Candy Store Courier, it was found money. Even if you only made a penny, that was good for a nice, large (for the price) Hooten Bar which was the poor man's version of Hershey's five-cents milk chocolate favorite. Or, for a penny, you could purchase a neatly-wrapped hunk of bubble gum along with a photo of a baseball player. These were called picture cards or, as we Brooklynites pronounced them, "pitcha-cahds."

The trick always was that you could discover a "hard card" by picking out a packet from about seven cards down on the pile. It was an interesting scheme but rarely worked.

In 1941 Alex Kampouris of the Brooklyn Dodgers was the hot card. Only one fellow on the entire block, Gilbert Birnbaum, had a Kampouris "pitcha card." For days, others went to the bottom of the pile in search of Kampouris but came up instead with Joe Vosmik, Babe Phelps or Pete Reiser, each of whom we had in doubles and triples.

Finally, Jerry Katzman, whose father owned the local kosher butcher shop, got a tip from his cousin on President St. that a candy store in Crown Heights had a ton of Kampouris cards. The news was tantamount to hearing that gold was discovered in California. We immediately sent an emissary, Irving Gottlieb, to the distant land that was Crown Heights. He was given carfare and a quarter and told to buy twenty-five cents worth of cards. "Gots" then received a royal sendoff as he boarded the Nostrand Ave. trolley to find the "hot" candy store next to the Talmud Torah of Crown Heights that supposedly had the cards.

We expected big things. If "Gots" returned with only two or three Kampouris cards it would be considered a bonanza. Even one would do. We waited at Al and Shirley's for Gottlieb's return secure in the knowledge that we had received a worthwhile tip. At last, an hour later, "Gots" alighted from the return Nostrand Ave. car and was greeted at the corner of Vernon and Nostrand like a conquering hero.

He emptied the brown, paper bag as if it was filled with jewels and, one by one, we each grabbed a neatly-wrapped bubble gum-card set, peeled off the covering, tossed away the gum (nobody ever bothered with chewing the stuff because the card was everything) and examined the cards.

One by one, the moans were heard. "Geez, another Pete Coscarart." "Damn, another Billy Herman." "Christ, who wants Dolph Camilli?"

Our special emissary to the Crown Heights candy store returned with nary a single Kampouris card. It marked the first and last time we ever accepted a hot tip from Jerry Katzman. Never again was "Gots" Gottlieb sent on the Nostrand trolley for "pitcha cards."

This trolley which stopped at the corner of Marcy and Myrtle is in the exact spot where it was when I nearly got run over crossing from the newsstand on the right. The truck coming up behind the trolley did so in the same way it is in this picture. The empty lots on the left are remnants of two classic tenement fires which I viewed from our living room window with abject horror.

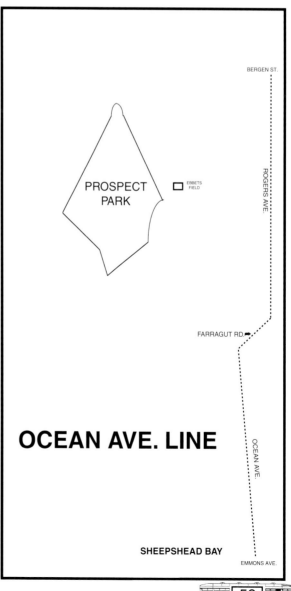

OCEAN AVE. LINE

BERGEN ST.

PROSPECT PARK

EBBETS FIELD

ROGERS AVE.

FARRAGUT RD.

OCEAN AVE.

SHEEPSHEAD BAY

EMMONS AVE.

Amid the arboreal splendor of Flatbush, the Ocean Ave. speed car never looked better than it did on Farragut Road en route to Lew Klotz's house at Ave. S.

CHAPTER SEVEN:
THE OCEAN AVENUE LINE/HIGH SPEED

Having the thrill of a high-speed trolley ride was a rarity in Brooklyn because of traffic conditions, generally s̶ ̶ks which required frequent stops and, most of all, the fact that nearly all the streetcars–with the exception o̶ ̶mliners–were not equipped for racing over the rails.

̶hus, when a Nostrand Avenue or Tompkins Avenue trolley had its controller pushed onto the highest speed poi̶ ̶ly rumbled over 20 miles per hour on a straightaway. The "thrill" in this case was merely the knowledge tha̶ ̶ey was going as fast as it <u>could</u> go and the best example of that was on Empire Boulevard, on the way to Ebbets F̶ ̶re a Tompkins Avenue 8000 series Peter Witt would have the luxury of several long block runs (between King̶ ̶ New York Avenues, for example) and would bounce along, straining to keep up with the automobiles. It ga̶ ̶ey buff like me a kick even though the streetcar wasn't reaching supersonic speeds.

̶ortunately, there were a couple of notable exceptions to this speedless rule and one of them was the Ocean Av̶ ̶. Wisely, the operators of the Brooklyn and Queens Transit System (BMT-owned), realized that there were a few ̶rooklyn where the distance between streets was abnormally long. On these avenues a trolley had a chance to r̶ ̶h better time if it had more powerful motors in the manner of the giant interurban trolleys that ran so rapidly a̶ ̶countryside between cities and towns during the early part of the century.

̶he B & Q.T. seized this opportunity and installed more powerful motors in the 8000 Peter Witts on the Ocean Av̶ ̶te although one would never know the difference just eyeing the vehicles from the outside. They looked every bi̶ ̶r slower cousins that plied Lorimer Street, DeKalb Avenue and Surf Avenue at a more leisurely m.p.h. and

Ordinarily, I would not have much reason to ride the Ocean Avenue Line because it was nowhere near my neighborhood. Its northern "terminal" was at the juncture of Rogers Avenue, Bedford Avenue and Bergen Street, across from the enormous and opulent Loew's Bedford Theater. On the southern side, the line terminated at Sheepshead Bay very close to the gaudy F.W.I.L. Lundy Brothers' Restaurant on Emmons Avenue. Lundy's, at the time, was the Taj Mahal of sea food restaurants and meant to Brooklynites, in a culinary sense, what Ebbets Field did in sporting terms.

But I had a very good reason to ride the Ocean Avenue Line because of my pal, Lewis Klotz.

While Lewis Klotz wasn't officially <u>family</u>, he was "family." His parents, Nat and Selma, were as tight with my folks as any four people could be. Without ever saying so explicitly, my father indicated in other ways that Nat Klotz was his best friend. My dad had an expression—"That man is a prince"—which he very rarely used. It was a form of Ben Fischler knighthood. If pop called someone a "prince," the subject of his admiration ranked somewhere in the vicinity of Jesus, Allah, Moses, Mohammed or Franklin Delano Roosevelt.

You're looking at Brooklyn's biggest and best seafood restaurant—F.W.I.L. Lundy Bros. at the foot of Ocean and Emmons Ave. in Sheepshead Bay. An ironic feature of Lundy's was the terribly officious and sometimes rude manner of the waiters. That's a Sea Gate Line car on the left and an Ocean Ave. Line car on the right. The Bay's fishing boats are not far away.

Nat and Selma had a daughter, Judy, who was a couple of years older than Lew. She was one of the happiest, funniest gals I've ever had the pleasure of knowing. Lewis, himself, who was my age, was a sweet fellow who sometimes seemed to be stepping right out of an Andy Hardy movie or an Archie Comic book.

Not that Lew was a fool (far from it) or anything suggesting one, but he did have a homespun Henry Aldrich quality about him that suggested Middle America rather than Avenue S and East 22nd Street. In Brooklynese, one simply would say that Lew Klotz was a "good guy" and a chap I enjoyed visiting as much as my father liked being in the company of Nat Klotz.

The only problem about being Lew's friend was geography. The Klotzs lived somewhere on the southern border of Flatbush, or, if you will, the northern border of Sheepshead Bay. Whatever, it was a heck of a long way from my Williamsburg abode and awfully difficult to reach via rapid transit because there was no subway (or el) stop within walking distance of <u>Maison Klotz</u>.

Which meant that the only "convenient" way of getting there was by trolley. No, make that plural; trolleys! First the Nostrand or Lorimer Street Lines and then the Ocean Avenue streetcar.

This was not an easy trip by our standards since the Klotzs lived in "Yenevelt," another world. As a matter of fact going to Lew's house was more

(LEFT) Lew and Judy Klotz in 1942. Lew and knickers were synonymous. As a matter of fact, he's the only kid in our crowd who actually wore knickers for his bar mitzvah.

(RIGHT) The man my father called a "Prince," Nat Klotz at home with <u>The Times</u>. Uncle Nat was the only travelling salesman I ever knew. I thought he had one of the most romantic jobs; traversing New York State by car, selling women's gloves.

like taking the New York Central to Albany, the Pennsylvania to Harrisburg, the Long Island Rail Road to Greenport or the Delaware, Lackawana & Western to Dover. In plain English it was by Brooklyn transit standards, a "trip." With luck, it would take an hour but likely more than that.

The hitch was that after you were on the Nostrand (or Lorimer) for about fifteen minutes and arrived at Bergen Street, it was necessary to get off and then "schlep" over to Bedford Avenue where the Ocean Line began its run.

Not that I minded the changeover. The area around Bergen and Nostrand had a special fascination for me because I could walk past Marta's Italian Restaurant on Bergen Street, between Nostrand and Bedford. Even then, Marta's had a mystical quality about it and, although I had never had the pleasure of entering its portals and partaking of the victuals, I was certain that this was one of New York City's best restaurants. Marta's had a modest white front and nothing else about it was especially prepossessing. Apart from never having eaten there, my other frustration was never knowing what the Marta of Marta's actually looked like; presuming, of course, that there was a Marta.

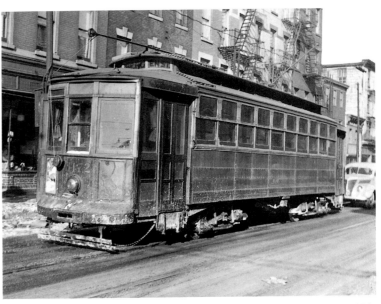

Wearing all its post-snow storm residue, Bergen Street Line's 1172 rumbles toward Bedford Ave. with a 1937 Ford bringing up the rear. One of the city's most famous Italian restaurants, Marta's of Bergen St., was located not far from this scene, near the Ocean Ave. Line's terminus.

Another neighborhood shop that always magnetized me to its windows was Jay's. This was situated on Nostrand, not far from Bergen and, although it was billed as a "stationery store," we youngsters knew it for its sporting goods and toys. (So many stationery stores are appreciated more for their non-stationery products and Jay's was right up there with the best.) I was especially enamored of Jay's because of its selection of outfielders mitts. There always seemed to be at least six in the window with autographed models from Joe Vosmik, Pete Coscarart, Ducky Medwick and Leo Durocher, all major leaguers when I was seven-years-old.

I actually wound up buying two different baseball gloves at Jay's. The first was a catcher's mitt. For a short time, I was hung up on being a backstop and pestered and pestered my father into buying me a catcher's mitt. As I recall, he continually nixed the idea but my Uncle Sid—married to my father's sister, Charlotte—who was quite a ballplayer in his youth, coughed up a few bucks and I got the mitt.

Sadly, it was was not nearly a big-league model with a deep, solid pocket. The yellowish hunk of leather was small and thick but the thickness made it almost impossible to create a pocket.

Not that I didn't try. I must have rubbed about half of Saudi's monthly oil production into the mitt futilely attempting to create some sort of permanent landing strip for the baseball. Alas, nothing worked.

Then, one day, Uncle Sid and Aunt Charlotte came to visit. Naturally, Uncle Sid inquired about my mitt. I told him about it and he suggested that we go outside where he could toss a few at me.

Now I knew Uncle Sid had been a semi-pro ball player but I had no idea that he would fire the ball the way he did. His first pitch sent me retreating about two yards down Vernon Avenue, just from the recoil alone. The sting from the horsehide coursed through my palm long after Sid wound up for the second pitch. This one had my bowels in an uproar because it had a curve on it and before I could center the ball, it caromed off the top edge of the mitt and then off my forehead.

I stuck it out for about five more pitches and then found an excuse to get back into the house. Sid's demonstration was impressive but my mitt was not and from that day on it saw very limited service–if any at all–among my sporting materiel.

The other purchase at Jay's was equally disappointing, but for a slightly different reason. One Sunday afternoon my dad and I found ourselves on Fulton Street in Downtown Brooklyn following a Bushwick's double header at Dexter Park. Pop liked to take me to Automat cafeterias which, in in the late 1930s and early 1940s, were fun eateries with quality food. (Creamed Spinach, mashed potatoes and baked beans were my specialties but the creamed turnips were terrific, too.) A half-block from the Automat, squeezed between a haberdashery and a woman's shop, and directly across from the Loew's Metropolitan, was a tiny sporting goods store on Fulton St. that carried high-quality equipment.

On this day we ambled past the store when I noticed right plumb in the middle of the display was perched the most beautiful outfielder's glove I had ever seen. It

That's Uncle Sid and Aunt Charlotte in the back row and my grandmother (on my father's side), Sarah and my cousin Sandee.

was a deep, rich ox-blood colored mitt with an oversized (for its time) webbing between the thumb and index finger which virtually guaranteed that a kid would snare any ball within leaping distance. The Spalding model even had the autograph of one of my favorite hitters, Joe (Ducky) Medwick of the Dodgers.

"Dad," I intoned as only a kid desperate for a gift that he knows he's unlikely to receive yet still holds out the faint hope that he'll get it, can intone, "I really would like that glove. I mean REALLY want that glove. Do you think I can get it?"

I didn't have to wait for the answer because the answer was hanging from the heel of the glove and, in exquisite script, said $6.

In 1942 a six-dollar price tag on a baseball mitt made as much sense to my dad as his purchasing a Rolls-Royce; and Ben Fischler didn't even know how to drive.

"You're not getting the mitt," my father replied on the short hop. "It's too expensive."

I never wimpered; never muttered another word as we walked over to the Automat. But I filed the image of the magnificently beautiful ox-blood Joe Medwick Spalding mitt in the back of my head, knowing full well that it would surface in one of my propaganda campaigns.

Craftily, I said nothing about the glove until I went off to summer camp a few weeks later, accompanied by some monstrously inefficient, old fielder's glove from another year. No sooner had I arrived at Camp Pythian in Glen Spey, New York, I launched a barrage of "gimme" letters to my parents.

While carefully articulating the joys–and sorrows–of camp, I also managed to weave at least one paragraph in which I insisted that my baseball career would come to a dismal and abrupt end if Dad didn't purchase that wonderful glove-of - my-dreams.

Absence usually made my parents' hearts grow fonder for their only child and they occasionally acceded to my long distance letter requests. But when it came to a six-dollar ox-blood mitt, Pop was as implacable as Winston Churchill defying the Nazi hordes. I intensified my campaign in the latter days of camp and finally achieved a breakthrough of sorts. Dad finally agreed that when I returned home, I could purchase a new glove, "but not the Joe Medwick model because it's too expensive."

Mistakenly, I harbored the idea that I could crack his resistance when I got home but when it came time to buy the glove—he directed me to Jay's on Nostrand Avenue near Bergen and not to my favorite little sporting goods store on Fulton Street. Dad put a three-dollar maximum on the purchase. Sure enough, Jay's featured a three-buck glove in its window. It was fairly good-sized with a not-too-bad pocket but it was yellow and was made by the Globe Sporting Goods Company which I had never heard of and that alone was a downer.

But it was the best I could get for three-bucks so into Jay's we went and down went the three bills on the counter. The mitt was wrapped and taken home, unwrapped and carried on to Vernon Avenue where it was immediately put into use. No way it ever could have been as good as the ox-blood Joe Medwick, six-dollar mitt but it was serviceable and gave me about three years of life before it was replaced by an ox-blood, first baseman's mitt, but that's another story.

After walking from Nostrand to Bedford, along Bergen Street, I then turned left to the Ocean Avenue trolley's point of departure. Usually, there was at least one car either rolling into view or one already there awaiting passengers; my signal to begin a new journey.

The beauty of getting on at the first stop was that I nearly always was guaranteed a spot in the front jump seat to the immediate left of the motorman. This was especially coveted on the Ocean Avenue Line because of the special "speed" cars.

From the moment I rested my derriere on the wooden bench and grabbed on to the slightly-movable upright seat end, an electric thrill moved up and down my body because of the anticipated ride ahead. For here was a trolley that was more like a thoroughbred. It didn't gallop, it raced!

You sensed the difference just by fixing your eyes on the controller. It was more imposing than its counterparts on the Peter Witts and so was the brake mechanism and even the floor. If memory serves me right, it didn't have the usual wood slats but rather was paved with a concrete-type composition that gave it a special quality.

The Ocean Avenue trolley's run was long, rich and varied. When the motorman finally jerked the controller, we moved through some of the grander sections of Bedford-Stuyvesant, still adorned with 19th Century mansions, older apartments and clean streets.

Here's where the Ocean line began it's run on Rogers Ave. where it intersects with Bedford near Bergen St. in Bedford-Stuyvesant

The speed car couldn't show its true stuff at the beginning because the streets were relatively short and there wasn't enough room to accellerate. Still, it was interesting as the Peter Witt car thump-thumped its way along Rogers Avenue, down the hill toward Empire Boulevard not far from Ebbets Field and then a levelling off as it hit the Tompkins-Lorimer lines crossover at Empire for the run into Flatbush.

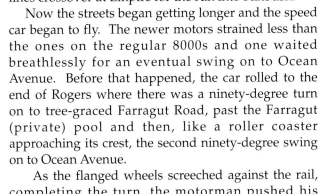

Now the streets began getting longer and the speed car began to fly. The newer motors strained less than the ones on the regular 8000s and one waited breathlessly for an eventual swing on to Ocean Avenue. Before that happened, the car rolled to the end of Rogers where there was a ninety-degree turn on to tree-graced Farragut Road, past the Farragut (private) pool and then, like a roller coaster approaching its crest, the second ninety-degree swing on to Ocean Avenue.

As the flanged wheels screeched against the rail, completing the turn, the motorman pushed his controller into high and the super-Peter Witt leaped into high gear. The tracks along Ocean Avenue were reasonably but not totally smooth and when the trolley got up to speed, the lurching, bouncing, click-clacking was just to the left of thrilling and just to the right of scary.

The speed car is heading home toward its Bergen St. depot past typical Bedford-Stuyvesant housing not far from Loew's Bedford.

Here's where I got goose-pimples as the trolley swerved off Farragut Rd. and developed its best speed along Ocean Ave.

Ocean Avenue was laid out in long, long blocks and the speed car was just perfect for the route. The contrast from a rail fan's viewpoint, was analogous to that of a subway car ride compared to a Long Island Rail Road passenger ride. Ergo; the difference in m.p.h. was as obvious as the Empire State Building.

I don't know whether any Ocean Avenue car ever derailed because of the intensely swift run but it certainly seemed possible, if not likely, that such an event had to have taken place. For a trolley gourmand like myself, the Ocean run was ideal because it seemed to have endless courses.

When we reached Ocean Avenue, the trolley went directly past the four-story apartment building where my folks lived after my mother had delivered me at Israel Zion Hospital in Borough Park. I have seen photos of myself being pushed in a baby carriage in front of the house which was situated just a block from Avenue H and Ocean where my father's parents, Sarah and Joseph Fischler,

lived. My Uncles Herbert and William (we always referred to him as Will) and Aunt Natalie (known as Tillie) shared the apartment with my grandparents. A floor above was Aunt Beatrice (Beadie), who was my father's kid sister, Uncle Sam Pelton (he with the fantastically neat and handsome pencil moustache) and my older cousin Judith, alias Judy.

I loved them all although, to be frank, I saw them considerably less than relatives on my mother's (Friedman) side of the family. Grandpa Joseph died when I was about seven and Grandma Sarah a few years later. Both were very sweet folks; gentle to a fault. After grandpa's death, grandma spent her last year or so at an old age home in East New York which I visited at least once with my dad via a ride on the Utica-Reid trolley.

Each of my uncles was affectionate but in a different way. Herbert was funny; Will was a fuddy-duddy but awfully nice; Sam was a laugh riot, exceptionally witty and Beadie (very pretty) always took a liking to me. I really liked my cousin Judy but because of the age difference, we spent less time together than usual; a fact that I always regretted. She inherited her father's wit and, to this day, is always quick with a laugh. Aunt Tillie was a gem; very funny–sometimes silly–always terribly kind to me.

Once we passed Avenue H, the trolley plied the rails through the heart of Flatbush over the Long Island Rail Road cut and south toward Sheepshead Bay. The speed was deliciously better than anything I've experienced on any trolley line and, interestingly, the joy never wore off right to my destination at Avenue S.

There I alighted, walked two blocks along Avenue S to East 22nd Street and then a right toward Avenue T and the Klotz residence, a two-story, white-wooded frame house that was as different from our Williamsburg brownstone as the Washington Monument is compared to Gracie Mansion.

We've just passed the apartment (to the left over the rear of the trolley) where my paternal grandparents as well as Uncles and Aunts lived.

Because of this difference, I liked the Klotz abode. I would even go so far as to say it had a "country" atmosphere compared to our "city" brownstone. Besides, the house was detached and almost reminded me of a farmhouse although that might be stretching it a bit.

It was on trips to Lew Klotz's house when I most often tantalized myself with the idea of committing the emphatically (by my mother) forbidden act of trolley-hitching.

For the unfamiliar, trolley-hitching is exactly what it implies; getting a free ride by fastening yourself to the streetcar's rear. The trick was to sneak up to the backside of the tram while it stopped for passengers. By carefully ducking under the window, you could stay out of the motorman's view although an operator with sharp mental radar knew exactly when kids were attempting a hitch.

Once the motorman engaged the controller, a trolley-hitcher would grab on to the cord-box or similar appurtenance and lift himself from the pavement. Off and rolling, the free-rider would enjoy his hitch until; a. The motorman spied the miscreant; b. An angry, self-righteous passenger intimidated the hitcher off the trolley; or c. The lad "made" a block or two and then decided to get off on his own.

Since most motormen experienced an avuncular feeling about their streetcars, they took a dim view of anyone daring to get a free ride on the trolleys. Hence, the driver would slam on the brakes, throw open the door and take four steps in pursuit of the fleeing lad. By this time, the trolley-hitcher was out of sight and the ride resumed.

The thrill of a free ride tempted me to try it at least once but not in my own neighborhood. That's why I figured I might gamble a hitch one day on the Ocean Ave. Line. But discretion was the better part of valor. Friends had warned me that the Ocean Avenue speed cars could stop very quickly, loosen my grip and send me hurtling under the rear wheels. Which explains why my trolley-hitching career began and ended

My adopted uncle, aunt and cousins. The Klotz family. (Aunt Selma, Uncle Nat, Judy and Lew) and the Fischlers were so close, I assumed for years that Lew and I were cousins. He felt the same way and it wasn't until we were teenagers that we realized the truth. We liked it the other way and still do, in fact.

with that chilling image.

Another ploy that drove motormen nuts was "pole-pulling," an act that was far more annoying than "trolley-hitching." A pole-puller executed his frustrating manuver much the way a hitcher would his; by unsuspectingly sneaking up to the streetcars derriere when it was at a stop.

The rapscallion then would tug on the rope attached to the trolley pole, pulling it off the overhead wire and effectively killing the vehicle's power. Unlike the trolley-hitcher who essentially antagonized the driver, the pole-puller infuriated all the passengers whose ride was disrupted—however briefly—by the dastardly act.

If a pole-puller succeeded, any self-respecting (in-shape) motorman would give serious chase for at least half-a-block. Heaven help the scamp who was within reach because he would have earned a half-dozen raps on the behind whether the American Civil Liberties Union approved or not.

Needless to say, I never even dreamed of pulling a trolley's pole. I considered it a heinous act, disruptive of service not to mention my favorite motorman's mental well-being.

The Klotz's were an interesting family. Nat was an easy-going quiet sort of guy who was hard to dislike whereas Selma–I generally called her Aunt Selma even though we were not related–was one of the most quick-tempered people I ever have met. Aunt Selma would fly off the handle at world-speed records and usually directed her wrath at Lewis or Nat although there was one afternoon when poor Judy got it but good. She had been sent to the grocery store with a ten dollar bill and lost it on the way. When Judy returned to the house minus groceries and minus ten dollar bill the Selma explosion could be heard as far distant as Paerdegat Basin.

Aunt Selma, about 15 feet away from the scene of the crime. That dining room table was the scene of many laughs many to the hostess' chagrin.

I was the target of an Aunt Selma blast on one memorable occasion. Lew and I were ten years old at the time–in 1942–and it was a weekend when I had slept over on a Saturday night and returned home on a Sunday. Nat and Selma went to the movies that night, leaving Lew and I alone in the house. After potchkying around with the usual run of games, we mutually agreed that it was time for a good, old pillow fight, an event that also could have taken place at 582 Marcy Avenue.

We decided to hold the pillow fight in Lew's bedroom which was a typical lad's sanctuary replete with a few banners on the wall, magazines stacked in racks and a box of marbles stashed on the side awaiting the season of "skellys," "roll-it-in-the-box" and other sidewalk, curbside marble games. (P.S. I once pilfered one of Lew's jumbolas brought it home, hid the marble and never looked at it again.)

The room was not very large. It accommodated a bed, a desk, a chair and not much else. Two was a crowd in Lewis Klotz's bedroom which made it perfect for a pillow fight because there was little space for retreat.

Lew supplied the pillows and then turned off the little wooden wall light that was attached to the plaster over the middle of the bed. Away we went, swinging high and low, having a raucous good time until IT happened.

Thoroughly exhausted and being battered heavily by Lew, I took a wild counter swing—and missed. The pillow glanced off the wall next to his bed and suddenly produced a "K-R-A-K" that gave each of us a temporary case of lockjaw. Almost simultaneously, we dropped our pillows and stared into the darkness to determine what damage had been done, suspecting that it had been colossal.

We were right. Lew dug out a flashlight and showed it on the wall. Where once there had been a smooth surface, adorned by a neat light fixture, there now was a gaping hole, a two-inch thick incision into the plaster and, of course, no lamp. The pillow had swiped the lamp right out of its home and took considerable roots with it.

Now there are some childhood misdeeds that can be covered up before the parents return. A spill on the rug often can be washed out and broken glass can be mopped up and tossed into the garbage. But there was obviously no repairing the dislocated lamp although we instantly thought of mixing some Plaster of Paris and attempting a quick patch job. The problem, naturally, was that no Plaster of Paris was obtainable at 10:30 p.m. on a Saturday night.

We each dug ourselves holes in our respective beds, secure in the knowledge that Sunday morning would be hell. And it was. When Aunt Selma discovered the ravaged wall, she let out a wail that would have made a banshee blush. I pleaded guilty with a poor explanation; the pillow fight.

Because Aunt Selma always had a soft spot for me, her wrath was gone almost as fast as it had typhooned into the room. She did inform my mother of the damage but by the time she had phoned Evergreen 7-1183, the incident was almost as amusing to her as it was horrific. I was allowed to spend the remainder of Sunday with Lew and then sheepishly walked to the Ocean Avenue trolley for the ride home.

I always felt a lump in the pit of my stomach when I left Lew's house. His neck of Flatbush-Sheepshead Bay appealed to me in a lot of ways but mostly because it seemed so countrified. More than that, I was sad about leaving Lew. Having neither sister nor brother, I occasionally suffered solitude pangs and mused about what it would be like to have Lew as a regular companion instead of a once-in-a-while type of pseudo-cousin.

But by the time I was back on the Ocean Avenue trolley, melancholy evaporated and I concentrated on the ride home.

One of the beauty parts of any Ocean Avenue trip was the block-to-block race with automobiles. Racing cars was no fun on the Tompkins Avenue trolley along, say, a stretch of Empire Boulevard because the standard Peter Witt simply didn't have the horsepower to keep up with the autos.

However, the Ocean Avenue speed car outsped just about every Pontiac, Buick, LaSalle or DeSoto that chose to keep pace and only wavered when it had to slow down for passengers. That a streetcar could still beat an internal combustion engine pleased me no end and I strained forward in anticipation whenever the motorman yanked on the rounded controller and pulled it to the high point.

A speed car produced better percussive sounds than its slower counterparts. Occasionally it would race over the Church Avenue crossover in high, delivering a da-dum-da-dum-dum-dum-dum that reminded me of drummer Gene Krupa executing a quick paradiddle on Tiger Rag.

The sights were also riveting; Brooklyn College's majestic Georgian architecture and library tower; the art deco apartments along Ocean Avenue; the enormous trees of mid-Flatbush and the red neon lights that signalled Toomey's Restaurant, Bar & Grill at Empire Boulevard near Ebbets Field.

The speed car was at its most muscular, climbing the relatively steep hill—caused by glacial moraine that marked the edge of the last glacier which ended its march at what is now Eastern Parkway—from Empire Boulevard up past Montgomery, Crown and President Streets and then into the heart of Bedford-Stuyvesant, terminating across from the Loew's Bedford and its massive marquee.

Then, the walk back down Bergen Street— Marta's was alive with people now—and the plodding ride home on either the Nostrand or Lorimer Street cars, depending on which came first.

After riding the Ocean Avenue speed cars, I have to say the switch back to the regular-motored Peter Witts was a bit of a letdown. Besides, the cars usually were crowded by the time they reached Bergen Street, so I usually had to move to the rear and hope that one of the window seats was available.

By the time I reached home there was the usual welcome from my grandmother and grandfather, Etel and Simon, respectively, in the ground floor living room. Sometimes my spinster Aunt Helen would be there. Then it would be up one flight of stairs—two steps at a time—then the second flight and into the waiting arms of mom and pop.

This time, Molly had only one thing to say, "So, you broke the plaster off the wall in Lewis's room."

"Sorry, Mom," I embarassedly replied, "but let me tell you about the great ride on the Ocean Avenue trolley..."

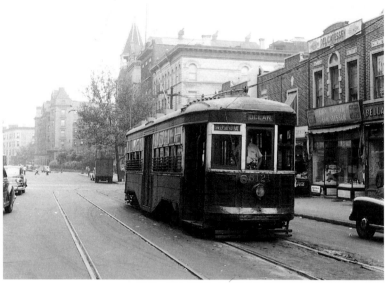

Here's where I got off for the one block walk along Bergen St. to catch the Nostrand car for the ride home.

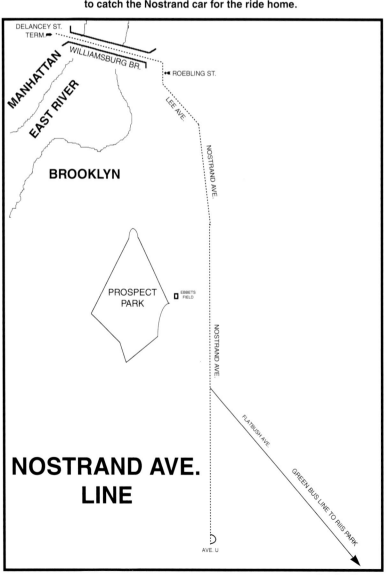

NOSTRAND AVE. LINE

One of the longest rides for a nickel, the
Nostrand trip begins here in Manhattan under
Delancey St. in the vast underground
terminal. This was an exciting moment when
the car switched on to the main track, and
headed toward daylight.

CHAPTER EIGHT:
THE NOSTRAND AVENUE LINE

crossing the Borough of Brooklyn, from Avenue U near Marine Park, all the way to the Williamsburg Br
d Avenue trolley gave a rider more than his nickel's worth. As an added fillip, it crossed the bridge over
d deposited remaining passengers at Delancey Street, site of one of vaudeville's oldest gags.

*A piano prodigy from Omaha, heading for the Carnegie Hall School of Music, gets off the train
at Grand Central and mistakenly takes the subway to Delancey Street instead of his proper
destination at 57th Street. When he climbs the station steps to the main drag of the Lower East
Side, he sees a rabbi. "Excuse me, sir," says the prodigy, "but how do I get to Carnegie Hall?"
The rabbi sizes up the young man and replies, "Mine boy, practice, practice, practice!"*

from the gag, the delights of Delancey Street were many and none more intriguing than the undergrou
the Bridge's end beneath the teeming thoroughfare.
endless number of Brooklyn streetcars–including the Tompkins, Sumner-Sackett and Utica-Reid–
sburg Bridge tracks and then barreled down into the tunnel where they switched off to one of the many t
entered the tunnel from Delancey Street just as one would for a subway ride. The difference in the troll
t there were no platforms. You walked along the tracks until you found the curve at which your tr
clambered aboard and then awaited the splendid climb out into the fresh air and the ride across the bri

Here's another view of the fascinating Delancey depot, the launching pad for several lines that went through my neighborhood, including the Nostrand run to Flatbush.

The trolley tracks looked different on the bridge than they did on the street. On any regular Brooklyn avenue, the tracks were embedded in the pavement and actually were comprised of two parts, the thick one on which the wheels rolled and a flange on the other side of the gap that essentially kept the wheel from derailing. But on the bridge, the trolley rolled along rails that duplicated those on the subway and elevated lines and therefore made for a very interesting ride while giving the Peter Witt an interurban quality not often available in the city.

Once out from underground, the motorman pushed the controller to high and Peter Witt groaned up the long incline to mid-point on the bridge. On the Williamsburg span, the trolley tracks were located on an inner roadway right under the BMT el tracks. A three-foot metal picket fence separated the Brooklyn-bound from Manhattan-bound rails. This differed from the Brooklyn Bridge where the trolleys ran

I got a special kick when the trolleys ran on pure rails sitting on exposed ties. This is on the Williamsburg Bridge run. Notice that promising vocalist Dinah Shore is featured at the Flatbush Theater.

shoulder to shoulder with a lane of automobile traffic in each direction.

Riding the trolley over the bridge provided one of the bigger thrills for a buff because the long uninterrupted run allowed the car to develop its fastest possible speed for the longest period of time. There were no traffic lights to contend with, just a straight run until the tracks dipped down to Bridge Plaza in Brooklyn. While the trolleys never developed the rapid click-clacks that, say, a BMT Brighton Line would at top speed rounding the Beverly Road curve, the Peter Witts did generate a pleasant enough staccato particularly after passing over the crest and gaining speed for the downward sprint.

It was then that the trolleys actually kept pace or even outran the autos which often were stacked up in

The base of the ramp at the Brooklyn end of the Williamsburg Bridge. #8509 has just left the bridge plaza and is heading toward Manhattan. The plaza is just past the trolley in the far distance where there was a veritable streetcar menagerie.

traffic while we had the luxury of an open track ahead. By the time we had passed over the East River and now were over the Brooklyn waterfront, the Nostrand Avenue car was going as fast it could go, swaying excitedly from side to side and, I'm sure, titillating the motorman as much as it did me.

The question always in my mind was how long would he wait before swinging the controller handle back to the closed position and, finally, applying the brake. This usually happened about fifty yards before the Broadway BMT Line curved to the right and headed towards Driggs Avenue.

Then the motorman played the brake handle on the right like a riverboat gambler shaking dice before the throw. Back and forth his hand gently–but firmly–pushed the wooden stump, producing that delicious hiss of air that pushed the brake shoes into place. At last the trolley passed from under the el tracks, slowing as it approached the lip of

Williamsburg and the plaza with its many semi-covered trolley terminals.

This was a true junction. While the Nostrand car lurched right from the switch to its proper plaza station, other cars of various shapes were taking on passengers or dropping them off as the case may be. The Bridge Plaza was a veritable menagerie of trolleys covered with a maze of tracks and an endless number of platforms.

Once we left the Plaza, the sensation of speed had gone and now we bounced along the more prosaic path through the streets of Williamsburg. The trolley made a sharp right turn on to Roebling Street, past the infamous Joe-Reds poolroom toward Lee Avenue and the equally notorious "Kitzel" (as in fondling a young lady) Park. A slight left at Lee left Roebling in the rear view mirror as the Nostrand line began its earnest jaunt across the spine of Brooklyn.

Others may have equalled it, but no line could outdo the Nostrand in terms of mileage. It bisected the borough, starting at the north end in Williamsburg, past Lorimer Street, Flushing Avenue, Myrtle and DeKalb before moving into Bedford-Stuyvesant. Then it was Gates, Putnam, Fulton, Atlantic, Bergen, Eastern Parkway and into Crown Heights followed by the dip toward Empire Boulevard and Flatbush.

The Nostrand Line crossed Flatbush in its entirety, eventually making its way to Avenue U at the very edge of Sheepshead Bay. A trip from the Delancey Street subway (trolley) terminal to Avenue U could consume an hour-and-a-half–and all for a nickel.

It would be impossible to detail all of my memories of the Nostrand Avenue Line because it played such an intrinsic part of my life. One of my favorite runs was from home (Nostrand and Vernon) to the juncture of Nostrand and Flatbush Avenue where one connected with the Green Bus Lines which operated the route from Flatbush to Jacob Riis Park on the Atlantic Ocean in the Rockaways.

This is the bridge plaza at the Brooklyn end of the Williamsburg Bridge. Just above the Wilson Ave. summer-sided car is the trestle of the Broadway BMT Line. The abandoned spur to the East River Ferry is still standing in this World War II-era photo.

This shot taken from the Myrtle Avenue el station shows the Marcy houses playground on the right where I practiced my roller hockey skills with Arnie Fox. Once we skated two hours in a torrential downpour.

I always knew that my family was "different" and I attributed that, in part, to the Hungarian genes on my mother's side of the family and my father's bulldog refusal to be like everyone else. He did not do this in an ostentatious way but rather subtly with catchy expressions like, "I'll Fix Your Wagon" (Beware or you'll feel my wrath) or "He's Busier Than A One-Armed Paperhanger With An Itch." Or, "Are you a wise guy or a Boy Scout?" (I never figured that one out.)

While just about every family in neighborhood would head out to Brighton Beach or Coney Island for their summer bathing, my parents doggedly refused to be caught at either of those briny havens. My Hungarian-bred mother considered them below her status, just as my grandmother–Molly's Hungarian mother–wanted no part of the <u>Litvaks</u> who lived next door.

Brighton and Coney Island were, as far as my folks were concerned, for the riff-raff. They were honky-tonk with bath houses like Storch's that were old and smelly and not the place where a self-respecting Hungarian-American would want to change clothes into a bathing suit. Raven Hall, which I loved for its punching bags, also got thumbs-down.

By contrast, Riis Park was spanking new and clean. Blueprinted by the City's supreme power broker, Robert Moses, the bathing beach was built during the Great Depression and completed when I was just out of diapers. I have a vague memory of being taken there one day by my mother when I was about three-years-old. My mother didn't trust letting me go into the men's bathhouse so she took me with her to the women's side and I can recall being enormously embarrassed–though only three–at seeing all the naked females, my mom included.

Riis Park was so new when we began going there regularly in the late 1930s that everything worked. It boasted wonderful outdoor showers with large buttons–not unlike those on the Peter Witts which were used to open and close the rear doors–that kept the water going for minutes on end before automatically shutting down. It had big, steel cubbies for clothes and neat tile shower enclosures. Most of all, Riis Park was spanking clean and that, among other things, was why my parents loved it.

But getting to Riis Park was a transit adventure. For starters, there was the long ride on the Nostrand Avenue trolley, usually on a Sunday morning. We generally left early enough so that I could get a window seat if I couldn't occupy my favorite spot next to the motorman.

A window seat had advantages, especially if it was summertime and the window opened. On the Peter Witts the windows opened wide and even though there were protective metal grates, one was guaranteed a grand breeze when the car was in motion with plenty of visibility for sightseeing.

Normally, a ride from home to the Flatbush-Nostrand intersection was uneventful on a Sunday morning but one such trip produced a vignette the likes of which I had never seen before and never seen since. We had just passed the Putnam Avenue switch, rumbled past ancient Girl's High School (which my mother had attended) and approached Fulton Street

(ABOVE) I got a big kick out of this spot—the Eastern Pkwy. crossing—because it led to Crown Heights and the exciting downhill run to Empire Blvd. It was the very spot where the glacier stopped ending the last ice age.

(BELOW) The cobblestone streets ran past the Loew's Kameo Theater which was just around the corner on the left and featured a roof garden.

when we stopped at a side street a block or two from Fulton. As the Peter Witt picked up its passenger, I sensed that something was going on farther down the block but, at that point, I could only hear the muffled chatter of persons still out of sight.

As the motorman pushed his brake handle into its off position and pulled on the controller, I was able to peer down the block. There in the middle of the street was a circle of mostly young people, surrounding two adult males who were about to engage in a bare-fisted fight.

It was an eerie and terribly frightening sight to me. I had never seen grown men slug it out anywhere but in a boxing ring with large gloves on their hands. This scenario had a "High Noon" quality about it as if an epic battle between two rival warriors was about to take place. I inadvertently held my breath as the car rolled past the intersection and the men moved toward each other. Before a blow had been struck, the trolley moved on to Fulton Street and, of course, I never learned the outcome of the fight.

The ride from Fulton to Eastern Parkway was generally slow although hardly boring. Nostrand Avenue is relatively thin at this point and there was heavy traffic because of the shopping areas. It seemed to open up at Eastern Parkway, the broad boulevard with its main thoroughfare and service road. At the southeasterly corner of Eastern Parkway and Nostrand proudly sat the Loew's Kameo Theater, one of my all-time favorite movie houses.

Since it was out of my neighborhood, I didn't frequent the Kameo but I was taken there from time to time by my parents or my Aunt Helen who shared the house with us or, during World War II, by my Aunt Lottie, whose husband (Uncle) Joe, was serving with the (U.S. Navy) Seabees.

What made the Kameo such a delight was the fact that during warm weather it opened its roof garden and showed films under the stars. Watching Eleanor Powell tap dance her way through "Broadway

Melody of 1940" (ably accompanied by Fred Astaire) in the Kameo roof garden was the ultimate in cinematic entertainment as far as I was concerned. After the showing, my Aunt Helen—who I nicknamed "Hale,"—invariably treated me to a a chocolate ice cream soda at one of the sugar bowls near the corner of Nostrand and Eastern Parkway.

After Eastern Parkway, the trolley moved south down the long hill (glacial moraine) toward Empire Boulevard. A notable–from a trolley buff's viewpoint–sight along the way was the maintenance depot on Nostrand near President Street. The original cobblestones were still in place, surrounding the wide curved rails that curled from the switch into the darkened interior.

It had always been my hope to spend an afternoon peeking around the old building, inspecting the snow sweeper or wrecking car but such an opportunity never presented itself, although I did have the good fortune of seeing a car or two leave and enter the mysterious barn.

Just south of Empire Boulevard there were a number of retail stores including a haberdashery shop that sold young people's clothes. On one occasion my parents and I walked past the store whereupon I got the crazy notion that I should wear a fedora like my father's. After peering at the window display, I noticed that there was, in fact, a greenish hat of the children's variety, which was fashionable in those days.

I urged my parents to go in with me and they acceded, never thinking that I would feverishly lobby for the fedora. My mother tried to dissuade me from buying such a head piece no doubt on the grounds that I would never wear it once we brought it home. No, no, I insisted, this will become part of my regular wardrobe.

I tried on the hat; liked the looks of it, persuaded my parents to make the purchase and happily brought it home.

This maintenance depot is of the kind I always wanted to inspect, but never did.

The hat shop was on the next block south just past the Empire Blvd. turnoff for the Lorimer St. line. The Nostrand plowed straight ahead.

A few days later, I took it out of the box, tried it on and decided that my mother was right. I never wore the dark, green thing again.

As the trolley approached Flatbush Avenue, I became increasingly more excited. Riis Park was part of the reason but the ride on the Green Bus Lines was just as appealing.

In those days, around 1938-43, a ride on a bus was rather special because it happened so infrequently. After all, we didn't have buses in the neighborhood and most of the street transit in Brooklyn was supplied by trolleys.

The Green Bus Lines was an exception. It was a private company that operated many routes in Queens but only appeared in Brooklyn as part of the run from Flatbush-Nostrand, down Flatbush Avenue, past Floyd Bennett Airport, over the new Marine Parkway Bridge and then to Breezy Point and finally the terminus at Riis Park.

There was always an air of excitement as the Peter Witt approached the Flatbush-Nostrand terminus

We're at the Nostrand-Flatbush intersection. The Green Bus Line queue for Riis Park is across the street.

There was always an air of excitement as the Peter Witt approached the Flatbush-Nostrand terminus because of the anticipation that preceded the bus ride. One never knew how long the lineup of passengers for the Riis Park bus would be on any given Sunday although there <u>always</u> was a line. Generally, we arrived when the line extended about one-and-a-half to two bus lengths from the entrance door. That meant we had to wait for about two buses to inhale the passengers before we were able to get on board.

The trick was to just manage to "miss" getting on the bus taking on the last group of people so that we were in good position for a choice seat on the next one. In those days of the early 1940s the Green Lines featured General Motors buses that held about 36 passengers and were in reasonably good condition. The major feature for me was a large window that opened from the bottom and did not have any guard rails as was customary on the trolleys. This enabled a kid to at least partially stick his head out of the window, collecting wonderful breezes as the GM bounced its way south toward Jamaica Bay.

Trolley buff though I was, the bus–at that time, at least–had an attraction all its own partially because it was so rare in the borough. (And a Green Bus, really was rare!) But the appeal far transcended its uniqueness. Unlike the trolley, a Riis Park-bound bus never stopped, except for red lights, toll booths before the Marine Parkway Bridge and the Breezy Point station just before the beach.

This guaranteed a fairly fast run along Flatbush Avenue and lots of wind in the face to boot. It was customary for the operators to jam the Green bus with plenty of standees which meant that those who were seated had a major advantage; and, somehow, we always managed to get a seat.

Sights along the Flatbush run were many, not the least of which were the Flatbush Avenue trolleys (6000 series) adorned with posters on the front end advertising the feature picture at Loew's Kings Theater and a second ad for Park Circle Roller Skating Rink. Since the trolleys had to stop at so many of the intersections it was no big deal for the Green bus to pass them but when a 6000 car had room to pick up speed, it gave the GM an even run for its money.

Flatbush was the best part of Brooklyn as far as I was concerned because it was middle-class, neat, had lots of trees, one-family houses and a more relaxed, rural quality than that to which I was accustomed in Williamsburg. The shops and restaurants along the run intrigued me especially a brand, new Chinese eatery with a shiny-black, mirror-like facade located on Flatbush, just below Kings Highway.

At the time it was the most popular restaurant I had ever encountered and the only one which had lines of people standing outside waiting to get in; a scene that always prompted my dad to utter his deathless: "They could stand on their hands but they'll never get me to wait in line for a restaurant!"

The Flatbush Avenue trolley terminated near Avenue U and since it was not a double-end car like the Lorimer, Nostrand or other Peter Witts, a circle was required to turn it back in the northerly direction. I always was taken by these trolley circles because we had so few of them in my part of Brooklyn. For the Flatbush line, the tracks curved right off the street, crossed the sidewalk and then described a left turn around an old shack over what amounted to a small sand lot. Then, it came around the other side of the shack and stopped to unload–and load new–passengers.

Once past Avenue U, the real fun part of the

The Nostrand car has just cleared the Long Island Rail Road cut and is heading for the heart of Flatbush. The streets are longer; the pace faster, the breeze stronger.

bus ride began because now we were approaching the shore and many interesting bits of marine life, from little fishing businesses to boat repair shops. The run from Avenue U south also was fast because there were no lights at all, and best of all, there was Floyd Bennett Field, which during World War II was a naval air station of considerable importance.

The airfield was on the left (east) side of Flatbush as we headed for the bridge and during the 1941-45 period was filled with a magnificent mix of craft from Grumman Wildcats to Hellcats to Catalina flying boats, to name just a few. Many of them were parked very close to Flatbush Avenue within easy viewing of the bus and others flew overhead. An immense surge of patriotism coursed through my body as we passed the field and it was enhanced by the fact that my dad was a Navy man (he served aboard the mine-layer USS San Francisco in the North Sea during World War I) and that my uncle Joe (my mother's kid brother) was serving in the Navy Seabees at that time.

At the far end of Floyd Bennett Field was the toll booth and ramp leading up to the Marine Parkway Bridge, adorned with two lift towers that gracefully bent in the center and a steel-grated roadway that created a soft humming sound as the rubber tires rolled over it.

Once over the span, the bus curved left and stopped at a small roofed-over station that served Roxbury (the far end of Riis Park) and Breezy Point. There were no bath houses at Roxbury so very few passengers alighted there. That done, the bus continued along the shorefront boulevard and curved right to the plaza where the imposing new Riss Park bath houses graced the shore front. Two large conical towers marked the pavilion which also featured a cafeteria (neat and new) and a chair rental stand.

Riis Park had many lures, starting with enormous waves that inspired me to dive into the base, clean sand and a recreation area that was my favorite. It featured a softball field with stands–some awfully good games were played there–shuffleboard courts, handball courts and a newfangled game (to me, at least) called paddle tennis. I generally played shuffleboard with my dad and, at least once, paddle tennis. Most of the time, I was either in the water, making sand castles or watching the softball games.

Robert Moses had seen to it that Riis Park had none of the honky-tonk ambience of Coney Island. It was well-planned, well-built and exquisitely clean in those days. And sometimes very crowded, although the beach opened up at the softball diamond where the boardwalk sharply curved inland and from that point to Roxbury there was so much sand one always could find a spot several yards from the next sunbather.

A good Sunday at the shore left one well worn from the beating dished out by the waves--which, incidentally, I loved-as well as the exertion from swimming. The trip home, therefore, was a time to unwind and by the time I clambered aboard the Nostrand Avenue trolley at Flatbush, I was ready to zonk out although I never did because there was so much to observe on the way back.

With luck, I usually managed to get a window seat or the jump seat on the ride home. I preferred the right side of the car if I was sitting in a regular window seat just for the sake of variety since I'd be staring out on the other side of Nostrand on the way out of Flatbush. I was fond of isolating ice cream parlors, sporting goods stores and parks along the route but most of all, awaited the crossing of other trolley lines. After Flatbush, we crossed Church Avenue (6000 series), Empire Boulevard (Tompkins Peter Witts), St. John's Place (speed cars, if I'm not mistaken), Bergen (the cranky 3000s), Putnam (6000s), DeKalb (8000s) and then home.

We usually walked the block back from Nostrand to Marcy along Vernon Avenue where a punchball game might be going on as we headed home. The temptation was to stop then and there and join in but my parents knew I had homework to do and the Fred Allen show to listen to on the radio, among other essentials.

By the time Fred Allen had said good-night to Portland Hoffa, Senator Claghorn and Mrs. Nussbaum, the surf-and-sun combo had fatigued me so that I was practically out by the time my head hit the pillow. But a few seconds before dozing into dreamland, I'd think about the trolley ride and muse to myself, "Gee, I'd love to be a motorman on the Nostrand Avenue Line."

By late Sunday afternoon I'd be unwinding on this Nostrand run back to Williamsburg after a day at the beach.

Here is some trolley action that I viewed many times in my youth at the corner of Nostrand and Flatbush. The Green Bus Line stop for Riis Park is located on the right just to the left of the Coca-Cola sign. Brooklyn College is two blocks to the left. That was my alma mater, circa 1950-1954. The Flatbush Avenue 6000 car is rumbling south over the Nostrand crossover. The IRT subway's Flatbush Avenue terminal is directly below the crossroads.

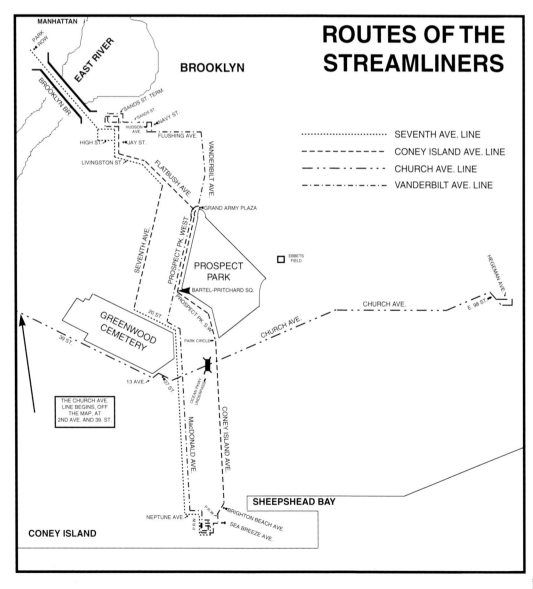

ROUTES OF THE STREAMLINERS

.... SEVENTH AVE. LINE

– – – – – – CONEY ISLAND AVE. LINE

– · – · – · CHURCH AVE. LINE

– ·· – ·· – VANDERBILT AVE. LINE

MANHATTAN

PARK ROW

EAST RIVER

BROOKLYN BR.

BROOKLYN

SANDS ST. TERM.

SANDS ST.

NAVY ST.

HUDSON AVE.

FLUSHING AVE.

HIGH ST.

JAY ST.

LIVINGSTON ST.

FLATBUSH AVE.

VANDERBILT AVE.

SEVENTH AVE.

PROSPECT PK. WEST

GRAND ARMY PLAZA

PROSPECT PARK

EBBETS FIELD

BARTEL-PRITCHARD SQ.

PROSPECT PK. S.W.

20 ST.

GREENWOOD CEMETERY

PARK CIRCLE

CHURCH AVE.

CHURCH AVE.

HEGEMAN AVE.

E. 98 ST.

39 ST.

13 AVE.

41 ST. ST.

COCO PATTERSON

MacDONALD AVE.

CONEY ISLAND AVE.

THE CHURCH AVE. LINE BEGINS, OFF THE MAP, AT 2ND AVE. AND 39. ST.

SHEEPSHEAD BAY

P.R.W.

BRIGHTON BEACH AVE.

NEPTUNE AVE.

SEA BREEZE AVE.

CONEY ISLAND

The trolley buffs call them PCC
(Presidents Conference Committee of Electric Railways) cars.
We called them streamliners and
you can see why.

CHAPTER NINE:
THE STREAMLINER ERA

No trolleys were more special in the borough of Brooklyn than the streamliners which ran along the Vanderbilt, McDonald Ave. and Coney Island routes among others. All you had to do was look at the rolling stock to know the reason why. Developed in the early 1930s by a consortium of streetcar companies to produce a vehicle that could compete with autos and buses, the PCC streamliner was the product of a conference of trolley presidents. The group's full title was President's Conference Committee of Electric Railways and its primary function was to orchestrate a program that would result in the perfect trolley.

Brooklyn played a large part in the PCC car's development, starting in 1931 when the Brooklyn and Queens Transit Company offered part of its Ninth Avenue Depot as a field laboratory. After considerable research and development a prototype streamliner was developed, tested, perfected and, finally, in 1935 the cars went to production. B&QT made an initial purchase of 100 PCC cars for use on the Smith-Coney Island, McDonald-Vanderbilt and Erie Basin trolley lines. One of the better runs was alongside Prospect Park in the Park Slope section heading towards Bartel-Pritchard Square.

B&QT followed up with a suitable promotion campaign including a multi-colored brochure titled, "Brooklyn's Modern Trolley Cars–The Last Word in Passenger Comfort." It noted in the introduction, "The development of these cars may truly be said to represent a fundamental advance in the science of street railway operation."

Truer words were never written.

The PCC car no more resembled the Peter Witt, 6000 Series or Bergen Street groaner anymore than Howdy Doody

(RIGHT) I particularly loved any trolley run that adjoined the park. The Coney Island car was a special treat as it sped along Prospect Park Southwest.

(BELOW) The "S" curve at Bartel-Pritchard Square occasionally got a squeak out of the otherwise quiet streamliner at the southern end of Prospect Park.

Its streamlining was so expertly crafted that, to this day, the PCC is more attractive than any of the "advanced" light rail vehicles (or cars) which have replaced it.

Apart from its luscious lines, the PCC offered endless advantages, starting with rapid acceleration (hitherto unknown with the possible exception of the Ocean Avenue "speed cars") and ending with a quiet ride unlike anything experienced on any other trolley, including the "speed car."

The original PCC (1000) with an old pal at West 5th Street. Note the slight difference in contours compared with other PCC cars.

The streamliner's body was mounted on rubber springs; it had wheels with rubber cores which insulated the axles against vibration and was equipped with an advanced braking system in which the motors were used to retard movement of the cars.

No less unique was the manner of operation. All the other trolleys were started when the motorman tugged on the controller handle, pushing it from point to point until he reached "high" speed. When he wanted to stop the trolley, he jiggled the brake handle until the car reached its destination and then pushed it forward to open the doors.

The PCC was so different from its cousins that the motorman—at least in the B&QT's literature—wasn't even called a motorman; now he was an "operator." And instead of a controller and brake handle, he manipulated three pedals with his foot. The one at left was a safety interlock and had to be pressed down at all times while the car was in motion. If it was released for any reason while the car was in operation, the brakes automatically were applied and the car brought to a stop. At the right of the motorman (oops! operator) there were two pedals—one to supply power to the control equipment and the other to apply the brakes.

Unlike the older, simpler cars, the PCC controller had 100 "notches" or starting points between low and high as compared with ten on the older types of control apparatus. As a result, the speed of the car could be imperceptibly graduated to a maximum speed and to a full-cushioned stop.

The inside was a veritable walkway of luxury. The form-fitting leather seats were all arranged to face forward. Bulls-eye lighting eliminated glare and shadow but provided high intensity light at the proper place for reading. There were picture windows and even doors that rotated to the side rather than spring back into the stepwell.

In short, it was as ideal as a streetcar could be—textbook wise—but it hardly was a trolley, as we knew and loved it so well.

Still, the PCC car was much admired by me because I saw so little of it. The streamliner remained a curio until the last one left Brooklyn's streets in 1956. From my house, the closest of the modern trolleys, geographically, was the Vanderbilt Avenue Line which ran along Flushing Avenue, past the vast Brooklyn Naval Shipyard (known simply as "The Navy Yard" to us) then on to Vanderbilt which was about a mile from my house.

Mostly, I'd see the PCC"s while riding either the Myrtle Avenue El or Myrtle trolley, which crossed Vanderbilt, or the Dekalb Avenue Line which did likewise. But every so often I'd ride either the Vanderbilt or Smith-Coney Island routes because of off-the-beaten-path destinations such as Dr. Sonenshein's office in Flatbush or Park Slope which the Vanderbilt Line paralleled. Once in a while I'd enjoy the luxury of a PCC ride across the Brooklyn Bridge.

Apart from its looks, the most striking aspect of the PCC car, to my senses anyway, was the sound, of which there was precious little. The groan of a Bergen Street 3000 or wail of a 8000 "speed car" was conspicuous by its absence. There was no perceptible hiss of the brakes or rumble of the electric circuitry. If, there was one sound consonant with the streamliner it was a "whoosh," muffled to be sure, but there nonetheless.

This was due, in part, to the remarkably silent resilient wheels used on the new car. A radically new method of vulcanizing rubber to metal made the new wheel possible. It consisted of a steel rim, the center of which fit between two inserts or "sandwiches" made of rubber vulcanized to steel and held by compression between two steel plates which formed the outside of the center of the wheel. Thus, the wheel had the appearance of a solid wheel when, actually, the rubber "sandwiches" formed a cushion between the rim of the wheel and the axle and carried the entire load. As the B&QT liked to boast, "the car may literally be said to ride or 'float' on rubber."

Instead of the weak, muted bulk that adorned the front of the older cars, the PCC's snout had a winged headlight and right above it a flashing red "next car" sign controlled by a switch lever on the motorman's desk. The rear had a pair of bullseye stop lights, similar to those on the modern buses. They glowed when the motorman hit the brakes.

The PCC car, heading for the Park Row terminal near Manhattan's City Hall, could outspeed an automobile heading down the Brooklyn Bridge incline.

While it was different seeing a motorman operate a trolley with pedals, I wasn't impressed by the newfangled procedure because, quite frankly, it took the fun away from running the car. With a controller which allowed you to feel each "point," and a brake handle that required the utmost sensitivity—and emitted a hearty "ch-ch-ch" when jiggled—you felt a part of the trolley car. The pedals brought the operator too many steps closer to automation.

Still, a ride on the Vanderbilt Avenue line had its moments, the best of which were the speedy ones. Man, the PCC could move! It easily overtook automobiles, trucks and taxis and gave the trolley a new feeling of pride that was unavailable on the Peter Witt or the 6000 series cars.

And it was new. The seats felt good, the sightlines were excellent and the turnstile up front added a subway flair unavailable on most other styles of trolleys.

Like the Ocean Avenue "speed cars," the McDonald-Vanderbilt and Smith-Coney Island PCCs were built for long blocks that were best exploited by the new motors. Some of the best Vanderbilt runs were experienced after the trolley moved south from Vanderbilt past Grand Army Plaza and along Prospect Park West to Bartel-Pritchard Square.

It was always fun to ride a streamliner under the McDonald Ave. el to see if the PCC car could stay ahead of the BMT trains above.

This set up another sweet sprint to Park Circle, site of the Parade Grounds. Designers of the Circle had thoughtfully arranged a 30-yard row of bushes on either side of the trolley tracks. By the time the car reached this point it was moving at a veritable gallop. The change from normal street running over to railroad-type tracks on an earth base surrounded by bushes gave the trolley a truly ethereal feel until it surfaced on the other side at the Park Circle Roller Skating Rink for the trek along Coney Island Avenue.

Like Ocean Avenue, not far away, Coney Island Avenue was another long-block street that enabled the PCC to reach high speeds for a reasonable length of time and gave the trip its special kick.

Coney Island Avenue itself was nothing special except for the fact that Dr. Sonenshein's office was there and my parents' friends, Joe and Irene Tick, lived around the corner from the doctor.

Although he was a mere general practitioner, Dr. Sonenshein was the favorite doctor of my young life. Moustacheod and fairly tall for his time, Dr. Sonenshein had the best bedside manner in the world, as far as I was concerned. His voice was like an audible powder puff, caressing you with every word, yet there was an inner strength about him that was immense. When Dr. Sonenshein talked, you not only listened, you automatically felt better.

Interestingly enough, Dr. S. made house calls, all the way from his Flatbush office to distant Williamsburg, yet I do remember taking the trolley to see him for examinations from time to time. During the summer of 1944, I had been visiting my Aunt Hattie, Uncle Paul and Cousin Ira Sheier in Albany when I was assailed by the worst earache of my life.

I spent days in a hot, air conditioned-less bedroom vainly trying to find a "comfortable" position to rest my ear. Aunt Hattie finally took me to an Albany doctor who prescribed some medicine that didn't work. Finally, she packed me on to a New York Central train for New York.

Upon my return, my mother resorted to the only possible solution; Dr. Sonenshein. THIS, I insisted, would be his supreme test. If Dr. Soneshein could eliminate the pain in my ear, he truly would be the greatest doctor in the world.

Mom and I took the DeKalb Ave. trolley which connected to the Smith-Coney Island Line. At least the streamliner distracted me from the ear pain and, finally, we arrived at Dr. Sonenshein's office. I had placed complete faith in him, with the knowledge his challenge was formidable.

With typical modesty, the good doctor calmly suggested that he might be able to take care of my problem. He took his ear-inspecting light to my left lobe, flicked on the bulb and searched around for a bit. That done, he put some drops in my ear, wrote out a prescription and told my mother to call in a couple of days if the pain persisted.

On the return trolley ride home, I was feeling better already. My mom took care of the prescription, I took the medicine and, within a day, I was feeling in mint condition. Dr. Sonenshein had done it again!

I might have been on this car heading home from Dr. Sonenshein's office after he cured my earache.

The other PCC line with which I was familiar ran from Vanderbilt down to McDonald Avenue, past Greenwood Cemetery, then the famed Gold's Horseradish plant and on to Coney Island, As far as I can remember, I never rode the PCCs on the Erie Basin Line, I knew nobody in the Red Hook section of town.

The PCC streamliner that ran to Coney Island had special significance to me because of 905 McDonald Ave. in Borough Park. That was the home of Gold's Horseradish, the firm owned by Howie Sparer's brother-in-law, Morris Gold who was married to Howie's sister, the beloved and consummately attractive Norma Sparer-Gold.

Actually, Gold's horseradish roots ran deep in Brooklyn and typified the growth of a company from a small family operation to a major, nationwide food corporation. It all started in the year of my birth, 1932, when Hyman Gold's cousin was jailed after a dispute with his landlord.

After being bailed out by nice-guy Hyman, the cousin gifted the benefactor with a horseradish grinder, Never one to look a gift horseradish grinder in the mouth, Hyman and his wife Tillie began grinding the stuff in their tiny Coney Island Ave. apartment overlooking the trolley line. Once the horseradish began selling, Hyman and Tillie impressed their three sons—Morris, Manny and Herbert—into the budding business. Using their bicycles as delivery wagons, the trio of young Golds toured the area and, in time, Gold's horseradish developed a following.

By this time a neighborhood pushcart peddler persuaded Hyman to sell his product to him whereupon the vendor then distributed them to the stores. "This was our first distributor," says Marc Gold, who now runs the company with brother Steven and cousins Neil and Howard.

When the Golds bought the Arrow Horseradish Co. in the early 1950's, the company took off, big-time and eventually moved into the red brick building on McDonald Ave. underneath the elevated tracks where the Coney Island trolley passed every few minutes.

For myself it always was a double-kick; riding the streamliners and then inhaling the pungent aroma of horseradish. Or, as Marc put it, "I can go in the back of the factory, inhale and go, 'AHHH!' and be perked up for the rest of the day. Horseradish recharges you. That's the way to live your life. Get a couple of little hobbies, eat horseradish and you're fine."

My memories of horseradish date back to the family Passover dinners. Both my grandfather, Simon, and my father devoured horseradish as if it was candy. I would watch in amazement as they'd gulp down a forkful without even wincing while the white stuff brought crocodile tears to my eyes.

(UPPER RIGHT) That's Morris Gold, in uniform, in front of 4127 18th Ave., the firm's second factory.

(RIGHT) This is what McDonald Ave. looked like from the front window of a PCC streamliner, between 18th Ave. and Ave. F. Gold's third plant (much expanded from the earlier two) is on the right.

No less fascinating was listening to another lover of the edible tear-jerker actually do a soliloquy to horseradish. If I didn't hear it, I wouldn't have believed it possible. Here's how Marc waxed giddily about the joy of horseradish-eating.

"The pores will open. You'll start sweating and you'll feel you're almost high. It perks you up. It gets the body ready for the day.

"It will increase your life expectancy. And your life will be better. It will burn up cholesterol and calories. It will slow up your eating and make you sweat and shake, like a good workout.

"It perks you up. I do a lot of traveling. I always keep a bottle in the car in a little insulated bag. On a long trip I open the bag and take a little bit. It wakes me up. I don't need to ride with the windows open.

"For lunch, let's say you have tuna, chicken or egg salad sandwich. Put on a little horseradish. I always sneak in a jar because not all restaurants have it fresh. Very discreet, I take out my little insulated packet.........

The tracks of the streamliners are also used by their more traditional brethren. Here a westbound Gravesend-Church Line 6000 is about to negotiate the switchwork that brings the South Brooklyn Railway onto MacDonald Ave. Behind 6038, the Macdonald Ave. line baloons out to make room for the descent of the Culver Line trestle into a tunnel. The Gravesend-Church line terminates in a loop a few blocks down MacDonald Ave. from this location.

"At Thanksgiving it's essential. Put horseradish in your cranberry sauce. Do you know what it will do? It will make your turkey gobble.

"Bagel and cream cheese? Mix a little horseradish with the cream cheese. Put it on the bagel. Your day is fine.

"Salad dressing. Whenever I have dinner at my mother-in-law's house, she knows she must make a salad dressing with horseradish, and it's delicious.

A meeting of the streamliners at Manhattan's Park Row at the base of Brooklyn Bridge with City Hall off to the left.

"When you have a piece of meat, use horseradish. If it's a cheap hamburger put on lots and lots. If it's a delicious, high quality piece of steak, put on less.

"Melt a bar of bittersweet chocolate and put in a teaspoon of horseradish. Let it harden again, and use it as chips in a chocolate chip cookie.

"Once you get hooked on horseradish, you'll spend all your time looking for uses for it. It's a windfall."

For Gold's horseradish alone it was worth a ride on the McDonald Ave. trolley. But the last car ran in the mid-1950's and it wasn't the same on McDonald Ave. after that.

A brief respite for pilots of the streamliners.

The B&QT had lofty hopes for the PCC and to this end began building new roadways to accommodate the streamliner. The company embedded steel rails in concrete along Prospect Park West between Union Street and 15th Street, providing one of the smoothest trolley rides imaginable. Downtown, at Livingstone and Bond Streets, it installed modern loading platforms which provided an isle of safety for pedestrians and passengers boarding or alighting from cars at that point.

But for the PCC's performing at their best, the Brooklyn Bridge run was the thing. The number 67 Seventh Avenue streamliner handled that, starting at Park Row (City Hall) in Manhattan. The tracks were in the outside lane, running side by side with one lane of regular automobile traffic, and brought the car to the distinguished Sand Street transportation center in Brooklyn from where the Myrtle Avenue El also crossed the bridge. The Seventh Avenue PCC flitted through Downtown Brooklyn to Flatbush Avenue, then past the borough's handsome Williamsburg Savings Bank skyscraper–biggest four faced clock in the world–and venerable Long Island Rail Road Station at Atlantic and Flatbush. It turned right at Seventh for the remainder of its run.

Many of us thought the PCC's were so beautifully efficient that they would be around forever. Unfortunately, forever ended on October 31, 1956 when the final streamliner whizzed along Church before heading for the trolley car's last roundup.

Not even Gold's horseradish could revive this baby.

P.S. In 1993, some 37 years later, Gold's moved to a new plant in Hempstead, Long Island. On Brooklyn Road!

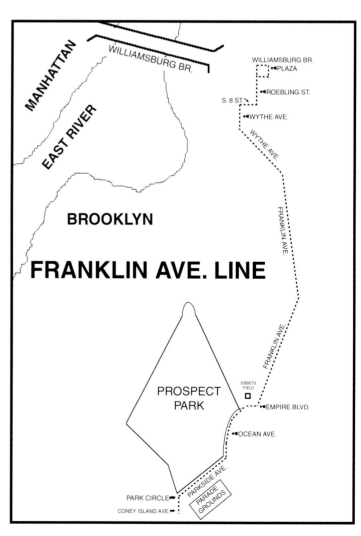

Occasionally I'd take the Franklin—instead of Tompkins or Lorimer—to our favorite ballpark, seen here overlooking Empire Blvd. near Flatbush Avenue.

CHAPTER TEN:
THE FRANKLIN AVENUE LINE

The Franklin Avenue Line spelled both pleasure as well as mental anguish for me. The pleasure part was Dodgers baseball. Like the Lorimer line, the Franklin route also went directly to Ebbets Field. The anxiety part because it took me to a ball field where I was humiliated in a rather innocent–but no less significant–incident involving my best friend, my father and a mis-thrown baseball. All of this occurred after a ride on the Franklin Avenue Line.

It was the only run within walking distance of our house that went directly to Park Circle and the Parade Grounds which had the largest collection of baseball diamonds in Brooklyn. We had none in our neighborhood. To those of us in Williamsburg, where baseball diamonds were non-existent, the Parade Grounds was holy (athletic) territory.

Not that our gang was obsessed with baseball; far from it. We were quite content with punchball, stoopball, triangle, box ball and and assorted other street games from Ringaleevio to hide-and-seek.

However, we recognized baseball as America's national pastime and felt it incumbent on ourselves to at least spend one or two days a year at the Parade Grounds, just to sort of pay our diamond dues.

Since I was an only child, my parents usually asked me to bring a friend or two with me when we took the Parade Grounds excursions and on this occasion my father herded, Howie Sparer, Gil Birnbaum and Jay Koslo along to the ball field.

We brought along a couple of bats, a new (but cheap) baseball and our assortment of ragtag mitts. Since there were so few of us, we had to get there early to nail down a diamond and play until one of the organized teams arrived. We

This is the corner, Myrtle and Franklin, where my father, Howie Sparer and I boarded the trolley for the infamous trip to the Parade Grounds.

To reach the Parade Grounds (we were satisfied to simply call it Park Circle), we had to walk along Myrtle Ave. about a half a mile to Franklin Avenue (past Bedford) to hail the trolley that went to the ball field. Like so many of the routes, the Franklin Line headed south from Williamsburg Bridge Plaza. It meandered through Williamsburg along Wythe Avenue which, at Flushing Avenue intersection, became Franklin Avenue. It rolled under the Myrtle Avenue El station where we usually waited for the Peter Witt. Then it continued on to DeKalb Ave. and passed the State Theater.

A ride on the Franklin Avenue Line had some special moments, not the least of which was the downhill run from Eastern Parkway within view of Ebbets Field and then the right turn on to Empire Boulevard. While the Tompkins and Lorimer Street Lines ended their runs at the junction of Flatbush and Empire, the Franklin Line continued over the fabled Malbone Street Tunnel (site of the worst subway crash in New York history, November 1, 1938 where 97 were killed), across Flatbush Avenue where one could smell the fresh bread from the Bond bakery and then for the

invigorating dash alongside Prospect Park, first on Ocean Avenue and then, after a right hand curve, to Parkside Avenue.

Along the Parkside-Ocean stretch, the tracks hugged the edge of the street, rubbing shoulders with the sidewalk. It is a run with very few stops but one that had a built-in Toonerville bounce that made it seem as if the car was racing much faster than it actually was, which I would assume was about 25 miles per hour, tops.

Before reaching Park Circle, the trolley stopped near Caledonian Hospital, a rather unimposing structure but one which had great importance to me–and other young baseball fans–because it was the "official" infirmary of the Brooklyn Dodgers. When Frenchy Bordegaray, Dolph Camilli, Cookie Lavagetto or Babe Phelps got hurt, they didn't go to Kings County, Beth Moses or Israel Zion (where I was born) Hospital, they went to Caledonian; and there it was, seen out of the Franklin Avenue trolley window, in all its plain, red brick glory.

After Caledonian, the Parade Grounds came into view. It was easy enough to see because it was an

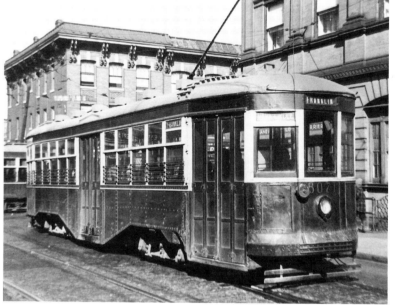

This is the intersection of Franklin and Dekalb, with the State Theater just around the corner.

immense stretch of Brooklyn prairie, surrounded by six-story apartment houses of various designs, many of them pseudo-English tudor but handsome nonetheless.

If memory serves me correctly, the Parade Grounds had a total of ten diamonds of which at least two were reserved for big-time semi-pro type games while the others were for more general use.

On this day, for some reason, all the fields were taken but Dad and the rest of us were able to carve out a niche of grass big enough for the bunch to have an improvised game of baseball.

The workout itself hardly was memorable but the aftermath was. After we had completed the game there still was time to toss the ball around, which we did. At one point, I threw the ball to Howie and he hurled it back to me, only this time the ball sailed over my head.

Whether he deliberately tossed a "bad" one or not will forever remain a moot point but suffice to say, my interpretation was that he meant it to be a lousy throw. The ball sat on the grass 30 feet from me and about 45 feet from Howie.

"YOU get the ball," I demanded. "That was a crappy throw and you know it."

"I'm not getting the ball," Howie shot back. "You shoulda caught it."

"That was way over my head and outside. You knew I couldn't catch it."

"Sure you coulda..."

We now were in a ferocious battle of wills and neither of us wanted to give an inch. My head was swelling with fury because I knew that my father liked Howie—sometimes I felt that he liked him more than he liked me—and I realized that Dad would soon have to be the arbiter in this dispute.

"Dad," I said imploringly, "<u>make</u> him get the ball."

This was a tough decision for Ben Fischler who had to choose between his son and what basically was the right decision.

"DAD! MAKE HIM GET THE BALL!!"

My father wouldn't budge. He insisted that it was not Howie's responsibility to get the errant hunk of horsehide, even though Howie didn't exactly throw me a strike.

By this time I was beside myself with fury; hate for my father who would not take my side; and hate for my friend Howie for making me look bad in front of my pop and my other friends.

To break the impasse my father finally walked over, picked up the ball and informed us that we were now heading home. Tears had come to my eyes in a moment of personal embarrassment that was rarely equalled in my life. I wanted no part of anybody, least of all Howie, my father or my friends but we were locked into each other's company for the duration of the trolley ride home.

As we waited at the Parkside Avenue curb for the Peter Witt to roll along, I tried desperately to separate myself from the others. I pointedly turned away from Howie and peered intently in the direction of Park Circle, as if my gaze would hasten the arrival of the streetcar.

In a few moments the maroon, grey-roofed car came into view replete with its attractive yellow striping. I quickly mounted the two steps and found a seat away from the others. It was obvious to me that I had dug myself a social hole from which extrication would be enormously difficult; but the damage had been done and I relentlessly dug deeper.

The trip home was an excruciating forty minutes during which I saw many things but remember little because my mind was so consumed with anger and despair. I felt utterly betrayed by my father and psychologically exploited and embarrassed by my friend. It was clear in my mind that I had to erase him from my consciousness if I was to survive.

When we arrived back at Vernon Avenue there were no good-byes. I climbed the two flights of our brownstone at 582 Marcy and headed straight for my room where I buried my head in my pillow. It was clear that I had let myself down and, more than anything, disappointed my father. But at that moment, at least, I felt disappointed by him.

For several days thereafter, I pointedly avoided Howie at P.S. 54. He was in class 3B and I was in 3A which made it somewhat difficult for our paths to cross but even during lunch hour I went out of my way not to encounter him; and succeeded.

This procedure went on for several days. One afternoon, right after my return from school, I walked into 582 where my grandmother usually had a glass of chocolate milk and graham crackers awaiting me. As I closed the door, she said, "There's somebody here to see you."

This is the car I took home in disgrace after my humiliating experience on the Parade Grounds located to the right. Prospect Park is across the street on the left. Notice how close the Franklin trolley is to the curb.

Before I even had a chance to ask who it might be, I turned into the living room and there was Howie, standing alone with his hand outstretched. Even If I wanted to run away, I couldn't. "Let's be friends," he said, pumping my hand and the armistice was immediately struck.

I was immensely relieved and immediately suggested we take a walk up Marcy Avenue just to get out of the confines of the living room. Howie agree and the two of us somewhat awkwardly strode toward Willoughby Avenue trying very much not to re-open the wound. Instead we discussed a number of inanities such as the state of the Dodgers, Leo Durocher's managing and the best flying model kit available at the Airplane Store. It was, of course, the British Supermarine Spitfire, best warplane in The Battle of Britain.

After about ten minutes of shooting the breeze, I understood that our friendship had mended and that it could conceivably be as tight as it once had been (which, incidentally, became the case). We finally walked into Goldberg's candy store, which was a block from my house, diagonally across Marcy Avenue sitting between Kay's (as in Konowitz) grocery store and the tiny (one short flight down) housewares shop which my parents humorously called Siegel-Cooper (after the giant department store of the same name that for years graced Sixth Avenue.)

Goldberg's was not a top-rated candy store in our view but it was handy. Mr. Goldberg was a man in his upper fifties (old in our view) with a thick Jewish accent and an impatient disposition. Howie and I ordered chocolate ice cream sodas and then decided that we should buy a punchball to cement our renewed friendship.

It was wartime and rubber was in short supply so it was not as easy as usual to get a ball for punchball. According to our informal regulations, three types of balls could be used for a game of punchball; a. A Spalding rubber, high bouncer known as a "Spaldeen," b. A "Pimpleball," which was a white ball that was adorned with a series of upraised rubber dots (ergo: pimples) which didn't bounce as high as a Spalding but was in many ways better; c. A used tennis ball which I often received from my Uncle Ed when he was finished with a match.

Having finished our sodas, Howie and I asked Mr. Goldberg whether he had any "Spaldeens." He said he did and then opened one of his dark brown cabinets which also contained a few old parlor games, which no right-thinking kid would buy, and pulled out a pink rubber ball that looked just like a Spalding.

I took it from Mister Goldberg and rubbed it in my hands, looking for the Spalding imprimatur. There was none. Then, I bounced the ball and it seemed not to have the same vitality as the "Spaldeens" we knew and loved so well.

"Are you sure this is a Spaldeen?" I demanded of Mister Goldberg.

"Don't vorry, mine boy," Goldberg assured us, "dis is the real <u>McChhoy</u>!"

How could we argue with "the real McChhoy?" We bought the ball.

Without fuss or fanfare, Howie and I resumed our friendship and even returned to Park Circle again- with my father–for another around of baseball at a later date.

This is Wythe Ave. in a run-down section of Williamsburg, from whence the Franklin car arrived.

The real purpose of this trip was to try out a baseball uniform that I had received for my birthday from my Uncle Sid and Aunt Charlotte, Unlike today's team-oriented outfits, this was simply a gray baseball uniform with a number on the back, no logo in front and a little grey peaked hat. If ever there was a generic outfit, this was it; but it was the only one on the block and it demanded to be used. Once again we awaited the Franklin trolley. Finally it came and we were on our way.

Off we went with Park Circle beckoning in the distance. We had left with some trepidation since it had rained heavily the night before, making it uncertain whether the Parade Grounds would be dry enough for play. Besides, it was still gloomily overcast with the threat of more rain at any moment.

I stared out of the front window of the Franklin Avenue car, looking for telltale rain drops. The Peter Witts, like all of the early trolleys, did not have windshield wipers which meant that the motorman had to really "fake it" in a downpour. (The PCC's thoughtfully were constructed with a big sweeping set of wipers that did an excellent job of cleaning the windows.)

When we arrived at Park Circle, there was no rain and few ball players. In fact, we were able to get a regular diamond to ourselves because all of the league games had been cancelled. And for good reason; most of the fields were undrained and the one we chose to play on had a huge puddle at second base, surrounded by an even larger circle of mud.

Not to worry. There was plenty of room on either side of it and there were only four of us. Besides, I had to show off my new uniform.

We took turns batting the ball around but since we lacked numbers, it was really the batter against the fielders. After hitting the ball, the batter would try to leg his hit as far as he could go. Then, another fielder would move in and take his licks and so on.

Nothing of note happened until my third at bat. This time I took a good cut at the ball and sent it flying over Howie's head in centerfield. I speedily rounded first and sensed that, with a bit of luck, I might actually stretch this into a triple.

I put my head down and sprinted for second. Suddenly, I realized that second base was buried under an inch of water and that the "new" second base had been moved to a new location ten feet from the original. When I looked up, there was the mud-surrounded puddle just ahead of me.

I swerved right and got around the fringe and then cut sharply to the left, heading for third. But I had made one colossal error; I had mistakenly focused ahead instead of concentrating on the ground immediately in front of me. As I passed second, my left sneaker stepped on a patch of mud that my radar had not detected.

In that millisecond, as I tried to regain my equilibrium, my mind rang the "Tilt" sign (as in you shouldn't have gone so close) and then blacked out when my legs shot skyward. In complete defiance of gravity, I did a somersault and plunged face-first into the mud puddle.

There were no if's, ands, or buts. I was right in the middle in every way. And as I pulled myself from the morass, I couldn't decide whether laughter or tears were the more appropriate response to the whole ugly mess. I began laughing uproariously until my father walked over and pointed out that he normally did not bring a change-of-clothes to baseball outings at Park Circle. "You," he said, "are out of luck."

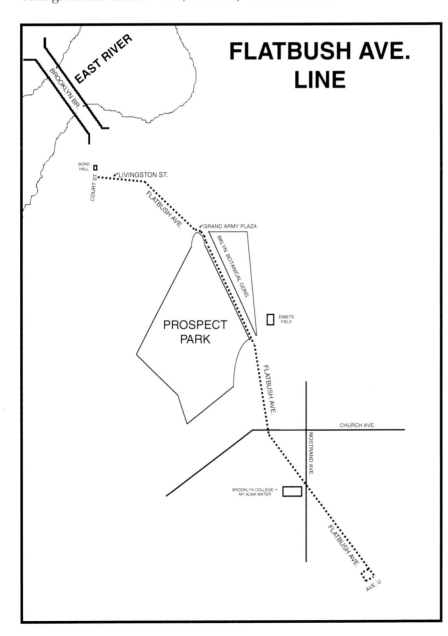

I scraped the mud off my cheeks, out of my ears, away from my eyes and spat an ounce or two out of my mouth. To say I was a mess would have been the understatement of the half-century. And now I had to take the Franklin Avenue trolley home.

My father thoughtfully pointed me in the direction of the Parade Grounds clubhouse where there was a men's room that had enough paper towels to enable me to at least partially dry myself off sufficiently to gain admittance to the streetcar. That done, we walked to the trolley station, my father keeping enough of a distance from the rest of us so that he would not necessarily be associated with the mud-caked kid with the once-new baseball outfit.

The motorman must have been accustomed to stranger sights because when we got on the Franklin Avenue car at Park Circle, he paid virtually no attention to Kid Mud. Still, I walked all the way to the rear of the trolley, hoping to be seen by as few people as possible.

Three things stand out about that trip; 1. It was the last time I rode the Franklin Avenue trolley; 2. It was the last time my father took us to Park Circle; and 3. It was the last time I wore that silly baseball outfit.

The Flatbush Ave. Line in all its glory, in the 1920's, with the Botanical Gardens on the left and Prospect Park on the right.

CHAPTER ELEVEN:
THE FLATBUSH AVENUE LINE

...ny ways the Flatbush Line was one of
... majestic of all the trolley runs,
... where it bisected the Botanic Garden
...ect Park.

...he thing it was a long run, traversing
... from the Borough Hall area on the
...stant Avenue U in the southern tier of
...nty.

...00 series cars seemed to look their best
...atbush run which may have been a
...f my imagination or might very well
... a function of their quasi-modern
...lding into the surroundings.

...000 cars that plied Flatbush Avenue
... handsome and they rolled through
...sant areas. Flatbush, in the late 1930s
...1940's, when I began to ride the line
...ewhat regular basis, was a very
...community in which to live, especially
...pened to reside in sub-middle class
...class, if you will) Williamsburg.

The Flatbush #6136 not only looked good, but smelled good, thanks to the aromatic baked odors that emanated from the Bond Bakery in the background.

Any 6000 series trolley that roamed our neighborhoods looked out of place. Williamsburg, Bedford-Stuyvesant and Bushwick were communities made for Peter Witts and the groaning 3000s. But the 6000s belonged with the upper crust and on runs that enabled the well-tapered car to get up to speed and stay there.

The Flatbush line could do that, especially if you were fortunate enough to get on board somewhere north of Eastern Parkway and then rode south through to, say Kings Highway or thereabouts. The Flatbush trolley took you past some wonderful vistas.

For openers there was Downtown Brooklyn which may not have equalled the Great White Way across the East River but jumped in its own right. Remember, Brooklyn once was a city all its own in the 19th century and the Fulton Street theater district was the equivalent of State Street in Chicago or any of the other big boulevards of a major American metropolis.

Fabian's Fox Theater, the Brooklyn Paramount, Loew's Metropolitan, RKO's Albee and Orpheum as well as the Majestic Theater (it actually ran a triple-bill one weekend) all were jammed in the Downtown community and some, like the Fox, were monstrously magnificent.

The Flatbush Avenue car rolled in the shadows of the Williamsburg Savings Bank Skyscraper, the ancient Long Island Rail Road Terminal at Atlantic Avenue, some classy restaurants and headed south toward Grand Army Plaza, our answer to Manhattan's Washington Square.

A Brooklyn College art teacher once mentioned to me that the Soldiers and Sailors monument arch at Grand Army Plaza was an example of overdone tastelessness and he may have been right. But I always found it an inspiringly heroic piece of work and never stopped gawking at it no matter how many times I rode the Flatbush Avenue trolley.

(TOP) A typical downtown Brooklyn scene in the late 1930's. Blue Barron's band was starring at the Flatbush Theater, one of New York's last vaudeville houses.

(MIDDLE) One of the biggest kicks was being on the trolley when the car rolled on temporary upraised tracks. With Fabian's Fox Theater on the left, the trolley plies its switch on its way towards Grand Army Plaza.

(LEFT) The Flatbush car, across from the L.I.R.R. terminal, is in third position behind a streamliner and a Peter Witt car with the Williamsburg Bank skyscraper directly behind the train station. The L.I.R.R. cars remained underground until they surfaced at Nostrand Ave. on to a trestle.

The majesty of the Flatbush Avenue Line became evident as the trolley approached Grand Army Plaza. Adorned with posh high-rise apartment houses, the Plaza impressed in many ways and not merely because of the Arch. Looking to the left, one could see the Brooklyn Public Library's tastefully modern main branch which, to our eyes, was every bit as big, handsome and classy as its 42nd Street counterpart.

Just around the corner to the left on Eastern Parkway–one of the rare boulevards in Brooklyn–was Brooklyn Jewish Center, THE synagogue of the rich and famous. Farther up along the Parkway was the entrance to Brooklyn Botanic Garden which rubbed shoulders with our cultural pride and joy, the massive Brooklyn Museum. (I shudder when I think back to the many P.S. 54 trips we took to the Museum where the objective was not to learn about Ancient Egypt, etc. but merely to

I always enjoyed the speed run starting here at Soldiers and Sailors Monument. The trolley is about to gallop toward Empire Boulevard. The Brooklyn Jewish Center is just to the right, out of the picture. The tall apartment houses were among the ritziest in Brooklyn.

"fool around." Ugh! Tutankamen, forgive me!!) And on the right, of course, was the best playground in New York City, Prospect Park.

Once the motorman thrust the controller to high, and the trolley rumbled across the Plaza and alongside Prospect Park, the real fun of the ride began. The steady uphill strain past the museum's rear was, in effect, the first climb of a roller coaster before the climactic dive to the bottom.

With the knowledge that he'd not face a light until the Prospect Park Zoo crossing, the motorman could keep his controller pushed on "high" while savoring the bucolic Botanic Garden scenes on the left and the tree-lined splendor of the park on the right.

If he was a daring driver, he would keep the controller in the far position as we traversed the crest and began barreling swiftly (for a trolley) down Flatbush Avenue toward Empire Boulevard ahead. The unfortunate part, for speed-lovers like myself, was the passenger stop and crosswalk half-way down where visitors entered and exited Prospect Park Zoo. Too many times the motorman was compelled to slow down–and stop–for passengers before resuming his run to Empire Boulevard.

The 6000 never could attain the m.p.h. of a Vanderbilt Avenue PCC streamliner but it sure did give a feel of rapid transit as it lurched between the park and the gardens to the junction of Flatbush, Empire Boulevard and Ocean Avenue.

What a splendid meeting of the roads that was. The main entrance to the Botanic Garden was on the left and behind that loomed the ancient columns of Ebbets Field. The corner of Empire and Flatbush featured big-time hot dog stands to service the commuters and fans. As I remember, the frankfurters were all right but not in the class of their chocolate egg creams (or is it cremes?)

One of the best things about the intersection was the aroma; not so much from the hot dogs, etc. but rather the sensuously sweet smell of bread wafting its way north from the Bond Bread plant directly across Flatbush Ave. from the BMT subway entrance. Culinary scents of any kind simply don't get much better than fresh white bread baking at Flatbush Ave..

The Flatbush run reaches its peak miles per hour here coming down the hill toward Empire Boulevard.

Facing the bread factory on the west side of Flatbush was the Prospect Park BMT subway entrance and Hugh Casey's Tavern. Casey was the tragic Brooklyn Dodgers hero-pitcher who had struck out the New York Yankees' Tommy Henrich in the classic 1941 World Series game. There were two outs in the ninth inning and the Dodgers were winning, when reliable Casey fanned the Yankee. The only trouble was that Brooklyn catcher Mickey Owen dropped the ball, Henrich scampered safely to first and the Yanks went on to rally and eventually win a Series we Dodger fans thought was in the palm of Owen's mitt.

There was something reassuring about Casey's Tavern and I imagine it had something to do with the fact that a Dodger cared enough about Brooklyn to actually have a business with his name on it just a stone's throw from the big ball park. Another Dodger, Freddie Fitzsimmons, owned a bowling alley on Empire Boulevard.

The Prospect Park BMT station was a curio in its own way. From Manhattan, via the Manhattan Bridge, came the Brighton Express as well as the local that plied the tunnel and Nassau Loop. In addition, the Franklin Avenue Shuttle fed trains from Fulton Street and all converged on the four-tracked station that began on the north end as subway and then flowered into an open cut platformed station. It was a train buff's paradise and if you also happened to be into chewing gum, Prospect Park Station was one of the precious few that featured Pulver's handsome bright red machines that vended gum not in the prosaic manner but with a flair.

Pulver gum came in three flavors, including Hot-Chu and Two-Chus. But more importantly the gum was delivered by a splendidly crafted device. The Pulver machine didn't have ordinary buttons but rather three thick, silvery sculpted plungers as well as a window behind which were a couple of performers. After you deposited your penny and pushed the plunger in one such machine, not only did you receive your Hot-Chu but also were entertained by a model of a cop hitting a robber on the head as your stick of gum plopped down to the receptacle.

Once past Prospect Park, the Flatbush trolley encountered serious traffic all the way south to Nostrand Avenue. The avenue was filled with shops and theaters including the Patio–a favorite of my parents–which was part of the vast Century Theater chain. My folks would receive a weekly brochure from Century Theaters which had such interesting movie houses as the Patio, Albemarle and Parkside, all far from my home and therefore all romantic in their distance. Each week I'd pursue the list of feature pictures and dream of someday spending a Saturday afternoon watching Basil Rathbone and Nigel Bruce doing Sherlock Holmes and Doctor Watson, not at the neighborhood Kismet Theater but the Albemarle on exotic Flatbush Avenue.

Hugh Casey's Tavern is just across the street on the right as is the Prospect Park BMT station. The building behind the trolley is the Bond Bread factory. Pulver chewing gum machines were a feature of the subway entrance with their bright red dispensers.

Not far past the Patio were two desirable locations, Lenox Road and Linden Boulevard, both admired for their relatively new and handsome apartment houses. My Aunt Frances and Uncle Ed--the latter being my mother's kid brother–lived on Linden Boulevard near Flatbush and I frequently visited them.

A long graceful garden plaza fronted their apartment at 201 Linden with paths that led both to the right and left. Ed and Frances lived in the building on the left. It had an elevator with buttons like the door-opener plunger on the Peter Witts (I liked that!) and other little niceties that went with modern apartment living in those days.

Ed and Frances always were very kind to me. Ed was an avid Dodgers' fan and took me to a game or two. He also liked tennis and, as mentioned, delivered an endless supply of used tennis balls to my house; balls which were than converted to punchball use on Vernon Avenue or at P.S. 54 Annex schoolyard on Sandford Street.

For a time Aunt Frances worked in an auto supply store on Bedford Avenue right in the shadows of Ebbets Field. That in itself made her very special in my eyes. Unfortunately, Uncle Ed worked for his father, my grandfather, Simon, and, therefore, alongside my dad at Lorimer Paint Works. Somewhere along the way Dad and Ed had a falling out which in the end had major repercussions and would forever modify–though not necessarily harm–my feelings toward my uncle.

I never discovered the root cause of the rift but I know that it was a bitter one and eventually resulted in my father leaving Lorimer Paint Works and having to find work elsewhere; which he did; but not without major unhappiness between the Friedmans and Fischlers.

Once past Linden Boulevard, the Flatbush line rolled toward the crossroads of mid-Brooklyn, Church Avenue and Flatbush Avenue. Prior to the outbreak of World War II it was a busy theater center as well. In addition to the Loew's Kings and RKO Kenmore movie houses there was the Flatbush Theater which featured stage shows as well as films.

I remember attending a stage show at the Flatbush in 1940 shortly after the Nazis had invaded Belgium. Louis Prima and his band rocked the stage show. Louie was young and vibrant then and his nasal tones and brassy sax epitomized Brooklyn swing. But for some reason, the major mental imprint of the night was provided by a newsreel shown as part of the movie segment. It was a chilling documentary about the invasion of Belgium accompanied by the constant chant of "La Livre, Belgique" (Long Live Belgium) that cut to the bone. It was powerful enough to take all the joy out of Louie Prima's splendid stage show.

The RKO Kenmore, located around the corner from Flatbush on Church Avenue, holds fonder memories. We only occasionally visited the Kenmore but on one afternoon during World War II, My Aunt Lottie–a major favorite of mine because she taught me how to play gin rummy when I was supposed to be at Hebrew school–took me there.

Actually, we had originally gone to Riis Park on this supremely hot summer day; just Lottie and I. Uncle Joe by now was a U.S. Navy Seabee, stationed in the Aleutian Islands, and Lottie had taken me under her wing, since she lived very near 582 Marcy.

Aunt Lottie was an excellent pianist who could knock out pop tunes as fast as you put the sheet music on the piano. She brought a whole bunch of them to our house and did some wonderful renditions of tunes like "My Heart Stood Still" (Rodgers and Hart) which thoroughly captivated me.

She also had a rich, hearty, easy laugh and an exuberance that appealed to a youngster like myself. In other words, Lottie was more like a kid than any of my other aunts who, in their individual ways, were just as much fun but at different times and places.

On this day Lottie had taken me to Riis Park via the Nostrand trolley and

(ABOVE) Post-World War Two Flatbush Avenue. The Loew's Kings was a showpiece theater here featuring Betty Hutton and Fred Astaire. Macy's Flatbush store was only recently opened but the 6000 series trolley was a venerable part of the landscape, dating back to the early 1930's. This one is moving towards Kings Highway and then Avenue U.

(BELOW RIGHT) Church Ave. and Flatbush, one of the best intersections in the borough. A pair of Flatbush Ave. 6000's are about to rock over the Church Ave. tracks. The famous Garfield's Cafeteria is at the near left and the fine Astor (foreign film) theater at the far left, adjoining Erasmus Hall High School.

(BELOW LEFT) Uncle Joe and Aunt Lottie in 1943.

A pair of Flatbush Ave. cars have completed most of the turn at the Avenue U terminal in preparation for the trip north to Downtown Brooklyn.

Green Bus. We returned by Green Bus but then got on the Flatbush line at Flatbush and Nostrand and headed for the RKO Kenmore. This was just after a marvelously fun day at the beach.

Riis Park's waves were danger-ously vigorous that afternoon but, hot as it was, I couldn't get enough of the water. I literally was pounded silly but kept coming back for more until the clock told us that it was time to go. The Flatbush trolley took us to Church Avenue where we alighted, stepped in to Garfield's famous Cafeteria for dinner (the cream spinach never could match the Automat's) and then walked over to the RKO Kenmore.

To this day I cannot recall the name of the feature picture which originally lured us to the Kenmore but that's irrelevant. Whatever it was, the film seemed like one we'd both like to see and it must have been good because the movie house was crowded enough for us to have to find seats way up inthe balcony.

The second film on the bill meant nothing to either of us. It was called "Prairie Chickens," featured nobody of note and would have inspired us to leave after the main flick except that we were so tired and comfortable in the theater that we just couldn't pick ourselves up to leave.

"Prairie Chickens" was, as we thought, an inconsequential comedy but that was not noticeable by my reaction to it. At best, it was a Grade B flick–more likely Grade C–but the combination of five hours of hot sun and relentless pounding of the Atlantic surf against my back, neck and legs had rendered me vulnerable to just about anything. But especially slapstick.

The humor of "Prairie Chickens" was banal and perhaps even gross for 1944 but at age twelve and under those weakened conditions, I was a perfect set-up for a bad line. About half way through the movie, some silly crack was made and it simultaneously hit me on the funny bone, my battered back and somewhere on my sundrenched brain all at once.

A split second after the supposedly funny line was delivered—I can't remember a thing about it other than it had to do with hillbillies—I erupted in laughter.

Now there is laughter and then there is LAUGHTER. What convulsed me at that moment was something beyond the latter. I roared louder than anyone else in the RKO Kenmore and certainly louder than Aunt Lottie. The difference, however, was that Lottie and the rest of the audience stopped laughing and I didn't; or rather, couldn't.

I literally fell off my seat roaring and dropped into the aisle. When laughter gets that deep in the body it ceases to be funny and becomes just short of dangerous but nonetheless multiplies. A number of theatergoers turned away from the screen to catch a look at this human hyena. Finally, exhausted, I had spent whatever involuntary energy I had and fell back into my seat, both to my own and Aunt Lottie's relief.

Since that evening a half-century ago, I have laughed uncontrollably from time to time—once when watching Laurel and Hardy; another time while reading a Jack Benny biography—but never to the extent that I did for that innocuous line from "Prairie Chickens."

A classic view of the Flatbush-Church ave. hub featuring the old Dutch Church tower on the right, along with Ellman's Tea Room. For some reason, tea rooms were a Brooklyn staple when I was a kid. The spires of Erasmus Hall High School—cousin Lois' "home"— are on the left. Around the corner to the right stood the RKO Kenmore.

By the time we reboarded the Flatbush Avenue Trolley for the connection at Empire Boulevard with the Tompkins Line, I felt as if an industrial pump had drained my arteries and veins. I was limp but happy and alive enough to take deep inhales of the Bond Bread when we got off the Flatbush 6000 car, changing for the Tompkins at Empire Boulevard for the comforting ride home. As I confessed to Aunt Lottie, "Prairie Chickens" was more fun than gin rummy. For some curious reason she didn't believe me.

This intersection of Flatbush Ave. and Empire Blvd. is one that I clattered through by trolley on numerous occasions while riding either the Flatbush, Franklin or Tompkins lines. The arch is the entrance to Brooklyn Botanic Gardens. Prospect Park is at the left, across from the Gardens while Ebbets Field is just behind the apartments on the far right. Kirsch Beverages, featured on the billboard, was a fine Brooklyn product for years and the first to produce a dieter's beverage called No-Cal. The Franklin Ave. trolley is on the left; the Flatbush Ave. cars are in the center and right and the Tompkins Ave, tram is just to the left of the Kirsch sign.

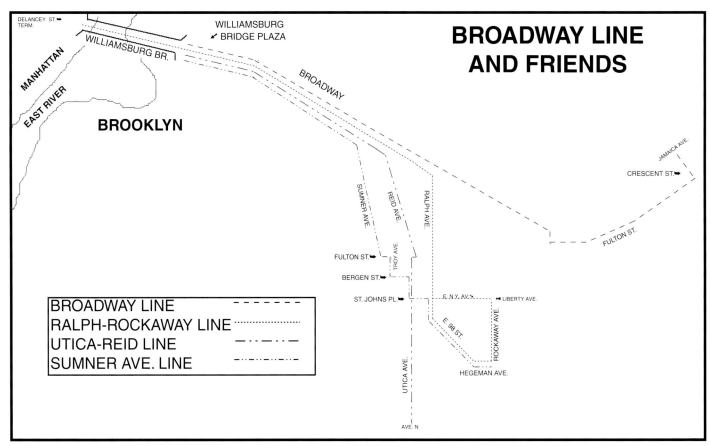

BROADWAY LINE AND FRIENDS

BROADWAY LINE — — — — —
RALPH-ROCKAWAY LINE ·············
UTICA-REID LINE — · — · — ·
SUMNER AVE. LINE — — · · — —

A Broadway car is making the turn into Williamsburg Bridge Plaza while a BMT Broadway Line set of 67-foot Standards roll towards Marcy Ave. station overhead.

CHAPTER TWELVE:
THE BROADWAY LINE AND FRIENDS

Perhaps this is cheating but at least I'm telling you up front that the Broadway Line, in my eyes, actually covered a multitude of routes that at one point or another began their runs at the Williamsburg Bridge Plaza and traversed Broadway but then turned right on to another street or avenue as the case may be.

Thus, when I discuss the Broadway Line, I'm not only going to tell you about Joe-Red's Pool Room, the RKO Republic on Keap Street, the Loew's on Broadway at the corner of Myrtle and Broadway and Eastern District High School but I'm going to toss in a few other delicious names as well.

Such as the Sumner Avenue Trolley that galumphed along Broadway but then headed my way along Sumner and passed the fascinating Schusterhoff and Kolodny Drug Store near Myrtle. Not to mention the Utica-Reid Line, which also was launched along Broadway but then cut right on Reid and finally Utica, that Casbah along the edge of Brownsville-Crown Heights that featured Sam Ash's colossal music store. And the Ralph-Rockaway Line which opened with an even longer stint on Broadway until it reached Ralph and later terminated not in the Rockaways–as I once had dreamed–but

That, of course, is not meant to upstage the Broadway Line itself which can stand on its own merits and evokes delightful memories; some harsh, some heavenly and, somewhere in between, the story of Muttle Bernstein and the Crunching Handshake.

The Bernstein Episode took place on Broadway, Brooklyn not far from the intersection of Flushing and Graham Avenues. This was a trolley buff's paradise because all of the above lines plied Broadway and several others were nearby. Travelling the Broadway Line to Muttle Bernstein, I would pass the Flushing and Graham Avenue lines with their wonderful fleet of 5000s that dated back to 1912 when they were center entrance cars replete with conductors.

It was a long walk to the Alba movie house but well worth it when "Omaha Trail" was part of the double-hill. We considered the Alba a cut above our neighborhood Kismet Theater on DeKalb Avenue. Great name, Alba.

The Flushing line passed the Alba Theater, close to Broadway. Unlike our local Kismet, which carried third or fourth-run films, the Alba was a second-run house and was revered as such by myself and my friends. It was a good ten-block walk from Marcy Avenue but we did make an occasional excursion to see what we figured was a special film that couldn't wait for its later arrival at the Kismet weeks or months later.

My rides on the Graham were few until I developed some strange foot problem and my mother sent me to a podiatrist—or is it chiropodist?—whose office was on Graham north of Broadway. That's when I really got to enjoy the 5000s, mostly because they were so different in style and character to my native Peter Witts. The 5000s had a groan that bordered on the erotic and I would have to say that if there was such a thing as a sexy trolley car—at least in my estimation—it would have to be one of the 5000s, not merely for the groan but the buxom lines as well. For my money, the 5000 was the Mae West or Marilyn Monroe of trams.

The 5000 under Broadway near Williamsburg Bridge Plaza. Is that sexy, or what? I considered the 5000 series the Mae West of trolley cars. It looked that buxom to me.

The 5000s also appeared on Sumner Avenue runs whereas Ralph-Rockaway, Utica-Reid and the plain old Broadway line had a mix of 2000s, 3000s and the standard 8000 Peter Witts.

Unlike the traditional runs along Tompkins, Nostrand, Franklin, et. al., the Broadway route had an exotic quality because it endlessly rolled in the shadows. Above it was the BMT Broadway elevated line that thundered over the Williamsburg Bridge, did a sharp left eastward toward Bushwick and eventually wound up in Jamaica.

The Broadway el was a three-track elevated with expresses running into Manhattan in the morning and out to Brooklyn and Queens in the evening rush hour. If featured the attractive 67-foot "Standard" car, arguably the best ever built for the New York subways, which caused quite a din as it rode high over the trolley tracks.

Sitting in the trolley's jump seat, I always got a kick out of looking upwards, staring at the underbody of the Standards as they roared over the Broadway streetcar. One little game I always played with myself was to see whether the Broadway trolley would be able to "catch" the el car at its next station.

This could happen at the junction of Broadway and Myrtle where the bigger Broadway el crossed paths—but not tracks—with the older Myrtle Avenue el. The Myrtle tracks actually were built over the Broadway station so one could walk down a flight of stairs from the Myrtle and catch a Broadway train; something my father and I often would do when we were heading to Dexter Park on Sundays to see the Bushwicks play semi-pro baseball.

That's the Broadway trolley on the far left while the Graham Avenue car moves across Broadway from Graham on to Flushing. The Loew's Broadway was a couple of blocks to the right under the el, not far from the Corn Exchange Bank located at Myrtle Ave. and Broadway.

Broadway-Myrtle was an interesting intersection with a solid, crunching trolley crossover. The northeast corner featured an ancient, towered building that housed the Corn Exchange Bank and Trust Company. (I always wondered what would happen if I brought a bushel of corn into the bank and asked a teller to hand over an equivalent amount of cash.) Just down the block sat the Loew's Broadway, one of the larger and older members of the theater chain and one we visited about as infrequently as the Alba.

There was one exception, however, and it occurred in the summer of 1944. Word had leaked out that the Loew's Broadway was featuring a very appealing "Chapter." In our lingo, a "chapter" actually was a weekly movie serial that accompanied the main features.

The one in question, if I'm not mistaken, was Bulldog Drummond; all about that dauntless detective. For inexplicable reasons, a couple of my friends—among them, Stuie Karger and Larry Schildkret—took a particular liking to Bulldog Drummond and we managed to catch the very first serial at the Loew's Broadway.

It was so intriguing that we made it our business to go every Saturday thereafter partly because Drummond was so unusual a detective and partly because the Loew's Broadway had a special deal going whereby if you saw each of the 13 serials—and had an appropriate round ticket punched each week—you would obtain a free ticket to the next feature at the conclusion of the series.

This was a delicious deal as far we were concerned because all of us fully intended to see every single "chapter"—Bulldog Drummond's health and welfare became a major concern by Chapter Two—and we enjoyed the trek and "schmoozing"on the walk to the theater.

There was only one problem; we were only up to Chapter Seven and already it was the end of June. This was bad, BAD because I was slated to leave for The Pythian Camp just before July 4th weekend and it meant I only had one more Saturday to go before departure.

The last Saturday bill was a dandy. The feature picture had Basil Rathbone and Nigel Bruce starring in Sherlock Holmes and The Secret Weapon. Holmes had become a big favorite of mine both on the radio as well as the screen and nobody, in my mind, could play Sherlock and Watson better than Rathbone and Bruce. (And nobody would portray the infamous Professor Moriarity better than Henry Daniell.)

As good as the Holmes flick was, the Bulldog Drummond chapter was even better. Toward the end of Chapter Seven, the indomitable detective was pushed down an elevator shaft by the bad guys. Drummond was at the bottom of the shaft, helpless, as the elevator plunged downward, sure to crush the beleaguered sleuth.

The way Stuie, Larry and I saw it, there was no way that Drummond could survive the impending doom. Just then; the action stopped and on the silver screen flashed the words, "NEXT WEEK, SEE HOW DRUMMOND ESCAPES TO PURSUE THE VILLAINS."

"NEXT WEEK!" I couldn't bear to wait until next week. In fact I wouldn't be around next week and I was dying to know how Drummond could possibly get out of this one. Actually, there appeared to be NO escape!

I tried to figure a way to miss at least the first days of camp so that I could return to Loew's Broadway the following week and learn how my hero had fooled his tormentors. But this was not to be. Off I went to Glen Spey, N.Y. and, to tell you the truth, I never found out whether Stuie or Larry ever went back to the theater again. By the time summer had ended I had forgotten Bulldog Drummond and was concentrating on Sig Jakucki, Mike Kreevich and the rest of the St. Louis Browns and their attempt to win their first American League pennant, which they did, beating the Yankees on the final weekend of the season.

Just past the Loew's Broadway and, of course, along the trolley route, there were a number of other shops but none with the magnetism of a Jay's on Nostrand Avenue or the Sugar Bowl on Tompkins and DeKalb. Except, of course, for Muttle Bernstein's hardware store.

Rare is the kid who can resist the romance of a hardware store where pliers, Three-In-One oil, fly paper and Sherwin-Williams paint cans sit side by side, magnetic in their own peculiar way. Muttle's store was old, had rickety wood floors, corrugated metal ceilings and barely enough light to enable one to see the directions on the back of the turpentine container.

Muttle, who was my mother's uncle as I remember it, was a short, stocky gentleman with white hair–but balding–who spoke with a strong, gruff voice. The first time I met Muttle, my mother had taken me by Broadway trolley after first transferring from the Nostrand line at Williamsburg Bridge Plaza.

The ride under the el, which began just after Bridge Plaza, was especially neat this day because there was a blazing sun that created wonderful designs on Broadway itself as the rays sliced through the track work above. We rambled along Broadway, first past the infamous Joe-Red's poolroom, near Havemeyer Street. Billiard parlors had always been off-limits for me, even as I grew older but there were wonderful tales told about Joe-Red's and I always resented the fact that I was forbidden to enter its portals; even for a clean game of snooker.

The trolley rolled under the Marcy Avenue station with the Commodore Theater (one of Williamsburg's biggest) on the right. A couple of blocks down we passed Keap Street which housed the RKO Republic Theater, one of the seedier houses run by the big chain. One my lesser ambitions was to visit the Commodore some afternoon and then have a Chinese dinner on Broadway before attending the RKO Republic at night. My parents assured me that, that would never happen and it never did.

Sitting in front of the Broadway car, I was able to enjoy the cavalcade of trolleys coming in the other direction; all Williamsburg Bridge Plaza-bound. I liked the double names–Utica-Reid; Sumner-Sackett, Ralph-Rockaway–better than simply Myrtle, Flatbush, Vanderbilt. They told you more and conjured up visions of distant lands, even though the land was just another part of Brooklyn.

We boomed over the Myrtle crossover and finally arrived at Bernstein's hardware store. It was totally unimpressive on the outside. The display window had some paint cans and other nondescript items but once inside your nasal passages were overwhelmed by the smell of turpentine and the mysteriously aromatic odor of the hardware.

Muttle walked out from behind the counter to greet us. My mother introduced me and the small but imposing man extended his hand for the traditional greeting.

"Shake hands with Muttle," my mother intoned righteously.

I reached out and suddenly felt a ham-like hunk of flesh envelop my fingers and palm. My hand had disappeared in Muttle Bernstein's and, as far as I could tell, would surely emerge as sawdust.

The crunch, I believed, must have set off the Fordham Seismograph on Rose Hill. I bit my lip in pain until finally, Muttle harshly remarked, "Young man, you must learn how to shake hands. THAT is not the way to do it. THIS IS the way to do it. And remember that for the rest of your life."

I did, just as I have remembered the lovely trolleys along Broadway. Whenever I shake hands, I think of Muttle Bernstein, gum terpentine and the joys of hardware store shopping.

A view of the Bridge Plaza complex. That's a Utica-Reid car about to depart. The trolleys have just come off the Williamsburg Bridge and will now head for all sections of Brooklyn.

Another view of the Williamsburg Bridge Plaza trolley complex. The vehicle on the right is a trolley bus. Manufactured by the St. Louis Car Company, the electric buses began replacing trolleys after World War II. They were well-built, silent and pollution-free. Maybe that's why they were soon replaced by the ugly, smelly diesels which began falling apart within days of their introduction.

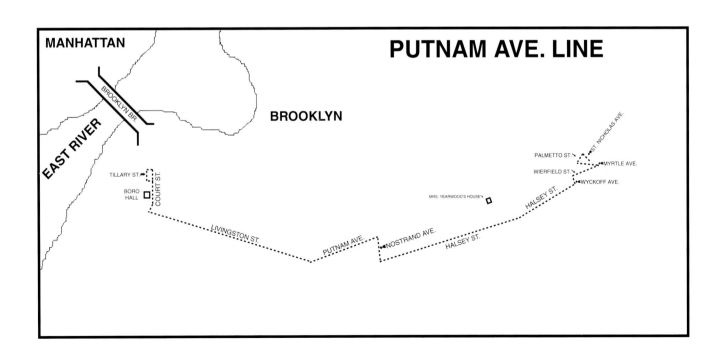

Trackwork forces the Putnam 6063 to switch across the temporary crossover by the Fox Theater in downtown Brooklyn. I always wanted to go to the Montauk Seafood Restaurant on the right but never did.

CHAPTER THIRTEEN:
THE PUTNAM AVENUE LINE

Putnam Avenue Line was just far enough from my house not to be ridden regularly but near en... e. As a matter of fact, the Putnam traversed Nostrand Avenue for a short spell before taking its 90° c... sey Street or Putnam depending on its direction.

...made the Putnam meaningful to me was my sixth-grade teacher at P.S. 54 (Annex), Anne Yearwood.

...st a word about the Annex. P.S. 54 was divided into two buildings. The main building, a typical, spra... ...was located on Nostrand Ave. (back entrance on Sandford St.) at the corner of Hart Street.

...sted, among other amenities, a large schoolyard, gymnasium, with wood flooring, a large assembly ...p room presided over by the infamous Mister Montague.

...trast, The Annex, dating back to the 19th Century, was a tiny two-story building located a couple of b... ...orth St. between Myrtle and Willoughby. There were many qualities to The Annex, not the least of wh... ...ss and its punchball court. And, of course, Anne Yearwood.

...ay it worked was that you started elementary school at the main building and switched to The Ann... ...rade. You did your third, fourth, fifth and sixth grades in the little building and concluded elemen... ...e big house.

...eference was The Annex mostly because of punchball. The "court" really was a narrow strip on the r... ...ing. The first base corridor was bounded by a nine-foot wooden fence while third base was boun... ...rick wall. Outfield ended at the side entrance to a pair of classrooms.

...s a terrific little court for either lunch hour games or an actual phys. ed. outing during school. But t... ...roblem. In order to play punchball, you needed a ball and, during those World War II years, balls we... ... Even worse, there was The Fence. It wasn't high enough to prevent foul balls from soaring into ...d next door but it was just tall enough for a kid to climb over in pursuit of an errant foul.

The ball dilemma was solved by my Uncle Ed Friedman (Mom's kid brother) who was an avid tennis player and who regularly supplied me with used tennis balls. Of course, the balls looked perfectly good to me and I never could figure out why Uncle Ed just didn't keep playing with them. But who was I to look a gift tennis ball in the fuzz so I accepted the cans as they were regularly delivered and used them for our punchball games.

However, The Wall was another story, mostly because of the teachers. We had no hesitation scaling The Wall—with three classmates providing a "boost"—but at least half the teachers who handled gym from time to time were militantly against our intruding into the private yard on the other side.

There were major and constant disruptions of our games: A. If the ball went over, I usually had only one replacement ball; B. If that went over, it was end-of-the-game; C. Even if there was a lenient teacher who let us climb over, enough time could be consumed in search of the ball to ruin the game anyway.

Suffice to say that when the balls remained within our limited boundaries we had some of the best punchball games in memory. When the ball went over, a good day could be ruined.

On the other hand, a day could be "made" with a successful effort in class. Which is where Anne Yearwood comes into the picture. Mrs. Yearwood, along with my fifth grade teacher, Frances Hochberg, had a keen appreciation for the teaching profession and a sensitivity toward her students above and beyond the call of duty.

Mrs. Hochberg had a way of reading to us that was totally mesmerizing. She treated each word with consummate care and seemed to show her appreciation for literature by the manner with which she turned the pages; slowly and passionately, as if it pained her to leave the last paragraph but with the expectation that the next one would be even better. I found Mrs. Hochberg's delicate page-turning as enthralling as her stories.

To the kids, Mrs. Hochberg was a relatively "easy" teacher. The word on Mrs. Yearwood, before we entered sixth grade, was that she was tough. She also was intriguing to the students because Anne Yearwood was the first Black teacher we had at P.S. 54.

Not that it mattered very much because it really didn't affect us in one way or another. What mattered was that Anne Yearwood was the quintessential teacher, She was tough when she had to be and soft at the appropriate occasion.

We also considered her good-looking. She had nice legs, a well-proportioned fuselage and a sweet face. It was tough not to appreciate Miss Yearwood—unless you hated arithmetic. She was demanding and I knew I had to shape up in her class or it would be, as my Aunt Lottie liked to say, "Ucchen Vay" (loosely translated: hopeless). So, I shaped up which meant that Anne Yearwood and I got on famously.

But the high point in our childhood romance developed over a crossword puzzle I worked on in 1942. Once a week we would receive a magazine called Junior Scholastic which carried all kinds of features including a sports column by Herman Masin, which I liked.

It also carried a Planter's Peanuts ad and a crossword puzzle in the shape of Mr. Peanut. During our weekly rest period, Anne Yearwood would occasionally work on the crosswords along with us.

For some reason I managed to breeze through most of the words until I came to a toughie at the end. The clue was "a part of the west." My classmates were having even more trouble with the Mister Peanut puzzle but Miss Yearwood went right down to the last word, along with me.

Mrs. Anne Yearwood, circa 1942.

By now, everyone in class realized that there was a contest of sorts between young Stanley and his teacher to see who could supply the missing word. With time running out, and regular class about to begin, I suddenly remembered a Randolph Scott western that had played at our neighborhood Kismet Theater. Not only that, but I could vividly visualize the billboard hanging on the wall of Jack's vegetable market on the corner of Marcy and Vernon.

The movie was "Badlands of Dakota" and I quickly counted the number of puzzle spaces in the empty boxes. "One, two, three, four, five, six, seven, eight." Eureka! It fit!!

I pressed my pencil into the Junior Scholastic, spelling out the word just to be doubly sure that it fit. It did.

"Mrs. Yearwood," I shouted with the high glee of one who had just smacked a bases-loaded home run, "I have the answer."

She looked at me with a mixture of dubiousness and anticipation. "What is it?" she asked.

"Badlands."

Anne Yearwood quickly gazed at her puzzle, counted the words and then smiled broadly. At the same moment, she catapulted out of her front of the room seat and walked three aisles over to me. The next thing I knew, Miss Yearwood leaned over and planted a kiss on my left cheek.

A teacher pressing her lips to my face in honor of an academic accomplishment! What could be a higher reward, short of knighthood or a job in the National Hockey League?

Never mind the day, Mrs. Yearwood had made my year.

From that point on, I vowed to work extra hard for Mrs. Yearwood, which I did, and we became true friends beyond the normal teacher-student relationship. In those days this was not often possible because teachers sat on a plateau in a realm far beyond their youngsters. They could be nice, all right, but that's about where it all ended.

Except for Mrs. Yearwood. Once, during Christmas holiday, she invited the students to visit her house. Egad! That was tantamount to being given an audience with the Pope at Vatican City. For some reason, my pals Ralph Hubbard, Neil Brown and myself accepted.

Mrs. Yearwood's house was right on Putnam not far from these 1947 blizzard scenes.

As it happened the Putnam Ave. trolley ran near Mrs. Yearwood's house—she lives to this day at 770A Putnam—in the heart of Bedford-Stuyvesant, so it was easy enough to reach.

Naturally, Ralph, Neil and I were queasy about going. After all, what does one do at a teacher's house? What does one say? And what is it like inside?

Until I had met Mrs. Yearwood, the only Blacks I knew were lower class poor who lived in the tenements around the corner on Myrtle Ave. or along DeKalb. Conditions often were on the poverty level and in the best of circumstances, not very attractive.

By contrast, 770A Putnam was other-worldly It was on one of the neatest streets in Brooklyn. The

houses were clean, well-appointed and could easily have been taken right out of Boston's posh Beacon Hill. Mrs. Yearwood's house was immaculate and I was particularly impressed with the living room because it was graced by a grand piano.

After Neil, Ralph and I untied our tongues, we chatted with Anne Yearwood as if she was a favorite aunt. She made us lunch, played the piano and otherwise gave us the royal treatment. By the time we headed for the Putnam Ave. trolley, Mrs. Yearwood and I were pals for life.

Ditto for me and Ralph Hubbard.

Of course, Ralph could have written me off as a buddy about 55 years ago, and I would have understood.

But I guess he understood as well that in 1940 we thought a lot differently about race than we do—in many cases, but not all—today. The truth was that while Whites and Blacks got along well in our neighborhood, there was an unspoken barrier of sorts and it manifest itself in a very painful way one day at our house.

This was March 31, 1940 and, as was the custom, my parents threw a birthday party for me. Naturally, I invited my friends—Howie Sparer, Lew Klotz, Jay Koslo, Gilbert Birnbaum, Abe Yurkofsky and Ralph Hubbard—to the house. At least I think I invited Ralph but I know that neither my grandparents nor parents knew he was coming.

What I do know is that Ralph was turned away at the door; probably by my grandmother. (I was two floors up and didn't know what was going on down below.) Whatever the case, the indelible vignette had Ralph standing in front of the house, unable to come in and my mother was tossing a brown bag filled with candy out the window to him. At that moment, I was unable to summon enough courage to berate whomever the guardian of 582 Marcy happened to be but shortly thereafter I made my feelings known and Ralph was then welcome in our house. Fortunately, Ralph, who could have been forever resentful, brushed aside the indignity and never thought about breaking our bonds. (Fifty-five years later, Ralph says, "That incident at your birthday party was long forgotton. More important, the amends made to me by your parents and grandparents produced a lifelong love for those four people.")

Our ties actually grew stronger through the school years. We continually joked around together and sent many a teacher to wit's end; but none more than Mister Montague, our shop teacher at P.S. 54, and Agnes McNeely, our third-grade teacher. With her white hair neatly tacked in a bun at the back, Miss McNeely alternately commanded attention as well as derision. Agnes—we affectionately referred to her as "Old McNeely Dame"— would periodically call a class to attention and then demand; "I want this room so quiet I can hear a pin drop."

Upon hearing the start of her command, either Ralph, Neil Brown or myself would push a pencil toward the edge of our desk. Once Miss McNeely said, "hear a pin drop," one of us would deftly push our pencil over the edge so that the otherwise quiet classroom atmosphere was interrupted by the "Plop" of the pencil, followed by laughter, followed by one of two classic McNeelyisms. She would either say to whomever dropped the pencil. "YOU IMPUDENT TOUGH!' Or, her other favorite, "THE ILLBRED OF YOU."

Putnam car #6005 is on Washington St. approaching Tillary St., northbound.

Either way, we felt it was well worth the effort and, besides, that's how I learned what impudent meant, not to mention, illbred. But much as we disliked McNeely, she never put the fear of God in us the way Mister Montague managed to do. The brilliance of Montague, the disciplinarian, was in his masterful understatement. Rather than raise his voice in anger, Mister Montague would do just the opposite. He would lower his voice to the finest Jimmy Cagney decibel count and then melt you with a stare.

On two separate occasions, Montague gave Ralph, Neil and myself cases of shell shock. Bear in mind, of course, that in 1940 the rules of decorum were significantly different than they are today. The primary mode of punishment was a demerit; which was tantamount to a whipping. Anyone who ran up five demerits over the semester was on the brink of being left back, which was the most humiliating fate that could befall any student at P.S. 54.

Ralph Hubbard, circa 1951.

Mister Montague knew this and wielded his demerits as prime intimidating weapons. Nevertheless, on certain occasions, the whimsical streaks which consumed the Terrible Trio of Brown-Fischler-Hubbard would overcome our fear of Montague. On the day that Hubbard pulled a prank, Montague caught him red-handed.

A hush fell over the shop class as the 15 boys wondered what manner of execution Montague would pull. Normally, a teacher would wither the pupil with a shriek or a harangue of some kind but Montague arrested attention with understatement.

"Mis-ter Hubbard," he began gently.

Ralph was riveted in his seat, practically breathless.

Ultra-softly, Mister Montague intoned, "Mis-ter Hubbard. D.,D.,D."
Then, a short pause while he extended, one by one, the fingers of his right hand. "One, two, three!"

Each one of us was overwhelmed with pity for poor Ralph. Three demerits on one pop. Hubbard had hit the disciplinary jackpot. He was up the creek for the rest of the year. Egad, Ralph had scored a demerit hat trick.

In a sense the fateful incident involving Neil Brown and myself was equally traumatic, if not more so because it involved something tangible that was near and dear to our hearts, bookends.

(LEFT) Principal Saul Bloomgarden of P.S. 54.

(RIGHT) The bookends in question.

(BELOW) Putnam #8212 has just turned the corner at Wyckoff and Wierfield, on February 12, 1950.

Each semester, Mister Montague would teach us how to build a specific item—once it was a silent butler, another time a tray made out of wood. The bookends were special because, A. They had our initials carved on each one; B. They were very useful; and C. Brownie and I had done a particularly good job with our carpentry.

As it happened we were just a couple of days from completing the job. The bookends were ready to use but lacked only a good shellacking. Brownie and I were ahead of the game, so to speak, when we chose to fool around in class and were spotted by the boss.

The usual hush fell over the class as Mister Montague announced—with extrordinary softness, of course—"Mister Brown and Mister Fischler, will you please come to the front of the room; and bring your bookends with you."

Trembling and frantic over the unknown, the two culprits marched up to Mister Montague's desk holding the precious bookends.

"Now," said Montague in almost a whisper, "I want each of you to give your bookends a big kiss."

We had no choice. Neil and I leaned over and gently bussed the bookends. The feeling of fear doubled. "Do you know why I had you do that?"

Without a clue, we shook our heads.

Montague calmly yet fervently went on, "You have just kissed the bookends good-bye because now I am going to take them to St. Lucy's Church and give them to the nuns."

Our heads fell collectively. "To the church...." The words rang in our ears. A year's worth of hard work on the darling bookends. As we marched with our heads lowered back to our seats, I recalled another word I was taught by a Miss French who once sent me out of the room for bad behavior. After I apologized, Miss French said, "Now you are penitent and now you have learned a new word—penitent."

Having plopped down into our seat, I realized how penitent I really was and, I presume, so did Mister Montague. After class, he walked up to Brownie and I, handed us the bookends and quietly said, "And don't let it happen again."

We didn't, although it didn't stop us from indecorous behavior elsewhere. Once, while we were watching the Hopi Indians rehearse their annual show in the school auditorium, we laughed up a storm. Unbeknown to us, the much-feared principal, Saul Bloomgarden, came up behind us and lifted me from my seat by the ears; virtually carrying me ear-borne and airborne straight to his office. I set a record for apologizing that morning.

Ralph, Neil and I collaborated on many a jape and in many a ball game. We generally played together although, from time to time, there would be some older fellows around who would welcome us in a neighborhood sporting event. One of my favorites was Abe Yurkofsky who was about two years older than me and whose parents, Max and Sara Yurkovsky, were among my favorite Vernon Ave. people. Max was a baker; a job that always intrigued me. I considered Abe very lucky to have a dad who would bring home free loads of what Sam Levenson once described as "mulutzuh rolls—bumbahs," which merely meant very large Jewish-type breakfast rolls.

Sara Yurkovsky is remembered for her sweetness—except for one occasion. This was the bitterest January Sunday in

(RIGHT) As you can see, the motorman on the Putnam Line had a softer seat than those who piloted the older models. They look like they're dressed for the worst.

(LEFT) That's Abe Yurkofsky. Right behind his left hand is the stone carving which we used for our daily stoopball games.

memory and I had traipsed down frigid Vernon Ave. to Abe's apartment which was a four-story job across from Howie's house. Apart from being a swell, warm fellow, Abe happened to own a table game that absolutely enthralled me. It was called "Lester Patrick's Hockey" and it featured a mix of real photos on the box with an oversized picture of Patrick, the manager of the New York Rangers. The box itself captivated me but the game was just as fascinating. The board resembled a hockey rink and the puck was moved by rolls of the dice.

On this incredibly cold winter day, ice had caked on the window of the Yurkofsky kitchen while Abe and I were playing Lester Patrick Hockey. It seemed to me that the only thing missing from the game was a scoreboard. I suggested to Abe that I scratch out the three period boxes on the icy window and then add the scores as we went along. Since Abe didn't disagree, I dug my fingers into the window ice and completed an elaborate—and what I thought quite neat—NHL scoreboard. My moment of satisfaction was fleeting.

Abe's mother wandered into the kitchen. looked up at the defaced window and blurted, "What's that!" The tone of the question required no answer. She believed that I had forever ruined her window; that it would have an NHL scoreboard imprinted on the pane throughout the summer and never would she be able to see clearly on to Vernon Avenue. I was banished to the cold, given a game misconduct in hockey terms, and it was a full month before I could return to Chez Yurkofsky.

The Vernon Ave. Gang with Howie Sparer (little guy with overalls in the middle), brother Gershy (kneeling to the right of Howie) and Abe Yurkofsky (kneeling to the left of Howie) among the stars. I was four at the time and not in the photo. Most of the guys and dolls here were good friends of mine.

Abe and I were involved in yet another incident which, for me, had a much happier ending.

The year was 1945. World War II had just ended but there still weren't many cars on the street; Vernon Avenue–my block–was like one long macadam football field. We didn't have television then so it was really impossible for a kid to comprehend the difference between a T-formation and the Statue of Liberty play–unless, of course, your father happened to be head football coach at Notre Dame.

Our variations on football could be broken down into three categories: very simple, simple and rough. The very simple version was called Association. In this two-against-two arrangement, each team had one down and all you had to do was tag the other guy with one hand to stop play. The simple version was two-hand touch. This required at least four persons on a side, two downs per team and two hands for a touch. The rough game, which we played only on the most masochistic of occasions, was tackle football. The problem with this version was not so much in the tackle as in the fall. Landing heavily (who ever lands lightly in football?) on city streets was something to wish on one's worst enemy.

Once the World Series was dispensed with, I yearned for the football season with a passion rivaled only by my anticipation of the next Sherlock Holmes or Charlie Chan movie. I followed the collegiate and professional results in the newspapers but found that the real fun of football was out on the streets. Vernon Ave. was our Rose Bowl and it was there, one Sunday morning, that I co-invented the reverse play.

I was lucky enough to own a real football in the pre-television era when not every kid on the block could make that claim. Like most of my athletic possessions, the football, though not the cheapest item in the line, was not of the best quality. (I always had the nagging feeling that one good punt would cause instant death for the pigskin.) Where I came from, we thought that footballs were meant to be thrown, not kicked. That's why Association was just right. There was no tackling, no kicking–just passing and running with the ball. Autumn weekends were never more delightful than they were in those early years.

Every Sunday morning, starting in September, I gobbled down my puffed rice fast enough to be the first kid out on the street. Invigorated by the chill air, I felt I could run for an eternity. That feeling of exhilaration was enhanced by the appearance, several minutes later, of Howie Sparer.

Me with football.

Within seconds, Howie and I would be tossing the ball around, awaiting the start of a game with a mixture of enthusiasm, and anxiety. We always were concerned that the next two fellows to appear on the street might be "big guys." By our definition, anyone a year or two older than us qualified for this designation. He could run a step or two faster, throw a yard or two farther and could certainly beat the sneakers off Howie and me in a game of Association.

On the historic day that Howie and I invented the reverse play, the first two chaps to make their appearance on the block were Abe Yurkofsky and Richie Mishkin, very definitely "big guys." The spring suddenly went out of my legs. I would have gladly settled for Monday, and school. But there was no ducking it; they wanted to play. Howie and I were doomed–or so we thought. Not only were Abe and Richie older, they were also two of the best athletes in the neighborhood, whether it was football, or stoopball, a game played in front of Abe's house. It was tacitly assumed that it would be the two of them against us. They threw off, Howie caught the ball and ran it to midfield before he was tagged.

Now the way in which we played Association a team had only one down. It made its play and either scored a touchdown or turned the ball over to the other team. Our idea of a pass was to throw the ball out of an opponent's reach. A running play was a simple matter of dodging the other guy.

On the morning in question, Howie experienced a brainstorm akin to Benjamin Franklin's discovery of electricity. "Look," he whispered, "when Abe tosses the ball to you, instead of running with it, hold still. I'll run back to you. Then you turn around so they can't see us and hand the ball to me. I'll run like hell and they'll think you still have the ball."

Such audacity. I suffered grave doubts about the revolutionary plan, but what the heck. I felt we were doomed anyway, so why not lose with flair? "Okay," we snapped at Abe, "let's go!"

I had goose pimples when the football left Abe's hands. It landed snugly in my palms as Howie sprinted toward me for our rendezvous with pigskin destiny. I wheeled away from Richie and Abe, uncertainly handing the ball to Howie as he completed his turn. That done, I ran at Abe, pretending that I had the ball in my determined grip.

The ruse worked. Abe and Richie tagged me with a vengeance, at which point they executed a lovely W.C. Fieldsian double-take as Howie galloped unmolested for a touchdown.

Having savored our triumph, we realized that the "big guys" would quickly tune into our ploy. "This time," said Howie, "instead of giving me the ball, pretend that you're doing it. I'll close my arm over it like I have the ball and keep running, but you'll keep it. They'll come at me–you go the other way."

Uncertain of the limits of our genius, we returned to the line of scrimmage. The ball was tossed and Howie arrived along the designated route. I handed him the ball; he grasped it momentarily, then thrust it hard into my stomach and continued on his merry way. Abe and Richie swerved left, lunging at Howie. I stood transfixed until I realized that I had a clear alley to the goal line. With every step toward the touchdown, I felt champagne in my blood. Two plays, two touchdowns against the "big guys."

We were batting a thousand. Now the question was whether or not we would enjoy the luxury of retiring undefeated. It didn't seem possible against such formidable opposition. But, lo and behold, a number of our friends had descended upon the field. That officially ended our game of Association. The rule was when the horde arrived, the four-man game was over and it was time for two-hand touch. The 'big guys" could never get their revenge–at least not on this Sunday.

Nothing was more gripping than a collision between a trolley and a truck. In this case the Utica Ave. car suffered a TKO after hitting the tanker, at Utica Ave. and Montgomery Street, on March 29, 1949.

CHAPTER FOURTEEN:
TROLLEY MISHAPS; (WRECKS, COLLISIONS, BREAKDOWNS AND STORMS).

   In the interest of fair and balanced reporting, something I always strive for in my hockey interviews and writings , I felt it incumbent on me to chronicle, through the visual record, the fact that trolleys have had their negative, though fascinating, moments as well.

Nothing was scarier than the sight of powerful electrical trolley wires falling to the street, as happened here under the Fulton St. el.

This is a newspaper photo of an unidentified collision between a Peter Witt and a PCC streamliner at the Park Row terminal in Manhattan.

Rugged 8176 is having a headache treated at the DeKalb Shops.

This is another collision between a truck and trolley that occured on November 29, 1948. This Putnam Ave. Line car met its match at Putnam and Classon Aves..

The blizzard of December, 1947 brought the entire city to a halt. Including this lineup of six Fifth Ave. cars near 42nd St., Brooklyn.

Not all snowstorms could grind the trolleys to a halt. This Flushing 6096 is gorging passengers on the way to Maspeth.

Here I am at the Branford Trolley Museum in East Haven, Connecticut, doing what I always wanted, operating the trolleys I could only dream about running as a child growing up in Brooklyn.

CHAPTER FIFTEEN:
TROLLEY EPILOGUE
(OR, YOU CAN GO HOME AGAIN)

As you may have imagined ny now, I spent all of my youth and much of my adult life wishing that I could get behind a controller and brake handle and actually operate a trolley car.

Then, in the spring of 1983, it finally happened. At the age of 51, I was touted by some transit nuts to <u>the</u> source.

I had just about given up when Howie and Suzanne Samelson, friends who then owned a New York railway antique store called Broadway Limited, came to the rescue. "If you want to try something really unusual," Howie offered, "why not trolley-car piloting?"

"Surely you can't be serious," I shot back. "Where are the trolleys? And how does one get to pilot them?"

With an "I'm glad you asked" wink, Howie explained that it was as easy as driving to New Haven, Connecticut. There in the sleepy suburb of East Haven, sits the Branford Trolley Museum (now known as the Shore Line Trolley Museum) where 104 real live trams enjoy the twilight of their lives in a rapid transit senior citizen's home.

"Best of all," chirped Suzanne, "these trolleys actually run a total of three miles on real track and you can pilot them. What could be more esoteric?"

I was hard pressed for an answer. "But," I wondered, "can trolley-car piloting be considered a sport?"

"It's no less a sport than riding motorcycles over a dirt track," snapped Howie. "Or driving automobiles around winding roads in Monte Carlo."

Suzanne added that the challenge was akin to solo golfing or riding down rapids in an inner tube. You can stake out goals–in this case bringing the trolley to a halt as close as possible to designated poles—and try to achieve them.

Convinced that they were serious, I phoned Branford. Yes, I was assured, I could operate any one of several trolleys dating back to the turn of the century after I had paid $20 and taken the training course. (For members of the museum, this privilege costs $10.) A week later, I was invited to Branford and introduced to my instructor, Henry J. Katz, a jovial, retired advertising executive, who had told me he had been operating streetcars as a hobby for more than 40 years. Henry led me to the carbarn and pointed out my machine-for-the-day.

There in gleaming cream livery, Montreal Tramways Car Number 2001 loomed majestically before us. Instructor Katz informed me that it was built in 1929 by The Canadian Car and Foundry Company, weighed about 17 tons and would carry more than 50 passengers. If I paid close attention, he promised, I would be operating the magnificent monster within ten minutes.

We clambered into the cab where Katz pointed out the vital elements required to propel and stop the streetcar. To the left was the controller and to the right, the air brake. The controller looks like a miniature avant-garde sculpture of an elephant. It has a long iron handle (the "trunk") jutting out from a body that sits on a circular base. To start the trolley one pushes down heavily on the wooden knob attached to the handle; the circular iron base is turned by yanking the handle from notch to notch until full speed (25 mph) is reached by the fifth and final notch.

Infinitely trickier than the controller is the air brake., which is manipulated by a wooden handle attached to a round steel brake valve to the right of the controller. Anyone can start a tram, but not everyone can make it stop; herein lies the sport of trolley-car piloting. The secret is to gather air (brake) pressure by skooching the wooden handle to the right, then sensitively moving it back to the left (but not too far) and then back to the right again.

"Okay," commanded Henry, "we're off!" A pungent whiff of ozone emanated from the electric motor as Katz tugged on the controller. He guided Old 2001–*thunk, thunk, thunk*–through a switch and onto a wooden trestle. The trolley groaned around a curve as though it were suffering from a hernia and then happily click-clacked into the straight-away. A moment later, Katz jiggled the brake handle and brought the vehicle to a gentle stop.

"Your turn," he said, inviting me to take the motorman's seat. Fretfully, I pulled hard on the controller and heard the plaintive wail of the old electric motor as we bounced forward on a trip through Connecticut woods, hills and meadows. It was just dandy until we rounded a curve and I spied another trolley sitting 25 yards ahead. Would I be able to bring Old 2001 to a stop without harming Car Number 1425? "You'd better start braking," urged Katz.

I moved the brake handle to the right and listened to the sweet hiss of air blasting through the pipes. The brake shoes embraced the eight wheels and the trolley ground to a safe halt several yards behind Car Number 1425. Triumphantly, I eased the brake handle to the left. "Not too far," cautioned Henry, "or you'll lose the air pressure altogether."

It was too late. I had lost the pressure and now the streetcar was rolling backward down a slight incline. "Don't panic,' chuckled Katz, "There's nobody behind us. Just tickle the brake again and we'll be all right." I nudged the brake and this time we came to a neat stop.

My first test was graded "P" for "Passing," if for no other reason than that I hadn't crashed into Car Number 1425. Not that I didn't suffer other moments of panic. Once I unconsiously eased my grip on the controller and nearly released the dead-man's switch, which activates the emergency brakes.

As the day wore on, my technique improved and I was able to bring the trolley to smooth stops within feet of the target poles. But I never did get over the fear that a derailment was just around the corner. Although the tracks at Branford appeared to be perfectly parallel and well spiked to the wooden ties, the trolley lurched like a drunkard, as if bent on leaving Connecticut for a return trip to its Motherland in Montreal.

Having successfully operated the Montreal tram, I decided to try another.

Despite my fears, Katz suggested that I try the Maserati of streetcars, a Connecticut Company trolley that runs twice as fast as Old 2001. It was late afternoon when he put me behind the controller of this open-air special. All the other trolleys had been returned to the barn. As I banged the iron foot piece, producing that immortal *clang, clang, clang,* the venerable goliath pranced along, swallowing up ties and track.

One challenge remained: I was to bring the trolley to a stop five yards before a switch near the carbarn. *Chuh, chuh, chuh,* the air released and halted the car within a few feet of the target. I gave myself a B+ for the effort. Henry gave me a hearty handshake and a motorman's cap.

A life's ambition had finally been realized.

Here I am posed with my two sons. Simon is on the left and Ben is on the right.

SPRINGFIELD
ROSEDALE
VALLEY STREAM
LYNBROOK
ROCKVILLE

Bob Presbrey
This photo of 18 year old Bob was taken in 1947 when he was stationed in Japan at the behest of Uncle Sam. Could he have forseen the historical mission he soon would be on?

Al Hirsch
Al is 17 years old here, on Feb. 28, 1942, expressing chagrin over the impending bus replacemnt of the Third Ave., Brooklyn trolley line, whose death notice is posted on the pole.

CHAPTER SIXTEEN:
TROLLEY SUPERSTARS
BOB PRESBREY & AL HIRSCH

BOB PRESBREY

 I originally encountered Robert Presbrey's name many years ago while leafing through a wonderful traction booklet called "The Tracks of New York." Photo after photo was credited to the Presbrey collection, inspiring me to wonder what manner of man this was and whether I would ever meet him.

   The opportunity finally presented itself early in June 1993 when Bob invited me and my researcher, Bob Hoffman, to his Valley Stream, Long Island home to check out his trolley photo archives.

   It was a memorable evening. Not only did Presbrey prove to be the ULTIMATE archivist but a warm host and, like myself, a keen fan of 1920s, 1930s and 1940s music.

   While we spent hours upon hours poring over trolley negatives, Bob played tape after tape of vintage Bing Crosby, Red Nichols and his Five Pennies, Connie Boswell and other musical stars of an era we sorely miss.

   Presbrey's patience was regal and his knowledge of the subject awesome. When it became clear that we couldn't complete the photo-securing assignment in one night, we agreed to meet again.

   Unfortunately, tragedy of a sort intervened. My then 15-year-old son, Simon, was unexpectedly felled with heart failure (cardiomyopathy), was hospitalized and eventually required a heart transplant in order to survive. My summer of 1993 was spent mostly at Columbia Presbyterian Hospital while the trolley book project was put on hold.

   Fortunately, Simon was released in late August 1993 and began his long recuperation. Friend that he had become, Presbrey remained in touch, dropped us the encouraging card while on vacation, and resumed his photo search when we were able to return our attention to the trolley book project.

   We convened again early in June 1994 and spent another wonderful evening together, pursuing pictures of the 6000 series, the Tompkins Avenue streetcar and other significant objects of our affection. Throughout, Presbrey entertained with lyrical cassette after cassette. It was more fun than the first time around. What I also learned early on was that

Presbrey developed his intense love for trolleys in the same borough of Brooklyn as I did and at almost the same time.

Thus, Bob's memories were as relevant as our's and worthy of inclusion in this book. Researcher Bob Hoffman sat with Presbrey one day and taped his recollections. The edited version follows:

My interest in trolleys started in the Flatlands section of Brooklyn, just off Flatbush Avenue, between Avenue J and Avenue K. There was a parade of some of the most marvelous trolley cars that went back and forth right before my eyes. My father once worked for the BRT in the East New York shops and he knew a number of people there. Then while he was going to college, he went to Virginia and operated some of the Brooklyn equipment that was sold to the Washington and Old Dominion Railway. This was a small traction company and he almost married the company president's daughter. It sounds like a Buster Keaton movie but here he was a professional engineer who invented the electric chassis dynamometer that road tests automobiles, trucks, and buses. It made him very observing of the transportation scene. Since he had the background in it, he would explain where things fit into place to me and I assumed my own interests. If that wasn't enough, one of my uncles had been a tower operator for the New York Central Railroad at many different locations, from the teens and the twenties. In 1932, when they opened the Independent Subway, they hired railway people with seasoned experience to run this new operation. He was one of them and he didn't retire until 1954. I visited him one time at the 168th Street Station on the A line.

My father explained to me that trolleys were liable to disappear from the American scene and that I should observe them while they were here. Then I had another uncle who came to the city and worked with the Public Service Commission, the Transit Commission after 1918, and with the Board of Transportation after 1924. He exposed me to all the old photographs of which I've become quite familiar. He also tipped me off that as soon as World War II was over, they were going to lay to waste all the trolley cars. It didn't matter how new they were, how new the track was, or permanently built in a right-of-way it had. No matter what their future was, they were going to see that they would be banished from the scene. They had just canceled orders for PCC cars to extend and replace the fleet. Some of the new track on Flatbush Avenue between Grand Army Plaza and Empire Boulevard was only six months old when they "bustituted" and gave us pollution instead of trolleys.

My family would point things out to me and then it was up to me. By that time I had gotten into photography and I tried to do wonders with my little box cameras. I covered all the different locations I could get to and tried to keep track of each day and every car and tried to find out if I had taken a picture of it. I think the earliest pictures were taken when I was still 13.

I was given the foresight to get out and do a photographic survey, find out where everything is, what it's like, and record the scene as I could see it, knowing that it was all going to go.

I remember standing out on Flatbush Avenue at Avenue K when my mother was shopping and suddenly there came "a half Nostrand Avenue Trolley" as I called it at age seven. It was what they called a Birney car, a four-wheel steel car that was used on the Holy Cross Cemetery Shuttle. That was its return trip with passengers, about 5:30 in the early evening, back to Flatbush Depot. I was determined to get a picture of it. While I was going to Public School 119, I had my camera in my briefcase and I got a shot of it coming and going in 1942.

In wartime 1943 I would get on my bicycle and head over to Flatbush Depot. My bicycle had a basket and in it I would put my school briefcase with the camera and film, along with my notebook and some photos. The Flatbush Depot was the end of the Utica Avenue line at Avenue N and all the cars would filter in through a series of reverse moves on switches to get into the yard. I would meet somebody in front of the depot and go back and take several pictures.

The 58th Street Depot was a considerable distance from my house but I went there too. I photographed what I could near it because it was a closed depot building. You would have to know someone there, convince them that you were not up to anything wrong, that you had an interest and you just wanted to go in and record what cars were there. This is before the general days of flash photography. They also stored cars there during 1940 and 41, reluctantly pressing many back into wartime emergency service.

What I would do is bring back some of the photographs to the trolley people. I would go and say, "Here, look at the pictures that I have taken. Is there anything around that I may have missed?" And all of a sudden, different people would open the pearly gates to me. They would say, "Oh, come on in! You can go back there as long as you don't get into any trouble. Just stay out of the way of anything moving!" I was an accepted person as I behaved myself, came out when I did my thing, got out of their way, and didn't give them any trouble.

There were dispatchers in front of the depot or in the shop. They were slightly charmed in what they were doing. They weren't there because they hated their jobs. I would hear a comment once in a while, "Oh yeah, that kid doesn't give us any trouble, he doesn't do anything wrong." I would be tolerated and given permission, as a favor, to go in there and take my pictures and not abuse the privilege.

My pictures were mainly taken at transfer points, but I did get to cover the entire Brooklyn car system. I rode the whole subway system by the age of 15. I had covered the entire Third Avenue Railway System in Manhattan and the Bronx as well as most Brooklyn trolley car lines and found just about every car. By 1944 I had taken an album full of pictures.

In my record book, as copied from the roster that was posted on the wall in back of the Ninth Avenue Depot shop, I would indicate in which depot cars should be located and what cars were supposed to be still in existence of the oldest types. I would go and find them and examine them inside to see how long ago they were painted as this information was printed inside the car. I would be able to determine what cars out of the 4500s should be saved. I had three--4573, 4588, and 4558—picked out as the best looking in outward appearance. I would talk this over with Henry Ruschmeyer, Leon Macie, and Al Hirsch. We decided that the 4573 was the best, so we joined forces to buy it and ship it to the Branford Trolley Museum in Connecticut.

While riding, I was in a very minor accident one time, in a particular Flatbush Avenue car (No. 6130), whose motorman had actually labeled it "fast wagon." It happened on a fine day in 1943, on Flatbush Avenue at approximately Beverly Road. Some woman backed her car out onto the tracks and the motorman just took her fender with him for about a block. He stopped unceremoniously and looked down at the woman and fumed. The trolley wasn't even scratched and her automobile was pretty well messed up, but she had asked for it. Accidents just don't happen, they're caused. The motorman's reactions were very sharp. I knew him from the neighborhood; he was a guy named Freddy who we all respected.

When I turned 18 my father advised me, "Get in the service and get it over with." So I just got under the GI Bill and I was sent to Tokyo for 13 months. It was an 18-month enlistment in the "regular army." I took 400 rolls of film in Japan's Tokyo-Yokohama-Kawasaki area where no one had film. I had the film sent from home.

Later on, while I was there, they were restoring abandoned lines by putting up steel trolley wire (during severe copper wire shortages) and they were happy to have them running again. They rebuilt war-ravaged trolley car bodies up from the ashes, having to run these cars with side windows mostly boardedup, due to the shortage of plate glass.

I witnessed a rail excursion trip of a Japanese group. They would get out at what would be a "picture stop" and then just look at the car with dejected expressions on their faces. Nobody had any film. So I took pictures for them and I rode along with them for a while. They were thrilled with the chances of things coming back to normal. Former enemies or not, I'm not an unfriendly sort, and I could make friends with people even with a language barrier like that.

Over there I was really able to run the trolleys because I was in uniform and they were a little afraid of American soldiers. They would bow to you and step backwards. They were very apprehensive having just lost a war not more than 15 months earlier. I was in the Army of Occupation that replaced the last of the wartime soldiers. One night, some fellows from the 7th Cavalry, who had been on a binge of some sort, were taking a trolley home to another section of Tokyo. They were really a disgrace; they had pushed the motorman aside and they were doing a terrible job of operating the car. I was so happy when they got off and I seized my opportunity. I stepped up as if I were taking my turn and I ran it properly. The motorman realized what was happening and he assumed the position of a forward conductor and collected fares. They gave me one bell to stop and two bells to go, and I observed the traffic lights. I did my thing and they were very happy. He thanked me when I was finished. That was the first time that I operated a trolley in Tokyo.

Many a time after that, I would operate a car that would stop nearby the Ernie Pyle Theater—the place where the GIs would see movies—and then take the trolley home. I would walk over to the stop and I'd be in the front of the car when it would pull into the end where they would reverse the car. I would take the reverse key, the brake handle, and the control handle and walk to the other end, put them in position, and stand there. This was the litmus test. If the conductor blew up and said, "No way Jose," I would step aside. But if he just cowered back a little bit, I would show him how a Yankee would run a trolley car and take it back to the corner near my regiment and get off.

I eventually came back to Brooklyn right after the big snow of December, 1947. I saw the last little glittering pile of that storm. The trolleys would have kept the City going if people didn't take their autos out and abandon them on the trolley tracks. Because of this, the plows and sweepers couldn't get through. Otherwise, they would have kept it open and people could have gotten places on the reliable trolleys. But everything got snowed in because some people didn't observe what was later going to be known as a "snow emergency street." I soon was able to enjoy trolleys again.

On a nice summer evening there was nothing like walking up to Flatbush and Farragut and getting on an Ocean Avenue car, an 8100 series speed car, and "flying" down to Emmons Avenue right outside of the then famous Lundy's Seafood Restaurant. Riding through the city streets at a fast clip with the front windows of the car pulled down was a very pleasant experience. 8100 through 8157 and 8186 were the speed cars, as well as the single end 8500 to 8534. They were a little heavier; they were two years younger and their brakes were a little bit more steady but they all gave you a good ride.

Going through the entire system, I had a hard time tying not to be biased when I came upon a different type of streetcar somewhere. Yet all of a sudden they were all my friends; you just couldn't differentiate. I accepted them all as they were, realizing how old some of them were. It's like respecting an elder. You didn't expect that much from some of the older cars, especially the ones that were not put back into passenger service, the ones that had gates on them in lieu of enclosed platforms. About trolleys being reliable, there is always one scene I will never forget. A group of 20 old cars were taken out of service and stored outdoors in the "dead yards" at Coney Island for over two years. Although it was illegal to destroy cars due to the war, it was declared that the city would sell the wheels and motors to lines in South America. These cars had new ropes attached to the poles on their roofs, and when dragged out to the street they ran under their own power to a planned "graveyard" in the Canarsie sandlots. Can you imagine any bus being able to do this? A year later these car bodies were burned up. The irony was that the ship that was to take vital parts to South

A group of trolley afficionados, Bob Presbrey included (fifth from the left), display their joy on a special run with the favored 8111.

America was torpedoed!

I was most used to the 6000s and the 8000s because they constituted 735 of the 1344 cars that were left in the fleet. But when in Rome, do as the Romans do. When you're in the Canarsie Depot, ride the 4100s or the 8100 speed cars, or if you're in East New York, the 2500s or the 1100s.

I was very familiar with the lines that emanated out of Flatbush Depot because I got there on a small sub-network of lines that were near me. A little later I got on over to Canarsie Depot and met people who had the run of the yard and rode all the lines out of there, as well as Ninth Avenue Depot.

I was very fascinated with the single-end Peter Witts on Flatbush Avenue. I really thought they were here to stay, and they were really something to ride in. Some of them were quite perky, quite fast. The motorman in one of them--6130--wrote "fast wagon" in pencil in the paint above his front window, as they didn't always have car numbers up front when he made his records out. I had to look around to see what car it was, but he put his little comment there. They really moved along and yet they were a very comfortable car. I could read a newspaper going through downtown Brooklyn and just ride along in perfect comfort. But that's all gone with the winds at this point. They were built after they began experimenting for the PCC car. They went back to 1930-31; they were a Depression gift to make work for people by building 200 newer cars. For their 20th birthday, the City had them scrapped by formula, not by necessity and not because they wore out. They would have been around a lot longer.

I always like the underdog. I would always find the older, smaller cars. Al Hirsch would talk about his 700 series--the light eight-window cars on the West End Line on the trolley underneath the El with the same name. I thought they were cute and I knew they were the most vulnerable to being gone, much more than anything else.

I met Al when I was still 14. He introduced me to some of those cars that only came out on special occasions. You know as you built up to rush hour they would bring out some of these older cars.

I met him on an Erie Basin-Park Row car, a 4100 series convertible with doors on it. We were on the same car by complete chance. He noticed that I was trying to be observant of everything coming at me and if I missed it I'd turn around to catch the car number. I was checking off the cars even before I really got into heavy-duty photography of them--getting out and doing the legwork of knowing where they were and getting a good view. He instantly recognized that I was there for the same purpose that he was; a friendship was struck up and we visited each other a couple of times. Al, being four years older than me, was draft vulnerable and he was soon in Europe as part of the army. He didn't get back until 1946 or so and I remember when he got back. We soon got involved in restoration of the cars at Branford.

I was able to read wiring diagrams and lighting circuit diagrams of the cars from the blueprints. We inherited the old BRT blueprints that were done on cloth in India ink. We had to replace or fix the wiring on our own at Branford.

Since we had been the ones who committed ourselves to bringing the car up there and we didn't have a car barn yet, we also had to be the ones who went up there on the laborious weekends to work on the car to get it back in shape so that we could run it. It was our objective to get it in service and get it as an accredited car, good for passenger use at the museum.

The Third Avenue cars were picked in 1947 while I was away in service and they were in Branford when I got back. It was the work of the Third Avenue group--Sid Silleck, Ronald Parenti, and Charlie Loinaz--and Eddie Blossom's guys who saved a car from the Westchester Lines. They were able to get together as young men, most of them were about 21, and legal to do something. It was a much smaller car and so it didn't give them many problems. We had the larger problems of choosing from an awful lot of cars.

Out of 1344 passengers cars, we did save three of them--PCC 1001, the first PCC, and the 8111. The 4573 was really a work car that we restored to passenger car status. We switched those rattan seats around with a few of the older cars and got the best ones going even though they were ages old. The car hadn't been touched; it hadn't been painted since 1934, maybe 1932. It really had to have been built out of something firm to be that good to last that long. That's what gave us the courage to be interested in it because we knew that somebody had done something right and we would rather have seen that continue than be destroyed. Then we saved about five or six work cars, two different plow cars, a sweeper, a gondola car, and two box motors--9421 and 9425, one of which was built in Middletown, Pennsylvania.

We held excursion trips on some of the trolleys we were planning to buy. You had to go down to the BMT head office and present your case. You had to look like you knew what you were doing and offer a trip that made sense. We told them that we were buying this car and that we wanted to run it, not to wear the wheels down but to have a safe and interesting trip and get people to support us in the car-saving activity. We selected 3 cars including the 8111, a car that had been out of service for two years. Immediately Don Harold and I went to the shop foreman in Canarsie Depot and told him, "Get the 8111 in shape! We're using it." Then the men in the shops painted it.

There were three trips with the 8111. I spearheaded the first one which was on March 11, 1951 (and then Don picked up on a couple of the others). It was a week after the Flatbush Line had quit and a week before the Utica-Reid line, which went on March 18th, and the Nostrand--the last line out of Flatbush Depot went on March 31. So by April 1, it was some April Fool's joke on everyone; there wasn't a car left operating in the Flatbush section of Brooklyn.

We had two cars on the trip; the other was 6180. Car 6180 was running on Flatbush at the time. I think it was the last 6000 series car that was painted. It was painted with a dull green ceiling. It has a night club atmosphere, a very quiet ride, and with that PC controller that thing would fly. In fact, I think it was faster than the 8111. (I had ridden it all the way to downtown Brooklyn to the Tillary Street Loop and back to Borough Hall to catch the subway on one of my commutes to College). I was absolutely enthralled with the operation of that car. So we asked for the 6180 and the selection three 8000 series, one of which was 8111. So they got 8111 ready and 6180 was in service and in operation. We went to Canarsie Depot, picked up 8111 and Don Harold, Ben Young, and I rode with the motorman. We parked Bill in Flatbush depot, picked up 6180 and took it back to Canarsie--a double bill move, which the excursion trip on the following day would serve to put these cars where they belonged.

Don knew a lot of the people in Canarsie better than I because he lived a lot closer. Whereas I had come to know the people of Flatbush Depot. We all sort of represented our areas. It was mini-provincialism of some sort but we all cooperated together.

So the trip started out of Flatbush Depot with 8111, went all around the place, came back to Canarsie Depot, switched, picked up 6180, flew down Wilson Avenue and back on Utica-Reid. It was a super trip where both cars behaved perfectly. Everyone had his full opportunity to get lots of nice attractive pictures with well-painted cars in different backgrounds. We brought 6180 at the conclusion of the trip after unwinding the two drill moves back to Flatbush Depot. They put it on the scrap track and did I feel lousy. I almost felt that I led it to its end and I still feel that way today..

I was involved with the car-saving committees of various organizations. I was seeking support from them, doing the legwork in getting permission to run the trips, designing the trips, selling the tickets for them, keeping track of everything, developing a mailing list for future trips, and having one heck of a good time. They were whole day trips with 40 or 50 people who were completely enchanted with what a convertible car that hadn't been in regular service since 1938 could do. Try that on a bus; take it out after 10 years after the fact and see if it will run for you.

Don ran two more trips with 8111 originating from Canarsie Depot. We needed spare windows and brake valves in order to rebuild 8111 and other cars when they got to Branford. We needed money and support and that's what the trips accomplished. Yet, all the while I knew that the empire was slowly closing in on us.

In the Spring of 1951, I went to a City Council meeting on trolley elimination. I stood up to question their thinking behind removing trolleys from a wide street like Ocean Avenue, along with the people that lived and depended on that line. I said that there was no reason to abandon it. We preferred the cars so just leave us alone. But the Council didn't listen at all. They had their minds made up. They had their own hidden agenda to buy reject buses from Detroit and Chicago. The ruse that the cars were in everybody's way and that no one wanted them

4573 is being prettied up for the August 22 trip on August 18, 1948 at the lower level of the Ninth Ave. Depot. There to supervise are (left to right) Ed Watson, Al Hirsch and Bob Presbrey.

continued. I just sat there and got railroaded.

The trolleys all went to Coney Island and were burned, except for the ones that we managed to save. I had that "Noah's Ark" instinct. I was trying to help save a little piece of something important.

I could always hear the cars at night. When the cars were abandoned and there were no more, I couldn't sleep. I was so used to the lull of an "owl" run going back to the depot. It was just like music to my ears. It didn't bother me a bit. The absence of it bothered me because I was aware of the consequence of not having trolleys anymore and having buses wander all over Flatbush Avenue. The buses wouldn't stop at the curbs, they would splash people with water on rainy days, and they would run in bunches. They accused the cars of running in a "banana line"--all ten cars running together and then nothing for a half-an-hour. The buses were no better.

In the next few years we ran four L.I.R.R. steam train trips from Brooklyn to eastern Long Island to raise funds for building carbarns at Branford to shelter the Third Ave. Railway and Brooklyn trolleys that we tried so hard to preserve.

Here we find Al Hirsch just before going overseas to Europe in World War II. He is inside a BMT trolley at the Ave. J sand pit near Rockaway Parkway. Its parts were needed for trolleys in Rio De Janeiro. This is what caused Al to start a trolley preservation effort.

AL HIRSCH

From his earliest years as a Brooklynite, Al Hirsch was a dedicated trolley buff. He translated his interest in many ways but, always, he displayed an overriding care and enthusiasm for streetcars above and beyond the call of mere fandom.

Nothing proves this point more than Al's pet project, the restoration and preserving of Brooklyn car #4573 which remains operative at the trolley museum in Branford, Connecticut.

In 1962, after he became a family man, Hirsch nonetheless found time between his job and home life to nurture old 4573 to its original, vibrant stature.

Because of Al's dedication, intelligence and overall enthusiasm for trolleys, we selected him as one of our two superstars. Research editor Bob Hoffman tape recorded an interview with Hirsch at Branford on March 3, 1993. Hoffman immediately was intrigued and delighted with his cooperative subject and conveyed those feelings to me on his return.

Before Hoffman completed his transcription, we learned that Al Hirsch had died of a heart attack at the age of 69.

A few weeks after the funeral, we conferred with Al's son, Bill, who by coincidence was an intense New York Islanders fan. We shared our enthusiasm at a game in early spring 1993 and remained in contact after that.

Bill Hirsch shared his father's enthusiasm for trolleys and has been a regular at Branford, overseeing the beloved 4573. Bill also supplied us with many photos from his father's collection.

To preserve the memory of Al Hirsch--and his trolley recollections--I hereby reproduce the original interview conducted by Bob Hoffman in March 1993.

BOB HOFFMAN: What memories does the 4573 bring back to you?

AL HIRSCH: I remember when I was a little kid in the last days of the two-man cars in Brooklyn. I used to look forlornly when these things ran on Church Avenue and wonder what they were like. I could never get close up to them. But later on my mother took me shopping to Namm's Department Store in Downtown Brooklyn. Lo and behold there were cars of this type and, in fact, it may have been this very car. It was switching back in front of the RKO Albee Theater where DeKalb Avenue meets Fulton Street. I started recognizing the old convertibles at that moment. In retrospect, that vignette proved to be one of my original inspirations to desire that a convertible be preserved.

BH: Do you remember the first time you rode in one of the 4573 types?

AH: I never really had a chance to ride them on the system when they were two-man cars; I never lived in that area. But I remember them running on the Rockaway Line and then they disappeared. There was a series of cars similar to this that had doors put on and those were the first cars of this type that I had the opportunity to ride. This was around 1941 when I started getting involved in this stuff. The first one I had an opportunity to ride was on the Erie Basin Line when I ran into Bob Presbrey. The cars were very similar to this 4573 except they were botched because pneumatically-operated doors had been put on them. They had been "modernized" in the 1920's. I always regretted the fact that they did that but it was done for economic reasons; they couldn't afford two men on the cars anymore. They had to make them operable by one man.

BH: What is it about the 4573 that you like in particular?

AH: It's a classic trolley car; anybody will tell you that. It's clean-looking. It's got a nice design to it. It was state-of-the-art in 1906 when it was built. You can see how solid it is. It had the first successful use of steel framing on a Brooklyn electric railway car. The whole bottom of the car was solid steel with some wood backing. The car was more solidly constructed than anything up until 1906. This particular prototype car was built by J.G. Brill in Philadelphia. Then there was a group of them built by the Jewett Car Company in Newark, Ohio. Laconia built the series of the 4500's, from 4550 up. From 4549 down to 4500 were built by Jewett. The 4100 and 4300's were built by John Stevenson. They used to get them from all different companies. This was a Brooklyn convertible because it was designed by the Brooklyn Rapid Transit. They bought a large quantity and since BRT designed their own car it had several different companies build from this same design. If you had four or five cars lined up here of that type built by four or five different companies they would all look alike. Except that guys like me would notice slight differences. The earlier cars were built in the days before there were laws about having windshields on cars and they came out in the ancient configurations. They didn't have any windshields on them. On open platforms the motormen had to prevail out there in the vilest of weather. They didn't put windshields on these cars until the union started to show its strength. So they started building the later versions in 1905 with windshields and in the cars that they retrofitted the windshields were set back a little, the overhang of the roof was a little more than this. So if I was standing there I could tell which had a retro fit and which had a built-in windshield when it came out of the factory. I knew if it was a Laconia or a Jewett because they had built-in windshields on them. If it had an overhang and without even looking at the number I could tell it was an earlier car, 3700 or 3900.

The end of the 86th St. Line. This is the last car arriving at its Coney Island terminus. On board to particpate in the funeral are trolley mourners; Jeff Winslow on the step, Al Hirsch holding the sign and George Horn, the motorman.

BH: Why was it specifically called a convertible?

AH: In the early years, when manpower was cheap and plentiful, they used to have two fleets of cars. One type of car ran with windows opened and was only used in the summertime. When the weather got bad you pulled the shades down on them. On another fleet of cars like the 1792 the windows were not open. They were permanently sealed. They were the winter cars and ran in the colder season. The intervening season, when the weather wasn't too hot or too cold, they would actually take the glass out on some of them and you would just pull the shade down. What they would do was store the winter cars in the summertime and the summertime cars in the winter time. They would utilize one set of electrical equipment for both cars and switch the equipment back and forth. In the summertime the winter cars would have all the electrical equipment taken off and put on the summer cars. There was plenty of manpower to do that in those days and it wasn't that expensive to do. Vice Versa in the other seasons.

BH: Why didn't the early cars have windshields?

AH: Everything was thought of in terms of the open carriages; the original horse cars that these evolved from. They never had glass in front of them. There had to be a place to carry the reins for driving the horses. The earliest electric cars were horsecars that had been electrified; motors put on them. The poor motormen had to stand out in the worst of storms. If it was cold they would tell him to buy an extra heavy coat or to grow a beard. It was just a real lousy job in those days. But as time went on and the unions became a little more organized, they started changing some of these things. It was not a horsecar doing three or four miles an hour anymore. They were doing 25 or 30 and this guy had to stand out front. The sharing of the electrical equipment got to be rather uneconomical and the cost of this every year was becoming prohibitive. It took up an awful lot of space in carbarns. So they came up with the state-of-the-art car, the convertible. It could run all year-round. They had heaters under the seats but wouldn't go so far as to put doors on the cars, it was too much of an expense. That lasted until the Thirties before it became impossible for a motorman to ride on an open platform like that because he was still subject to weathering (and these cars could only function with a two-man crew.

BH: How did you get the cars to the Branford Trolley Museum?

AH: In my teen years I had these things in the back of my mind and always was inclined to be a railroad fan. In those Depression years it was difficult for a youngster to go riding trains for hundreds of miles. But I was constantly reminded of the trolleys at night by the noise of the West End Line which was right near my house. So I got curious and decided to take advantage of an expert on getting mileage on five-cent fares and transfers. Sometimes as I roamed around I got braver and started investigating the carbarns and saw these cars in dead storage. It was after 1934 when they scrapped a lot of them but kept a handful around as service cars. They used to use them as sand cars, tow cars and salt cars. On the tow cars to tow other disabled cars there were very heavy motors to make it easy for them to pull. Salt cars and sand cars were another service. They put salt bags in these cars and they ran them on the line in the wintertime in the icy conditions. The open platforms came in handy. They shoveled out the salt from the interior of the cars to the adjacent tracks. The sand cars were used on places like Farragut Road where there were a lot of trees and the tracks were slippery from the leaves dropping. They would run up and down there and drop sand on the tracks. That's how 1792 was used for over twenty-five years at various places. I started noticing these service cars and I realized subsequently that there was quite a fleet of these things. They had a considerable number up until the very end. But they were all out of service, sitting in the back of the car barns all dirty with broken windows. In the early years when they converted them to these uses, especially the 4500's, they figured they were still useful cars although they were occasionally still used in rush hour on the Canarsie Shuttle.

BH: Were they considered speed cars?

AH: No, they weren't fast. They were useful but not so much for speed. You couldn't speed that much in Brooklyn anyway. When they converted them to work cars, they nailed canvas on the floor to protect the undercarriage from the salt and the sand. But as time went by they finally saw the handwriting on the wall and got a little careless about maintaining them and started running the cars into the ground. They looked like derelicts as they sat in the back of the car barn. You would swear they would never roll a wheel but then you would see them out in the wintertime. This 4573 was lucky, in a way. Very early in its life it was being used as a tow car. Tow cars also had sandbags inside of them to give them the extra weight for more traction. The 4573 was well protected; it had canvas all inside of it. Early in its use as a sandcar-saltcar-towcar, it broke a coupling and it abbreviated its practical use as a towcar. They were not going to spend time to repair the 4573 when they could just put another car in service. But the body had not been abused to the point where it was derelict-looking. I'm talking about 1935, 1936. Here's how it was saved: In the 58th Street Depot there was a drafty area in the back of the shop where they did maintenance. In the wintertime the men back there were complaining that it was too God-damned cold. There was no heating in that big, cavernous place. The unions were in a position of a little more power so they demanded a place for the men to keep warm during lunchtime. As a result, they put 4573 in the back of the 58th Street Depot Shop area and the guys used it as a place to eat and sit and throw the bull, warm up if it was chilly and take a break. It sat there for years and years, nice and brightly painted where the others all had their windows broken.

BH: How did the 4573 get saved?

AH: Two men, Leon Macie and Sid Silleck, were around at the time when the Branford Museum was started (Aug., 1945), a little bit after World War II. Silleck concentrated on the Third Avenue cars from the Bronx and he was very successful in getting a few cars up here. Macie knew Sid through the National Railway Historical Society and learned about the museum movement and what was going to be done for Brooklyn. Macie, having lived near 58th Street Depot, knew of the existence of 4573, which had a characteristic dent in the front. My involvement came this way: After the war, I ended up at the University of Miami and received a solicitation from the Branford Electric Railway so I sent ten bucks in. During Spring recess, when classes were out, I jumped into my friend's 1934 Ford and went up North. One of the first things I did was get hold of Sid and go up to the Trolley Museum. Meanwhile, the 4573 sat and sat at 58th Street until I got together with Bob Presbrey. We figured that the reason the preservation of the 4573 was stalling was because no one knew how to raise the money. At this point Ed Watson came into the picture and he became interested in the preservation. He was well employed at the time so we agreed that he would fund purchase of the car if we would fund the shipping or vice versa. Presbrey and I approached some of the officials of the Surface Division of the Brooklyn and Queens Transit Company. We requested permission to use the 4573 on an excursion to raise money and to our surprise, we got the okay on that.

On its first excursion, August 22, 1948, the car ran without the windows in it and the window grill panels in, so there would be a cool and comfortable place for the crew. The excursion was momentous and we were thrilled because everyone knew the car was going to be saved. We made a good start raising money to ship the car. Watson paid $300 or so dollars to purchase the car at scrap value and we had to raise $800 dollars to ship it. So we took a big chunk out of that $800 bill and arranged for a second trip. We were on the Trip Committee at the Electric Railroad's Association and we had to plan all these routes. It got to the point where I knew the Brooklyn trolley system like the back of my hand. I could tell which switch we were going to take here and what switch we were going to take there. We then had to run the car in the cold season because you weren't going to run a closed car in the warmer seasons. So we went back into the shop and took the grill panels out and installed all the windows which we had placed back in the Ninth Avenue Depot. They were really shoddy, real terrible and the car itself had gotten to be a bit seedy. Sometime before the first trip we sneaked in during the middle of the night and worked all night on the car. The crews would just turn their heads because they knew what we were up to. I remember one time going there at three in the morning; me with a red brush, painting and George Horn, who stood 6-5, painting the upper parts with a yellow brush. We had tried cleaning off the grills which had shit, pigeon crap, and dust all over them, but the rags wouldn't do the job, so we decided to paint them black. I had to go through the back recesses of the depot looking for black paint until finally I came across a two-gallon can of black paint and we painted all of the grills. The people who went on these trips really weren't aware of all that we went through to get these things running. After a while, I noticed passengers with stripes all over their arms. Suddenly it dawned on me that the stripes were coming off the paint. Then, I thought, this was three or four days after the paint job so it couldn't be the paint. It turned out to be the car barn lubricant, graphite. Everybody on this trip was marked with it. Later on, we went down to Ocean Avenue and were hit by a sudden summer thunderstorm. Some of the guys were pulling the shades down and about half of the people got soaked to the skin because their shades didn't work. Still, they enjoyed every minute of it.

A week later we got the third trip going (October 10, 1948). We had to go down to Brooklyn Boro Hall and pick up people on Tillary Street. We had some time so the motorman, Sam Fairchild, took us on a special trip. Instead of going to Boro Hall by the direct route, we wandered around Vanderbilt and Myrtle Avenues and took switches that were not regularly used. It was a big thrill to go over a switch that didn't have any wire over it. We made one crucial switch turn at DeKalb but the car partly derailed and went off the track. So there's 16 experts out rerailing the car with the rest of the people waiting for us at Tillary Street. But all the experts prevailed and we got the car back on track in less than 5 minutes. We got down to Tillary Street where everybody got on and we took off. I remember going through Boro Hall where Brooklynites hadn't seen a car in this type of condition in years. This was Brooklyn personified. In the end, we covered every bit of Brooklyn trackage that was still operable.

We made three trips in this car and finally raised enough money. The following year there was so much momentum that after the car got to Branford in 1948 they wanted to run some more. The trips were so successful, we went after car 4550, another car just like the 4573. It wasn't in as nice a shape as 4573. We went after this car not to get it here; we had enough time with the 4573. We couldn't put any grill on the 4550 and we could run it only in the colder weather. We ran that for three successful trips and the money we made on those we put into this car. We raised money every way possible, even going to the guys running stag movies; it was the only way to do it then. The 4550 ended up lingering in the carbarn and eventually as a waiting room car on Park Row and then back to the carbarn and then it became a saltcar.

When Freedomland was started up in The Bronx, the owner wanted to start a trolley line there and 4550 was available. He bought the car and stored it on the train tracks at Shell Road and Ave. X near Coney Island; the tracks that led in off the streets where the South Brooklyn Railway would run freight trains and sometimes run a freight car in there without looking. The car wasn't protected and several times they ran freight cars into the end of the car, bashing in the end of the car. The owner of Freedomland had no experience with trolley cars but wanted to get it up there before it got completely demolished by these freight cars. He hired a trucking crew to come in and get it. These people had no experience handling trolley cars. They came there with a big flatbed truck to load the car. But how the hell are you going to load the trolley car with those wheels on it? So they went under the car to cut off the air compressor, the resistance bank, and all the piping. They removed the trucks and anything under the car that protruded. They dropped the car flat on the flatbed truck.

But by the time Freedomland had disappeared, they took the 4550 to Edaville, in South Carver, Massachusetts. It sat out in South Carver for many years, weathering and deteriorating. They gave it a couple of cursory coats of paint but it still looked terrible. Then Alex Pollack was hired by the Mayor of Detroit to participate in a downtown rehabilitation effort and part of that effort, the hallmark, was to be an old time trolley line and he was looking for trolley cars. One of our members, Ed Blossom, told him about this place and he came down here and got wind of the fact that 4550 was in Edaville rotting away. I think he bought it for $4000 but they weren't ready to receive it in Detroit so they had it stored out in the open in Pennsylvania and it rotted away out there.

In the meantime Alex Pollack found out that the city of Lisbon in Portugal was disposing of some of its historic trolleys. So I believe he bought four or five cars from Lisbon and he put down narrow gauge track in Detroit. The trolley line runs these American-made cars from Lisbon on this Heritage Line. He couldn't use the 4550 anymore so it was sold to the Penelli Railroad Station in Pittsburgh. They hired a carpenter who had no knowledge of what a trolley is supposed to look like and he did a "restoration" job on it and the last I heard it looks like a horror show. It's the sister of the 4573 and it's sitting in Pittsburgh. It's the only other car like it, except for the 4547 up in Kennebunkport, Maine. They bought that one in later years when the car was completely shot. The man up there, Fred Maloney, is dedicated to restoring completely shot trolley cars. Over the last five or six years he became obsessed with 4547, one of the Jewett cars. He tore that car apart to the ground and built it up like new, very accurate. So there's another one existing but the running gear isn't restored that well.

The 4573 has been in steady service since 1948. I don't think there's any trolley in any other museum in the world that has been in continuous service as long as this one. It was out of service for a period of a year or two. It was technically in service but it was in maintenance. The trucks had started to fall apart because a lot of salt had gotten into them. The trucks got so bad that it became a hazard to run the car anymore. So, Teddy Eichmann, our dedicated shop man, advised us that the car couldn't run anymore unless we rebuilt the running gear. So they brought it into the shop, put it up on horses, and pulled the running gear out. The trucks were completely dismantled and completely replicated with new metal. Everything you see down there is brand new except for the bearing houses and the journals. He did it in a very accurate way, because we were able to get some of the original drawings.

BH: Do you have any memories of the original motormen?

AH: I remember when I was going to Utrecht High School, on the West End Line the motormen got to know me pretty well. I used to go down to Coney Island and every time a car would pull up to the end of the line, I would put the poles on the wires for them. Or if it was one of the later model cars, I would flip the seats over for them and save them an awful lot of effort. After getting down to Coney Island they would be pretty tired and they would appreciate that. So some of the motormen, in fact a good many of them, I got to know. I would have to walk from my house to 66th Street and Utrecht Ave. and wait for one of these cars to come along. Nine times out of ten the motorman would open up the doors, I would get on, and he would have his hand over the fare register. He's paying me for working at Coney Island. I hardly paid a fare on the West End Trolley Line on Utrecht Ave. for a good three-and-a-half to four years, all the time I went to Utrecht. The one thing I regret is that we never saved the old wooden box cars.

As a result of preservation efforts, 4573 is seen here departing the DeKalb shops on a flatbed trailer on November 30, 1948, for the Branford Electric Trolley Museum, where it resides today and is available for your viewing pleasure. The participants on this mission of mercy were, left to right: Al Hirsch, Sid Silleck, Mr. Hensler, the Transit official, and Everett White accepting posession.

A Fulton St. car, 6169 leaving the Sands Stree Station in 1941.

CHAPTER SEVENTEEN:
A BRIEF HISTORY OF STREETCAR OPERATIONS IN BKLYN.

If a community's baseball team can be named after trolleys then you know what an impact the streetcar had on tha city. Which is precisely why the trolley car meant more to Brooklyn—and vice versa—than any metropolis in the world Let us not forget that Brooklyn already was a metropolis in the late 19th century, not to mention a city unto itself until its politicians made the colossal mistake of incorporating with greater New York City.

But back to the rails. When the electric streetcar revolution hit America in the late 1800's, it was Brooklyn tha embraced the clang-clangers with more enthusiasm than any community between Portland and Philadelphia. There were so many electric vehicles in the borough that Brooklynites became commonly known as "Trolley Dodgers," an endearing erm that soon was adopted by the area's major league baseball team. From Brooklyn Trolley Dodgers, the denizens o Ebbets Field soon shortened their title to Brooklyn Dodgers—all because of the streetcar influence.

So, you may ask, how did Brooklyn become so heavily-sprinkled with trolley cars, from Williamsburg to Mill Basin from Flatbush to Flatlands; from Sea Gate to Bensonhurst?

It all began with horse cars; specifically on July 3, 1854. Tracks were laid along Myrtle Ave. from Fulton Ferry to the stagecoach stable at Marcy Avenue. (Interestingly, the intersection of Marcy and Myrtle is only a half-block from the house where I grew up at 582 Marcy Avenue.)

The Myrtle Ave. line was one of the four original horsecar rail lines owned and operated by the Brooklyn City Railroac which had been incorporated on December 17, 1853 and supplied with a lump sum of 2.5 million.

Brooklyn was a boom town at that time and mass transit was necessary to move the ever-growing population and tc provide an alternative to the relatively infrequent service of steam locomotives that chugged from the East River south tc the Atlantic Ocean.

When Brooklyn's original horsecar line opened, the fare was four cents on one of the dark, brown-painted cars. Fou horses were required to pull cars on the Myrtle Ave. line and each was adorned with rows of bells to alert Brooklynites o their presence.

Just three days after the Myrtle Ave. line made its debut, yet another route was opened, this one along Fulton St. from Fulton Ferry to City Hall (now Borough Hall). This was followed on August 8, 1854 with the debut of the Greenwooc Line (Later the Court St. Line) which began its run at the Fulton Ferry and terminated at Third Ave. and 60th Street. The last of the original four—the Greenpoint Line— premiered on October 1, 1854. Like its predecessors, it became ar nstant hit and spurred a network of horsecar runs throughout Brooklyn that lasted forty years.

Intense competition for ridership resulted in a battleground for several competing companies, each of which believed a bonanza could be reaped from mass transit. In no time at all lines were heading for Flushing, East New York, Bushwick Ridgewood, Williamsburg and Greenpoint.

Although the Brooklyn City Railroad was first on the scene it soon faced competition. Some of the rivals included: The Broadway Railroad which began at the Broadway Ferry (on the East River) in Williamsburg and ran along Brooklyn's version of Broadway toward Long Island. The Atlantic Avenue Railroad which had Brooklyn's South Ferry as its termina and Atlantic Ave. as its principal axis. The Coney Island and Brooklyn Railroad opened the first line to the seaside resor n 1862 along the old Coney Island Plank Road.

Several smaller companies appeared from 1860 to 1865 but these, with precious few exceptions, were gradually swallowed up by the big companies. By 1892, they had developed into a vast network of horse, steam and elevated lines which reached all the major communities between the East River and the Atlantic Ocean.

As the decades passed in the 1800's, technology improved the quality of service on these lines. In the beginning the horsecars were no more than urban stage coaches set on cast iron wheels. Eventually, the car's design was modified into a double platform vehicle which had such amenities as a pot-bellied stove and eight windows. But the most significant "high-tech" advance which changed the entire fabric of Brooklyn surface transit was the advent of electricity as a streetcar propellant. Steam engines, which had pulled elevated trains in both Manhattan and Brooklyn, had been replaced by the new-fangled electric cars.

The first Kings County line to electrify was the Coney Island and Brooklyn Railroad. On April 20, 1890 the CI&B went the trolley route from Park Circle, in Flatbush, to Brighton Beach.

Its immediate success inspired the majority of Brooklyn rail companies to abandon dobbin and turn to electricity as their power source. By 1895, nearly all of Brooklyn's horsecar railways had been eliminated. The cable exceptions to the rule were the Park Ave. and Montague St. lines.

Interestingly, Park Avenue's run was a cable car which lasted only a short time before the switch to the more practical electric rail method. However, the relatively insignificant Montague St. Line would stand firm in its reliance on cable for nearly twenty years before the change to trolleys.

By the early 1900's the electric streetcar was the primary means of transportation in Brooklyn and a golden age of trolleys would last the next four decades through World War Two.

During this period there were several problems to resolve, not the least of which was the glaring need for some kind of uniformity in the control and operation of the Brooklyn trolley system.

A major step toward centralization was taken by the Long Island Traction Company which, in 1893, bought out the small one-line Brooklyn Heights Railroad Company. The LITC, via the BHRC, obtained a 999-year lease on the Brooklyn City Railroad System, which had just absorbed seven small companies. Thus, Long Island Traction boasted twenty-seven lines. Next the holding company bought the Brooklyn Queens County Suburban Railroad. But the Long Island Traction Company overspent itself and in 1895 ceased operation due to foreclosure. Out of the ashes of the LITC rose the Brooklyn Rapid Transit System on January 18, 1896. By acquiring the lines originally run by the LIT, the BRT was on its way to becoming the largest transit system in the world!

The BRT's takeover of the Nassau Electric Railroad Company (a conglomerate of five companies including the Atlantic Avenue Railroad) in 1899 meant that only five Brooklyn companies remained independent of the BRT giant. In time BRT would acquire two of the five holdouts, the Brooklyn and Rockaway Beach Railroad in 1906 and the Coney Island and Brooklyn Railroad in 1914. The three remaining companies—the Van Brunt St. and Erie Basin Rail System, the Marine Railway Company and the Manhattan Bridge 3-Cents Line—were never to become part of the BRT empire.

During the golden years, the trolley became an integral and vital part of the Brooklyn culture and provided generation after generation with fond memories. The morning and evening rides became a ritual for business commuters who travelled the Williamsburg and Manhattan Bridges on their daily exodus to and from Manhattan. And, of course, there were the wonderful lines—Tompkins, Lorimer, Franklin, Flatbush, Ocean—which delivered fans to Ebbets Field. Not to mention those which carried millions to America's favorite amusement park, Coney Island.

But underneath the facade of trolley gaiety, there was a darker side of the streetcar operation under the BRT. According to author, historian Edward B. Watson ("One Hundred Years of Street Railways in Brooklyn"), the BRT encountered problems ranging from, "Worn out tracks and equipment....unsuccessful routes, costly strikes and (dealing with) every conceivable type of electric surface and elevated car then in use." Many of the problems were solved, especially that of standardization of cars. As Watson noted, "new and more efficient power plants were built, labor agreements were drawn up; equipment, tracks and elevated structures were improved and modernized."

However, the bugaboo of overcrowding remained an unsolved dilemma. No matter how many more lines, cars and bridges were built, Brooklyn's population kept exploding and, obviously, more and more people were riding the streetcars.

Under the circumstances, it would seem that the BRT made handsome profits but there were strong forces working in the other direction and upkeep of the forty lines became almost impossible to maintain on a grade-A level.

Even more fiscally damaging was the infamous Malbone St. (Empire Blvd.-Prospect Park) disaster on November 1, 1918. A BRT Brighton Beach Express was operated by a poorly-trained scab during a motorman's strike. The train sped out of control down the hill leading to the 90-degree tunnel portal curve and crashed into the concrete wall. The wreck killed 97 passengers during the rush hour (but not the motorman Edward Luciano) and signalled the beginning of the end of the BRT. Outstanding damages and reconstruction costs forced the BRT into receivership.

This, of course, directly affected the BRT's trolley operations and now the task of running the forty lines would fall into a number of hands during the 1920's. Eventually, the lines of the bankrupt BRT were merged into a new holding company. By virtue of this takeover, every line but one–the Brooklyn Heights Railroad—was able to emerge from receivership.

On June 1, 1929 the streetcar lines once and for all were reorganized under the massive Brooklyn and Queens Transit Corporation. The B&QTC, in turn, was directly affiliated with the Brooklyn Manhattan Transit (BMT Lines) which had taken over the subway and elevated operations from the BRT. Thus, the many railroad companies which had existed for nearly seventy years ceased operation and the B&QTC took complete control of all Brooklyn's trolley and elevated lines.

Like its twin brother, the BMT, the B&QTC was a progressive operator in many ways but faced a major challenge, Both the passenger automobile and the gasoline-powered bus had become increasingly popular and were luring riders away from the streetcar. Aware of the problem, the B&QTC leaders took action and became part of a nationwide group of trolley operators which formed the Electric Railway Presidents' Conference Committee.

In 1929. the ERPCC—later shortened to PCC—agreed to pool its resources and design a modern streetcar that would compete with the automobile and motor bus. During the early 1930's two experimental trolleys—Twin Coach Company's 5200 and Pullman's 5300—were used in Brooklyn to test the various components for the proposed PCC car. Authors George V. Arnoux and E. Alfred Seibel ("A Glimpse of Brooklyn trolleys: 1934-1940"), reported, "Eventually the two cars were placed in regular service on the Flatbush Avenue Line for a short period of time, being taken out of service in 1935." By this time the PCC car had been fully developed and in 1935 the B&QTC ordered 100 of the streamliners from the St. Louis Car Company. This enormous vote of confidence for the trolley appeared justified when car 1027 was put on public display at Albee Square in Downtown Brooklyn, on October 1, 1936.

Brooklynites were impressed with the PCC car's clean lines, high-tech (for its time) improvements and speed. The cars were soon put in service on the McDonald-Vanderbilt Ave. Line as well as Seventh Avenue, Erie Basin-Park Row and Smith-Coney Island routes.

The public loved the new streamline streetcars and it appeared the trolley would remain the transportation king of Brooklyn for decades to come. But unknown to the public, there were hidden political forces working irreversibly against the PCC's and their older brethren. The New York City Board of Transportation had quietly developed a hidden agenda of replacing trolleys with gasoline-powered buses. Technically, it came under the heading of New York City's proposed plan of "Transit Unification"—consolidating all mass transit lines and placing them under public ownership. Even more unfortunate was the fact that the city's popular mayor, Fiorello LaGuardia, was not a trolley fan and endorsed a plan that would rid the city of electric streetcars.

On June 1, 1940 the city's "Transit Unification" plan was realized. The three subway lines (IRT, BMT, IND) would now be operated by the city's Board of Transportation. In addition, the task of operating and maintaining the vast 3000-car, 500-mile track trolley system also was handed over to New York City. But it was a task the City had no intention of honoring.

There were many who realized the advantages of trolley operation and attempted to persuade the city fathers not to abandon the streetcar. Before the city takeover, the B&QTC prepared a detailed study emphasizing that there were clear economic advantages in retaining trolleys on at least 28 of the 49 Brooklyn trolley lines in 1940. Of the remaining routes, the plan recommended 12 for conversion to trolley bus and 9 to motor bus routes. But an insidious nationwide campaign conducted by the General Motors Corporation, a bus-manufacturer, to rid America of streetcars, had helped persuade City Hall that the trolleys must go. The B&QTC study, sound as it was, made no impression at all.

However, the onset of World War Two provided a reprieve for the trolleys. Wartime gasoline restrictions limited automobile and bus use enabling streetcars to become a necessary and successful aspect of the city's transit system. The period between 1941 and 1945 was a second golden age of trolleys in Brooklyn as virtually every usable piece of rolling stock was trotted out of the carbarns to fill the demand.

But war's end accelerated what streetcar buffs call the trolley holocaust as line after line was replaced by buses or, in some cases, electric coaches. To trolley fans the horrible sight of Peter Witt cars, the 6000 series beauties and their cousins being dumped in their burial ground at the Canarsie Sand Pit was an awful experience.

Authors Arnoux and Seibel explained the burial process, "Canarsie contained a steep banked, water-filled pit, with a track on the top edge. The condemned trolley, stripped of all salvageable parts at the Rockaway Depot, would be towed to this location, then shoved by the Judas Car to the track running along the top of the pit. Here another unusual piece of equipment, mounted on a single truck and fitted with a long pole jutting from one end, (Numbered 9960) would run forward, the long heavy pole catching the victim under the belt rail and tip it over down into the pit. Number 9960 was mounted on a portable track in order that the pit would not become cluttered with car bodies at one location."

A century after the "opening day" of horsecar operation, only three trolley lines remained in operation on the streets of Brooklyn—the McDonald Avenue route, Coney Island Avenue and the Church Avenue run. The final death knell was sounded on October 31, 1956, the last day of Brooklyn trolley service.

Edward B. Watson: "Trolley passenger service ended in Brooklyn forever in the small hours of the morning and a gray and sad morning it was! The last McDonald Avenue car #1042, left 9th Avenue depot at 2:27 AM (Run 13) and from Coney Island Terminal at 3:04 AM. The McDonald Avenue Line became a shuttle from the 16th Avenue Loop on Run 145. The last full McDonald Avenue run (#13) ended at 9th Avenue at 3:34 AM. The last 16th Avenue run (#14) ended at 9th Avenue at 5:20 AM, the finale!

"On 'he Church Avenue Line the last car to run in regular passenger service in Brooklyn, thus ending 102 years of surface rail transportation, was #1039. The last run was #63 which left the Bristol St. Loop at 4:50 AM amidst newspaper photographers...Car #1039 left the 39th St. Ferry Loop at 5:36 AM and finally ended the last run at McDonald Avenue and Church at 5:52 AM. Hail and Farewell!"

With that, Brooklyn's lovely time of the trolley ticked to a close.

SIGNIFICANT BROOKLYN TROLLEY MILESTONES
(Courtesy of ERA *Headlights,* July 1954)

Transit innovations. experiments and accomplishments of the forty-seven years
of B.R.T.-B.M.T. control and operation (1893-1940)

1893-1936   Over 5,000 cars for both passenger and work service were built for Brooklyn between 1896 and 1936 —an average of 125 cars per year for forty years.

1893   The Eastern Power Plant was built on Kent Avenue in Williamsburg and in it was installed the largest General Electric generator ever built up to that time.

1894-1895   The premier trolley car used for mail service in the United States was launched by the Atlantic Avenue RR on August 8, 1894 to Coney Island via Fifth Avenue and the West End Line. This was followed on June 3, 1895 by the Brooklyn City RR which began the first combination mail and passenger service from the Brooklyn Post Office to Flatlands via Flatbush Avenue. This mail and passenger combination served no additional purpose, therefore, in 1899, seven all-mail cars were built and continued in mail service until 1914.

1895   During the strike of 1895, which grew so serious that it was necessary to call out the State Militia for property protection, President Rossiter imported cars from the Roxborough, Chestnut Hill and Norristown Railway Co. of Philadelphia. They were yellow and operated in Brooklyn with red lettering and colors. The maiden voyage of the newly-illuminated open cars designed for trolley parties took place in August, 1895. At the same time the construction of the first trolley parlor cars in the country was initiated by the Barney & Smith car Co. The Brill Co. built an even more elaborate parlor car in 1895. They named them after Brooklyn Theaters—Amphion, Columbia and Montauk—and painted Marseilles royal blue with lettering and ornaments in gold leaf. They could be hired for $15-$25 per evening for twenty people. Routine parlor car service began in 1910 from Park Row to Brighton Beach.

1900   The BRT formed the American Railway Traffic Co. under Colonel Piper as a subsidiary corporation to operate the substantial fleet of flat cars in a far-ranging ash removal contract with the city. Contracts had already been made with both the National Express and American Express Companies to provide box freight cars for freight delivery throughout Brooklyn and parts of Queens. The BRT had over 90 flat cars and 50 boxcars. The freight department was operated by the subsidiary company—South Brooklyn Railway Co. under Lt. Col. Van Etten.

1900-1901   Eugene Chamberlain, Equipment Supt., designed a semi-convertible car of which the first five (2700-2704) were constructed at the company's shops. Among the innovations were a removable window sash for summer use, push buttons provided for signaling motorman and a new type of car seating named after Chamberlain himself. The "Chamberlain Chairs" were cane-backed in groups of two and could be swung close to the side or out into the aisle of the car. However, this seating arrangement was done away with by 1915.

1905-1908   During this period trolley and elevated car equipment were standardized and renumbered for more convenience and clarification. All trolley work cars were renumbered in the 9000-9999 series to avoid duplication. Over 1,500 closed cars were vestibuled by order of the city. Installation of the modern air brake was begun.

1911   Four cars were remodeled for pay-as-you-enter service. Two parlor cars (796 & 797), a semi-convertible (2700) and a convertible car (4100) were also converted.

1912   The BRT created a center-entrance, stepless car (3557) which proved successful enough to order 100 more of this type, which were assembled in the 39th Street Bush Terminal shop.

1913   September 27, 1913 the BRT incorporated its operating company, The New York Municipal Railway Corp., for the purpose of operating the subway lines of the BRT. They signed extensive contracts on March 19, 1913 with the Interborough Rapid Transit Co. and New York City for the Dual Subway System, for which the BRT was to spend $70 million as its part of the cost of one of the greatest municipal transit developments ever undertaken. Most of this work was completed by 1920, so that today it is basically the BMT-IRT Subway Divisions of the present New York City Transit System.

1916   An articulated car unit (4900) was placed in service, made up of two single-truck cars and a low vestibule in the center, similar to the type used in Boston. This experiment failed because of too much length and too little weight.

1919   The BRT was among the first companies to introduce the trailer car for rush hour operation and the Birney car, a new type of small single-truck safety car.

1924   A duplex safety car (4600) was placed in service on February 6, 1924. It was made up of two convertible car bodies connected by means of a drum-type vestibule, permitting passage between the two sections. This was the largest and longest car ever used in Brooklyn and had a passenger capacity of 142.

1928-1929   The BMT introduced the first car (4800) ever adapted to the subway method of fare collection by automatic turnstile.

1929   A motor steel coach car (5200), built as a demonstrator by Twin Coach, was used as an experimental car from 1929 to 1935.

1934   The BMT introduced the forerunner (5300) of the present modern streetcar known as the Presidents' Conference Committee car, built by Pullman. It was the initial car built from the ground up, to the specifications of the Committee by whose initials that type of car (the PCC) came to be known.

1936   Brooklyn was the premier city in which an ample number (100) of the modern cars were operated. These cars were the first of a huge fleet of almost 3,800 PCC cars which were used in practically all the larger cities of North America. (Note: In 1995 PCC's were still operating in Newark, New Jersey ,Toronto, Canada and many other locations.)

On the far right is a Birney Safety Car sitting in a siding at the St. John's. Place terminal. At one time the Birney was a popular vehicle on Brooklyn streets. This one became a rail-grinder.

Bergen Avenue at Bergen Beach in the early 1900's. Approaching car #1427 was built by John Stephenson in 1901. This portion of the line was closed in 1929.,

This is the corner of Nostrand and Atlantic Avenues, circa 1900. The crossing gates are down for an approaching Long Island Rail Road train. The summer car in the foreground, #253, was built by John Stephenson in 1898. Its run originated at Bergen Beach. The smaller car up front, #405, was built in 1898 at the Brooklyn Heights Railroad Shop and is operating as a special from Prospect Park. The Nostrand Ave. L.I.R.R. station is on the far right and the sign above trolley #405 states that the Rockaway Beach trains will also stop at Troy and Utica Avenues. A few years after this photo was taken the L.I.R.R. was elevated above the Avenue and is to this day.

(RIGHT AND BELOW) Cars #1 and #7 were built by Lewis and Fowler in 1890 as cable cars. They were electrified in 1909 and placed in postal service.

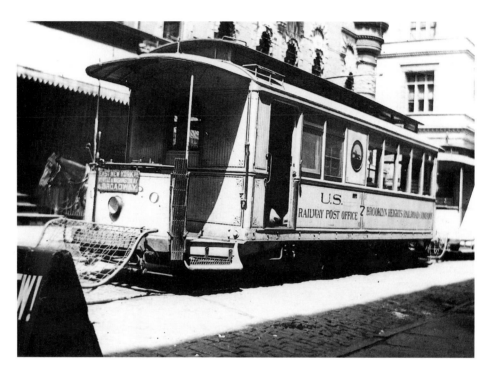

(RIGHT) Car #2700 was the first in a series built in 1900 by the Brooklyn Heights Railroad Shop. Here it was found operating on the Putnam Line in 1901 .

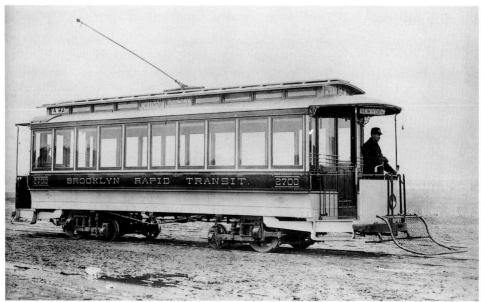

This is the 1928 "master"-type car built by Kuhlman, a division of J.G. Brill. It was housed here at the DeKalb Depot while being used on tests. It served for less than a year before being returned to the manufacturer.

APPENDIX
FISCHLER'S FAVORITE'S

****   1. NOSTRAND: It had the longest most varied run; from Delancey Street across the Williamsburg Bridge; through Brooklyn's spine, concluding with long, high-speed spurts through Flatbush to Avenue U.

***$^{1}/_{2}$ 2. OCEAN: The speed cars were in a class by themselves, especially from Farragut Road south to Sheepshead Bay. The 8000 series design remains perfect to this day.

***$^{1}/_{2}$ 3. NORTON'S POINT: Because it rolled across back alleys, along standard track and descended the ramp at Stillwell Avenue, this was extra special. The 5000 series cars had an attractiveness all their own, despite their age.

***$^{1}/_{2}$ 4. VANDERBILT: Any PCC route is in a special niche, but this one, cutting around Prospect Park and through the bushes at Park Circle was a special favorite. In its original tan and red coloring, the streamliner was as handsome as any piece of rolling stock, anywhere.

***$^{1}/_{2}$ 5. TOMPKINS: Like its Nostrand cousin, the Tompkins line crossed the Williamsburg Bridge; a big plus. It was my route to both Ebbets Field and my Bar Mitzvah lessons at Kingston and Park Place. Nuff said. The best part of the Tompkins run was from Eastern Parkway down the hill to Empire Blvd. and then on to Ebbets Field.

***   6. FLATBUSH: This was the longest and best run of the 6000 series cars. Its most memorable sprint was from Grand Army Plaza to Empire Blvd., along Prospect Park. Once south of Nostrand Ave., it galloped smartly to Avenue U.

***   7. LORIMER: Certainly not the prettiest route but it did run to Ebbets Field and to my grandfather's putty factory, Lorimer Paint Works, (26 Lorimer) and McCarren Park Pool.

***   8. FRANKLIN: It gets a high rating for the next to-the-curb speedway from the Parade Grounds (Park Circle), along Prospect Park to Empire Boulevard. And it served Ebbets Field with an especially exciting downhill run from President St. to Empire Boulevard.

**1/2   9. BERGEN: The route wasn't much but the ancient, groaning cars gave it an antique quality all its own.

**   10. MYRTLE: It was hard to like any line that was —literally and figuratively— overshadowed by a BMT el overhead. Besides, the 6000 cars were out of place on Myrtle.

**   11 BROADWAY: Same reasons as the Myrtle line except for the car styles.

*1/2   12. GRAHAM: Apart from the fact that it bumped past the Alba Theater (near Broadway) and featured the curious hobbleskirt cars, it was a tough sell.

*1/2   13. PUTNAM: Its virtue was that the 6000 series cars went to Mrs. Yearwood's house. Otherwise, it was an unimpressive ride.

ROSTER OF BROOKLYN TROLLEY ROUTES, CIRCA 1925, DURING THE GOLDEN AGE.

AVENUE C—From Cortelyou Rd. and Flatbush Ave. to Cortelyou Rd. and Coney Island Avenue.

BERGEN ST.—From Woodhaven, via Liberty Ave., East New York Ave., St. Johns Place, Buffalo Ave., Bergen, Boerum Place, Adams, Sands, to Park Row and to Flatbush–Atlantic and the Fourth Ave. subways.

BERGEN BEACH SHUTTLE—From Bergen Beach, via East 76th, Avenue U, Coney Island Ave., Avenue N, to Ave. N and Utica Avenue.

BROADWAY—Williamsburg Bridge and Ferry only, via B'way, to East New York, also from B'way Ferry.

BROOKLYN BRIDGE LOCAL—From Park Row to Bklyn. Terminal, via Bklyn. Bridge.

BUSH TERMINAL LINE—From the 39th St. Ferry to 1st ave., through private property to Pier 1, at the foot of 51st St.. Then from 28th St. to 41st St. on 2nd Ave., through to 1st. Ave., and then on 1st Ave. to 63rd.

BUSHWICK AVENUE— from Myrtle and Wyckoff, via Myrtle Ave., Bushwick Ave., Meserole, then South 4th, to Roebling and South 4th.

CALVARY CEMETERY—From Greenpoint Ferry, via Greenpoint Ave., to Calvary Cemetery.

CHURCH AVENUE—From Canarsie Depot, via Hegeman, E. 98th, Church Ave., 37th, 13th and 39th, 2nd Ave. and private right of way to the 39th St. Ferry.

COURT STREET—Bush St. depot to Park Row, via Hamilton Ave., Court, Fulton, to Park Row.

CROSSTOWN—From Erie Basin, via Richards, Woodhull, Columbia, Atlantic Ave., Court, Joraleman, Willoughby, Raymond, Park Ave, Washington Ave., Kent Ave., B'way, Bedford Ave., Manhattan Ave. and 4th, to Long Island City. The return route was the same, except Driggs Ave. was used instead of Bedford Ave. and Navy instead of Raymond.

CYPRES S HILLS— From Wyckoff and Myrtle Aves., via Myrtle, Cypress Ave. and Cypress Hills St..

DEKALB AVENUE—From Park Row to Sands St., to Washington, to Fulton, to DeKalb Ave., to Seneca Ave. with a branch to the Fulton Ferry and extensions to Grandview Ave. and Stanhope.

DEKALB-CONEY ISLAND—During summers on Saturdays, Sundays and holidays, from Ridgewood (Seneca and Elmhurst Ave.,) via Seneca, DeKalb, Franklin, Empire Blvd., Ocean Ave., Parkside Ave., Park Circle, Coney Island Ave., Brighton Beach Ave., Sea Breeze Ave., West 5th to Coney Island terminal.

EIGHTH AVENUE—From Bay Ridge Ave., via 8th Ave., 39th St.,, to the 39th St. Ferry.

EIGHTY-SIXTH STREET— From Bay 19th and Bath Ave., via Bath Ave., 14th Ave., to 86th St and 5th Ave..

FIFTEENTH STREET—Hamilton Ferry, via Hamilton Ave., 15th to Prospect Park West and 20th..

FIFTH AVENUE—From Ft. Hamilton, via 4th, 5th and Atlantic Aves., to South Ferry; shuttle, Atlantic Ave., to Fulton Ferry, via Boerum Place and Adams, also Flatbush-Atlantic subway loop.

FLATBUSH AVENUE— From Park Row, via Fulton, Flatbush Ave., Ave. N to E. 49th.

FLATBUSH AVENUE SHUTTLE—Flatbush Ave. and Ave. U, via Flatbush Ave. to Nostrand and Flatbush Ave..

FLATBUSH AVENUE—From Park Row, via Sands, Navy, Flushing Ave., Grand to Maspeth Depot; to Park Row, runs via Hudson Ave. and Nassau instead of Navy.

FLUSHING-RIDGEWOOD—From Ridgewood, via Lutheran Line, Fresh Pond Rd., to Flushing Ave., to Grand, to Corona Ave. to Lawrence Ave., to Bradford Ave., Empire Blvd. (Willing entrance to Prospect Park). Circle to Boulevard, to Coney Island during summer months.

FULTON STREET—From East N.Y., via Fulton, to Fulton Ferry. During rush hours operates some service to Park Row.

FULTON-CRESCENT—From East N.Y., via Fulton, Crescent, to Cypress Hills.

GRAHAM AVENUE—From Park Row to Sands, Navy, Flushing Ave., Graham Ave., Driggs Ave., Manhattan Ave., Newtown Creek Bridge, Vernon Ave. to L.I. City.

GRAND STREET—North Beach, to Bowery Bay Rd., Junction Ave., Corona Ave., Grand, Marcy Ave., S. 4th, S. 4th and Roebling.

GRAND ST. SHUTTLE—From Grand and Marcy Ave., via Grand, Kent Ave., to B'way Ferry.

GRAVESEND AVENUE—From Coney Island, via Gravesend Ave., 10th Ave. to 19th and Prospect Pk. W.

GREENE AND GATES AVENUE—From Park Row, via Fulton, to Greene Ave., Franklin Ave., Gates Ave., Myrtle Ave., to Myrtle and Wyckoff Aves., Ridgewood.

GREENPOINT—From Manhattan Ave., via Commercial, Franklin, Kent Ave., Classon Ave., Myrtle Ave. to Boro Hall. Operates to Classon and Myrtle Aves. only except during rush hours on weekdays. and does not operate on Sundays and holidays.

HAMILTON AVENUE—From Hamilton Ferry, via Hamilton Ave., to 3rd. Ave., to 65th.

HAMILTON FERRY LINE—From Hamilton Ferry, on Hamilton Ave. to W. 9th, 9th, Prospect Pk. W., to Coney Island Ave. and Park Circle to W. 9th and Smith only, except during rush hours.

HOLY CROSS—From Nostrand Ave., via Tilden Ave., to Holy Cross Cemetary.

HOYT AND SACKETT STREETS—From Bergen St, depot, to Hamilton Ferry, via Bergen, Hoyt and Sackett.

JAMAICA AVENUE—From Jamaica, via Jamaica Ave., to East N.Y..

LORIMER STREET—From Box, via Manhattan Ave., to Empire Blvd., to Prospect Park Loop.

MANHATTAN BRIDGE 3-CENT LINE—From Flatbush Ave. and Fulton through Flatbush Ave. Extension to and across the Manhattan Bridge. Returns same route.

MARCY AVENUE—From Marcy and Fulton, via Marcy and Metropolitan to Lorimer and Metropolitan Ave.

MEEKER AVENUE—From Newtown Creek (Calvary Cemetary), via Meeker Ave., Graham Ave. to Metropolitan and Graham.

METROPOLITAN—Williamsburg Bridge Plaza, via B'way, Marcy Ave., Metropolitan Ave., to Jamaica Ave.

MYRTLE AVENUE—From Park Row, via Fulton, Myrtle Ave. to Ridgewood. To and from Boro Hall, except during rush hours.

NASSAU AVENUE—From Manhattan and Nassau Aves., through Nassau, Varick and Meeker Aves., to Newtown Creek (Calvary Cemetary).

NEW LOTS AVENUE—Rockaway and Hegeman Aves. to Berriman, via New Lots Ave..

NORTON'S POINT LANE—From Railroad Ave. and W. 37th, to Railroad Ave. and Stillwell Ave..

NORTON'S POINT SHUTTLE—From Railroad Ave. and W. 37th, via private right of way to Nortons Point Dock.

NOSTRAND AVENUE—From S. 8th and Roebling, via Roebling, Lee, Nostrand Aves., to Flatbush and Nostrand Aves.. Some B'way Ferry service also operated.

NOSTRAND AVENUE SHUTTLE—From Flatbush and Nostrand Aves., to Kings Highway, via Nostrand Ave..

OCEAN AVENUE—From Rogers Ave. and Bergen, via Rogers Ave., Farragut Rd. and Ocean Ave. to Sheepshead Bay.

PARK AVENUE—From Bklyn. Br., via Washington, to Concord, to Navy, to Park Ave., to Park, to Beaver, to Evergreen Ave., to Jefferson, to Central Aves., to Cooper.

PUTNAM AVENUE AND HALSEY STREET—From Park Row, via Fulton, to Putnam Ave., Nostrand Ave., Halsey to Wyckoff Ave.

RALPH-ROCKAWAY AVENUES—From Canarsie Depot, via Rockaway Ave., East N.Y. Ave., St. John's Pl., Ralph Ave. and B'way into Delancey, via Wmsb. Br..

REID AVENUE—From Bridge Plaza, via B'way, to Reid Ave., Fulton, Utica Ave., to Church and Utica Aves..

RICHMOND HILL—From Ridgewood, via Myrtle Ave., to Richmond Hill.

ROCKAWAY PARKWAY—From Canarsie Term., via E. 94th, Rockaway Pkwy., Rockaway Ave., to Canarsie Depot.

SEA GATE—From Sea Gate, to Sheepshead Bay, via Surf Ave., W. 8th, Neptune Ave. and Emmons Ave.. During summer months, also runs bet. Sea Gate and Coney Island terms..

SEVENTH AVENUE—Greenwood Cemetery, 20th, via 7th Ave., Flatbush Ave., Livingston Court, to Boro Hall; returning via Joralemon, Fulton and Boerum Pl.. Subway service also to Atlantic Ave. and 4th Ave. subway loop.

SIXTEENTH AVENUE—From 16th Ave. and 63rd, to 16th and Gravesend Aves., via 16th.

SIXTY FIFTH STREET-BAY RIDGE—From 65th and 3rd Ave., via 3rd Ave., 13th Ave., 86th, 25th Ave., to Ulmer Pk..

SIXTY FIFTH STREET-FT. HAMILTON—From Ft. Hamilton to 65th and 3rd Ave., via 4th Ave., 99th, 3rd Ave.. Some trips operated to 39th and 2nd Ave., a.m. and p.m. rush hours via 2nd Ave..

SMITH STREET—From Park Row, Mhtn., via Bridge, to Washington, through High to Jay, to Smith, to 9th, to Prospect Park W., to Prospect Park S.W., to Coney Isl. Ave., to Neptune Ave., to W. 15th and Coney Island.

ST. JOHN'S PLACE LINE—From Buffalo and St. Johns Pl., via St. John's Pl., Rogers Ave., Sterling Pl., Washington Ave., Atlantic Ave., Livingston, Court, Borough Hall, returning via Boerum Pl., Livingston.

SUMNER AVENUE—From Bridge Plaza, B'way, Sumner Ave., Fulton, Troy Ave., Bergen.

THIRD AVENUE—From Borough Hall, via Fulton, Flatbush ave., 3rd Ave., to 65th.

TOMPKINS AVENUE—From S. 8th and Roebling, Roebling, Division Ave., Harrison Ave., Tompkins Ave., Fulton, Kingston Ave., Empire Blvd., Prospect Pk..

UNION AVENUE—From Greenpoint Ferry, via Greenpoint Ave., to Manhattan, Driggs, Union Aves., B'way, Throop, Flushing, Knickerbocker, Myrtle aves., to Ridgewood.

UNION STREET—From Hamilton Ferry, to Hamilton Ave., to Union, to Prospect Pk. W., to 20th. Return same route to Court, to Sackett, to Ferry.

UTICA AVENUE—From Church Ave. and Utica Ave. to Ave. N and Utica Ave..

VAN BRUNT STREET AND ERIE BASIN LINE—Hamilton Ferry to Erie Basin. Route: From Hamilton Ferry, through Hamilton Ave., Van Brunt, Beard, Hallock to Columbia, Erie Basin.

VANDERBILT AVENUE—Prospect Pk. W. and 20th to Park Row, via Prospect Pk. W., Vanderbilt and Park Aves., Navy, Concord, Washington and Brooklyn Bridge.

WEST END—From 39th and New Utrecht Ave., via New Utrecht Ave., Bath Ave. and Stillwell Ave., to Coney Island.

WILSON AVENUE—From Canarsie, via Rockaway Ave., Cooper, Wilson, Morgan, Johnson Aves., Union Ave., S. 5th, Marcy Ave., B'way, Wmsbg. Br., to Plaza.

CARS AND CAR BUILDERS
THE BIRTH, LIFE AND DEATH OF THE TROLLEYS

BARNEY & SMITH:

Barney & Smith produced all types of street railway and railroad cars for the United States and various foreign countries. They are also one of the few car builders to produce their own line of trucks.

Car Name: AMPHION; built: 1894; owner: Brooklyn City RR; type: PARLOR; life and death: reblt. 1929 to #797, scrapped 1947

Car Name: MONTAUK; built: 1894; Owner: Brooklyn City RR; type: PARLOR; life and death: reblt. 1929 to #796, scrapped 1938

J.G. BRILL:

The monarch of all electric railway car builders, J.G. Brill was founded in 1868, in Philadelphia. With the maturity of electric railways in the 1890's, J.G. Brill cars were sold in great abundance throughout the United States and almost every other country in the world. They were also greatly popular with trucks and all other car types especially the semi-convertible developed early in the century. J.G. Brill was a master in keeping up with the competitive threats of other companies. When the PCC was created in 1936, Brill created the "Brilliner" which was only slightly inferior. When Brill produced its last trolley cars in 1941, it left only Pullman-Standard and St. Louis Car Company remaining in the trolley-building business.

Car Name: COLUMBIA; built: 1895; owner: Bklyn City RR; type: PARLOR; life and death: reblt. 1915 to medical inspection car 798, converted to one man car in 1929, scrapped 1946

Car Name: DIRECTORS; built: 1897; owner: Coney Island & Bklyn. RR; type: PRIVATE; Life and death: re-numbered 799 in 1920, sold Penn-NJ in 1926, converted to passenger car #6, scrapped in 1934

Car Numbers: 139-151; built: 1894; owner Bklyn. City RR; type: ST-8-WD; life and death: scrapped 1904

Car Numbers: 420-499; built: 1898-99; owner: Bklyn. City/Nassau Electric RR; type: DT-13-BENCH; life and death: scrapped 1928-33

Car Numbers: 530-549; built: 1899; owner: Bklyn. City RR; type: DT-8-WD; life and death: scrapped 1928-33

Car Numbers: 787; built: 1898; owner: Bklyn. City RR; type: DT-8-WD.; life and death: orig. Brill sample, scrapped 1933

Car Numbers: 788; built: 1898; Owner: Bklyn. City RR; type half opened & closed; life and death: scrapped 1930

Car Numbers: 789-795; built: 1895; owner: Bklyn. City RR; type: half mail & pass.; life and death: scrapped 1933

Car Numbers: 900-999; built: 1896-99; owner: Coney Island & Bklyn. RR; type: DT-8-WD.; life and death: scrapped 1925

Car Numbers: 1100-1178; built 1903-04; owner: Coney Isl. & Bklyn. RR; type DT-10-WD.; life and death: scrapped 1948

Car Numbers: 1650-1659; built: 1897; owner: Coney Isl. & Bklyn RR: type DT-12-BENCH; life and death: scrapped 1925

Car Numbers: 1160-1699; built: 1898; owner : Coney Isl.&Bklyn RR; type: DT-12-BENCH; life and death: scrapped 1925

Car Numbers: 1850-1899; built: 1898; owner: Nassau Electric RR; type: ST-10-BENCH; life and death: scrapped 1925 (renumbered 2400-2449)

Car Numbers: 2260-2299; built: 1898; owner: Nassau Elec. RR.; type: ST-10-BENCH; life and death: scrapped 1930

Car Numbers: 2398-2399; built: 1894-95; owner: Nassau Elec. RR; type: DT-8-WD.; life and death: scrapped 1938

Car Numbers: 2450-2499; built: 1896; owner: Nassau Elec. RR; type: ST-10-BENCH; life and death: scrapped 1924

Car Numbers: 2600-2604; built: 1896; owner: Nassau Elec. RR; type: ST-10-BENCH; life and death: scrapped 1924

Car Numbers: 2621-2641; built: 1896; owner: Nassau Elec. RR; type: ST-10-BENCH; life and death: scrapped 1924

Car Numbers: 2662; built: 1896; owner: Nassau Elec. RR; type: ST-9-BENCH; life and death: scrapped 1924

Car Numbers: 3700-3799; built: 1905; owner: Nassau Elec./Bklyn., Queens County and Suburban; type: DT-12-WD-CONV.; life and death: scrapped 1950

Car Numbers: 3900-3999; built: 1905; owner: Bklyn., Queens Cnty & Sub.; type: DT-12-WD.-conv.; life and death: scrapped 1950

Car Numbers: 5000-5099; built: 1912; owner: various; type: CENTER DOOR; life and death: rebuilt 1930's, 5000-5079 single end, 5080-5099, double end, scrapped 1946-48, motorized scrapped in 1946-48, (one man 1932)

Car Numbers: 5100-5153; built: 1925; owner: various; type: CENTER DOOR; life and death: motorized scrapped 1946-48 (one man 1932)

Car Numbers: 6000-6099; built: 1919; owner: Bklyn, & Queens Transit Co.; type: CENTER DOOR TRAILER; life and death: 6054-6099 scrapped 1930's

Car Numbers: 6050-6099; built: 1931-32; owner: Bklyn & Queens Tr. Co.; type: SINGLE END CAR; life and death: scrapped 1951

Car Numbers: 6100-6199; built: 1931-32; owner: Bklyn.& Queens Tr. Co.; type: SINGLE END CAR; life and death: scrapped 1951

Car Numbers: 7000-7199; built: 1919; owner: various; type: BIRNEY SAFETY CAR; life and death: scrapped 1937.

Car Numbers: 8000-8099; built: 1923; owner: Bklyn. City Dev. Corp. (holding co.); type: PETER WITT; life and death: scrapped 1951

Car Numbers: 8300-8399; built: 1925; owner: Bklyn. City Dev. Corp. (holding co.); type: PETER WITT; life and death: scrapped 1949-56

Car Numbers: 8400-8449; built: 1925; owner: Bklyn. City Dev. Corp. (holding co.); type: PETER WITT; life and death: scrapped 1949-56

JEWETT CAR COMPANY:

Jewett's initial production was assigned mostly to horsecars but later the firm was renowned for well-built and proportioned cars for Midwestern railways. Shortly after 1900 Jewett constructed several elevated cars for New York, Brooklyn and Chicago. Jewett went bankrupt and ended operation in 1918.

Car Numbers: 1-20; built: 1904-05; owner: (Bridge Co.); type: DT-8-WD; life and death: used on the Williamsburg
        Bridge local line from 1905-1920, scrapped 1927
Car Numbers: 4550-4599; built: 1906; owner: Dev. Transit Corp. (holding co.); type: DT-12-WD-CONV.; life and
        death: scrapped 1930-56

PULLMAN:

The firm was created by George Pullman in 1867 and merged with the Wagner Palace Car Company to create the Pullman Co. Pullman became a streetcar builder in 1891 when its trolley department produced every sort of electric railway equipment. Examples of early Pullman streetcars were double-deckers and the spacious "big, red Pullmans." The closest thing to Pullman (as in railroad) luxury in the streetcar vein was the experimental PCC Model B that had art deco written all over it. The magnificently designed trolley premiered in 1933 at the American Transit Association Convention in Cleveland. Pullman's well-crafted product was dubbed B&QT 5300 when it ran in Brooklyn. Unfortunately, it was retired in the 1940's, well before its more traditional PCC cousins manufactured by the St. Louis Car Company.

Car Numbers: 100-103; built: 1893; owner: Bklyn. City RR; type: ST.-8-WD.; life and death: scrapped 1904
Car Numbers; 1300-1349; built: 1893; owner: Bklyn. City RR; type: ST.-7-WD.; life and death: scrapped 1904
Car Numbers: 5300; built: 1934; owner: Bklyn.& Queens Tr. Co.; type: PCC MODEL A; life and death: scrapped
        1940

PRESSED STEEL CAR CO.:

Originally a builder of steel freight cars, the company began turning out steel passenger cars starting in 1906 and then got into the railway car business. The company continued in the car-building business until 1954.

Car Numbers: 3556; built: 1906; owner: Tr. Dev. Corp. (holding co.); type: DT-12-WD-CONV.; life and death:
        all steel version, scrapped 1933

ST. LOUIS CAR CO.:

St. Louis Car was second only to J.G. Brill in the number of trolley cars constructed. St. Louis, like Brill, designed its own line of trucks and trolley car accessories along with manufacturing thousands of streetcars of every description. After 1936 St. Louis remained the principal PCC car builder after producing one of the first PCC cars.

Car Numbers: 104-117; built: 1894; owner: Bklyn. City RR; type: ST-8-WD.; life and death: scrapped 1904
Car Numbers: 152-160; built: 1894; owner: Bklyn. City RR; type: ST-8-WD.; life and death: scrapped 1904
Car Numbers: 169-176; built: 1895; owner: Nassau Elec. RR; type; ST-8-WD.; life and death: scrapped 1904
Car Numbers: 370-399; built: 1898; owner: Bklyn. City RR; type; DT-8-WD.; life and death: scrapped 1929-33
Car Numbers: 510-529; built: 1899; owner: Bklyn. City RR; type; DT-8-WD.; life and death: scrapped 1929-33
Car Numbers: 600-674; built: 1899; owner: Bklyn. City RR; type; DT-13-BENCH; life and death: scrapped 1929-34
Car Numbers: 1700-1749; built: 1899; owner: Bklyn City/Nassau Elec. RR; type: DT-8-WD; life and death:
        scrapped 1925-31
Car Numbers: 1800-1849; built: 1898; owner: Nassau Elec. RR; type: ST-10-BENCH; life and death: scrapped 1925
        (renumbered 2400-2449)
Car Numbers: 2200-2259; built 1898; owner: Nassau Elec. RR; type: ST-10-BENCH; life and death: scrapped 1930
Car Numbers: 2400-2449; built: 1898; owner: Nassau Elec. RR; type: ST-10-BENCH; life and death: scrapped 1924
Car Numbers: 2605-2620; built: 1896; owner: Nassau Elec. RR; type: ST-10-BENCH; life and death: scrapped 1924
Car Numbers: 8100-8199; built: 1923; owner: Bklyn. City Dev. Corp. (holding co.); type: PETER WITT; life and
        death: scrapped 1949-56
Car Numbers: 8200-8299; built: 1923; owner: Bklyn. City Dev. Corp. (holding co.); type: PETER WITT; life and
        death: scrapped 1949-56
Car Numbers: 1001-1099; built: 1936; owner: Bklyn. & Queens Tr. Auth.; type: PCC; life and death: 1002-1099
        scrapped in 1956, 1001 in museum

JOHN STEPHENSON:

The Stephenson shops began as a carriage-building firm in 1831 and the next year the company built the world's first streetcar, the *John Mason* for the pioneer New York & Harlem Railroad. It wasn't until two decades later, during the New York street railway boom, that Stephenson came into its own as a car builder. Between 1876 and 1891 the firm produced 25,000 streetcars and a full line of trucks for street railway service. In 1904 the Stephenson firm was purchased by J.G. Brill but operated under the Stephenson name until Brill ceased car building in 1941.

Car Numbers: 163-168; built: 1894; owner: Bklyn, Queens County & Suburban; type: ST-8-WD.: life and death:
        scrapped 1904
Car Numbers: 200-299; built: 1898; owner: Bklyn City RR; type: DT-12-BENCH; life and death: scrapped 1929-33
Car Numbers: 1400-1499; built: 1901-02; owner: Nassau Elec./Bklyn, Queens County & Suburban; type: DT-13-
        BENCH; life and death: scrapped 1908

Car Numbers: 1600-1649; built: 1902; owner: Bklyn, Queens County & Suburban; type: DT-13-BENCH: life and death: scrapped 1925
Car Numbers: 2300-2366; built: 1894-95; owner: Nassau Elec RR; type: DT-8-WD; life and death: scrapped 1938
Car Numbers: 2500-2599; built: 1907; owner: Tr. Dev. Corp. (holding co.); type DT-10-WD; life and death: scrapped 1948
Car Numbers: 2905-2954; built: 1902; owner: Nassau Elec RR; type: DT-10-WD; life and death: scrapped 1934
Car Numbers: 3155-3199; built: 1903; owner: Tr. Dev. Corp. (holding co.); type: DT-10-WD; life and death: scrapped 1933
Car Numbers: 3300-3304; built 1903; owner: Tr. Dev. Corp. (holding co.); type DT-10-WD.; life and death: scrapped 1933 (3300-01 1946)
Car Numbers: 3555; built 1904-05; owner: Tr. Dev. Corp. (holding co.); type DT-12-WD-CONV.; life and death: prototype of the class, scrapped 1937
Car Numbers: 4100-4199; built 1906; owner: Tr. Dev. Corp. (holding co.); type DT-12-WD-CONV.; life and death: scrapped 1949

LACLEDE CAR CO.:

Best known for its diligent building of street railway equipment, the firm also built a large number of trucks and cars for horse, cable and electric railways. The firm was purchased by the rival St. louis Car Co. in 1903.

Car Numbers: 500-509; built: 1899; owner: Bklyn City RR; type: DT-8-WD.; life and death: scrapped 1929-33
Car Numbers: 550-554; built: 1899; owner: Bklyn City RR; type: DT-8-WD.; life and death: scrapped 1929-33
Car Numbers: 1750-1799; built: 1899; owner: Nassau Elec. RR; type: DT-8-WD.; life and death: scrapped 1925-31
Car Numbers: 2705-2799; built: 1902; owner: Nassau Elec. RR; type: DT-10-WD.; life and death: scrapped 1930-38
Car Numbers: 2900-2904; built: 1902; owner: Nassau Elec. RR; type: DT-10-WD; life and death: scrapped 1934
Car Numbers: 2955-2999 built: 1902; owner: Bklyn, Queens County & Suburban; type: DT-10-WD; life and death: scrapped 1934
Car Numbers: 3100-3154; built: 1902; owner: Tr. Dev. Corp. (holding co.); type DT-10-WD; life and death: scrapped 1933

AMERICAN CAR CO.:

One of the premier builders; American Car Co. was purchased by J.G. Brill in 1902 but continued to operate under the American name until 1931. American manufactured the first Birney Safety Car in 1915 in both single and double-truck designs. The plant closed permanently four months after it was reorganized by J.G. Brill in 1931.

Car Numbers: 5555-5579; built: 1899; owner: Bklyn. City RR; type: DT.-8-WD. life and death: scrapped 1928-33
Car Numbers: 800-849; built: 1900; owner: Nassau Elec. RR; type: DT-13-BENCH; life and death: scrapped 1924-34
Car Numbers: 1000-1009; built: 1899; owner: Nassau Elec. RR; type: DT-13-BENCH; life and death: scrapped 1925
Car Numbers: 1900-1949; built: 1899; owner: Nassau Elec. RR; type: DT-8-WD; life and death: scrapped 1930

BRIGGS CAR CO.:

Briggs entered the streetcar-building arena and supplied cars to almost every system in New England. Briggs began as a carriage and wagon builder. Production ceased in 1903 when Briggs was replaced by the Southern Car Co.

Car Numbers: 675-699; built: 1899; owner: Bklyn. City RR; type: DT.-13-BENCH; life and death: scrapped 1929-34
Car Numbers: 850-899; built: 1900; owner: Nassau Elec. RR; type: DT.-13-BENCH; life and death: scrapped 1924-34
Car Numbers: 2175-2199; built: 1899; owner: Nassau Elec. RR; type; DT.-8-WD; life and death: scrapped 1930-33

LACONIA CAR CO.:

Laconia was formed from the Ranlett Manufacturing Co., a carriage building firm, in 1881. The company turned out a large number of electric cars as well as its own line of trucks for street railways in New England. After 1915 Laconia also produced cars for steam railroads. It was forced to end its operation due to the decline of electric railways.

Car Numbers: 2175-2199; built: 1900; owner: Nassau Elec. RR; type: DT.-13-BENCH; life and death: scrapped 1928-33
Car Numbers: 2000-2099; built: 1900; owner: Nassau Elec. RR; type: DT.-13-BENCH; life and death: scrapped 1930-33
Car Numbers: 4300-4349; built: 1906; owner: Tr. Dev. Corp. (holding co.); type: DT-12-WD-CONV.; life and death: scrapped 1930-55
Car Numbers:4500-4549; built: 1906; owner: Tr. Dev. Corp. (holding co.); type: DT-12-WD-CONV.; life and death: scrapped 1930-55

G.C. KUHLMAN:

J.G. Brill acquired the Kuhlman firm in 1904 although it continued to produce under the Kuhlman name. Its most notable accomplishments were the first "two rooms and a bath" cars, the first "Peter-Witt"-type cars and several advanced design lightweight streetcars. As the trend toward modern cars intensified in the late 1920's, Kuhlman (owned by Brill) designed a sleek "master"-type car which nested at the DeKalb Depot. Despite its attractiveness, the unit lasted less than a year before being returned to the manufacturer.

Production ended in 1932.

Car Numbers: 3308-3354; built: 1904; owner: Tr. Dev. Corp. (holding co.); type: DT-10-WD; life and death: scrapped 1933

STANDARD STEEL CAR CO.:

Formed in 1902 by "Diamond Jim" Brady and chief engineer John M. Hansen of Pressed Steel. SSC is most noted for its production of electric car trucks of all types and steam railroad cars. Standard Steel was acquired by Pullman Car & Manufacturing Co. in 1930.

Car Numbers: 3557; built: 1912; owner: Nassau Elec. RR; type: CENTER DOOR; life and death: prototype of the class rebuilt in 1930's, scrapped 1946

OSGOOD-BRADLEY:

An original carriage builder, Osgood-Bradley produced its first railway cars in 1833. At one time it was second in size only to Pullman. The plant was purchased by Pullman in 1930.

Car Numbers: 6000-6049; built: 1931-32; owner: Bklyn. & Queens Tr. Co.; type: SINGLE END CAR; life and death: scrapped in 1951
Car Numbers: 8450-8499; built: 1925; owner: Bklyn City Dev. Corp. (holding Co.); type: PETER WITT; life and death: scrapped 1949-56
Car Numbers: 8500-8534; built: 1925; owner: Bklyn City Dev. Corp. (holding Co.); type: PETER WITT; life and death: scrapped 1949-56

CINCINNATI CAR CO.:

Cincinnati cars were found on many street and rapid transit railways. They were well-designed vehicles, the most popular of which was the special curved-side lightweight car. Cincinnati cars were predominantly found on electric railways in the Midwest. The firm ceased production in 1931.

Car Numbers: 7200-7205; built: 1918; owner: South Bklyn. Railway; type: BIRNEY SAFETY CAR; life and death: scrapped 1940

CLARK EQUIPMENT CO.:

Clark wasn't a notable car builder, but it did develop the B-2 type truck used under the PCC streamliner. It also was noted for an experimental "standee" window PCC car built for Brooklyn in 1936 and six rapid transit trains for Brooklyn subway-elevated lines and a streamlined railway gas car built in 1930.

Car Numbers: 1000; built: 1936; owner: Bklyn.& Queens Tr. Co.; type PCC: life and death: museum

LEWIS & FOWLER:

Car Numbers: 1-8; built: 1890; owner: Bklyn. Heights RR; type: ST-8-WD-CABLE; life and death: electrified 1909, scrapped 1924
Car Numbers: 14-16; built: 1890; owner: Bklyn. Heights RR; type: ST-8-BENCH- CABLE; life and death: electrified 1916, renumbered 2663-65, scrapped 1924
Car Numbers: 118-138; built: 1894; owner: Bklyn. City RR; type: ST.-8-WD; life and death: scrapped 1904
Car Numbers: 161-162; built: 1894; owner: Bklyn. City RR; type: ST.-8-WD; life and death: scrapped 1904
Car Numbers: 1350-1399; built: 1894; owner: Bklyn, Queens County & Suburban; type: ST-7-WD; life and death: scrapped 1908
Car Numbers: 2800-2888; built: 1895; owner: Various; type: ST-10-BENCH; life and death: scrapped 1924

JONES CAR CO.:

Car Numbers: 17-20; built: 1895; owner Bklyn. City RR/Bklyn. Heights RR; type; ST.-8-BENCH-CABLE; life and death: ex horse car, electrified 1910, renumbered 2666-2668 in 1916, 17-19 scrapped 1917, 20 scr. 1905

BROWELL CAR CO.:

Car Numbers: 2367-2397; built: 1994-95; owner: Nassau Elec. RR; type: DT-8-WD; life and death: scrapped 1938

TWIN COACH:

Located in Kent, Ohio, Twin Coach is better known for its manufacture of buses. Nevertheless, the firm did have a trolley industry function as well. The outfit built three experimental cars, culminating with 5200 which anticipated the PCC's foot—rather than hand—controls. After the B&QT bought 5200 in 1930 it ran on both Flatbush and DeKalb Avenue routes. It later was donated to PCC planners for experimental purposes and was designated PCC Model A. It lasted through 1934 and was scrapped in 1939.

Car Numbers: 5200; built: 1929; owner: Bklyn. & Queens Tr. Co.; type: PCC MODEL A; life and death: scrapped 1939

BROOKLYN HEIGHTS RR SHOP:

Car Numbers: 400-419; built: 1898; owner: Bklyn. Heights RR; type: DT-12-BENCH; life and death: scrapped 1928-33

Car Numbers: 2700-2704; built: 1900-01; owner: Nassau Elec. RR; type: ST-1O-BENCH; life and death: scrapped 1924

DEKALB SHOPS:

Car Numbers: 4600; built: 1923; owner: Bklyn.& Manhattan Tr, Corp.; type: DUPLEX CARS; life and death: rebuilt 1929 as 4528, scrapped 1933
Car Numbers: 4700-4707; built: 1927; owner: Bklyn.& Manhattan Tr, Corp.; type: ONE MAN CLOSED; life and death: ex-3900's, scrapped 1946
Car Numbers:4800; built: 1929; owner: Bklyn. & Queens Tr. Co.; type: ONE MAN CLOSED; life and death: ex-3900, scrapped 1946

FRESH POND SHOPS:

Car Numbers: 4900; built: 1915; owner: Bklyn. City RR; type: TWO UNIT CARS; life and death: scrapped 1924

COMPANY SHOPS:

Car Numbers: 97 BRIGHTON (Pontiac); built: 1897; owner: Nassau Elec. RR; type: PRIVATE; life and death: rebuilt as pay car in 1907, renumbered 9900 in 1916, scrapped 1933
Car Numbers: 98; built: 1899; owner: Nassau Elec. RR; type: PRESIDENT; life and death: converted to transfer car 9903 in 1915, scrapped 1924
Car Numbers: 99 AMPHERE; built: 1898; owner: Bklyn. City RR; type; PRESIDENT; life and death: scrapped 1902

VARIOUS BUILDERS:

Car Numbers: 177-194; built: 1895; owner: Nassau Elec. RR; type: ST-8-WD; life and death: converted to sand cars-sold to N.Y. State Ry. in 1924, (180,182,186,188,190,192,194 all scrapped 1930)
Car Numbers: 700-786; built: 1897-98; owner: Bklyn. City RR; type: DT-13-BENCH; life and death: scrapped 1929-34
Car Numbers: 796-799; built: 1895; owner: Bklyn. City RR; type: HALF MAIL & PASS.; life and death: see parlor cars above
Car Numbers: 1500-1599; built: 1893-94; owner: VARIOUS; type: ST-8-WD; life and death: scrapped 1908

A Norton's Point Car climbing the grade to the Stillwell Ave. terminal.